The
Big Book
of
HOPE

Published 2010
by Poolbeg Books Ltd
123 Grange Hill, Baldoyle
Dublin 13, Ireland
E-mail: poolbeg@poolbeg.com
www.poolbeg.com

A catalogue record for this book is available from the British Library.

ISBN 978-1-84223-467-9

Typeset by Patricia Hope in Sabon 11 / 15.5
Printed by CPI, Mackays, UK

www.poolbeg.com

The
Big Book
of
HOPE

Compiled by Vanessa O'Loughlin
with Hazel Katherine Larkin

POOLBEG

Contents

In order to keep the wonderful blend of contributions, in the eclectic spirit of the book we have interspersed the non-fiction among the fiction – we hope that this will surprise and entertain you and keep you turning the pages!

Fiction * Non-Fiction ** Poetry ***

Preface

*It is difficult to say what is impossible, for the dream of
yesterday is the hope of today and the reality of tomorrow.*

ROBERT H GODDARD (1882–1945)

∽ ↶

*Hope, like the gleaming taper's light,
Adorns and cheers our way;
And still, as darker grows the night,
Emits a brighter ray.*

OLIVER GOLDSMITH (1730–1774)

∽ ↶

This collection has only been made possible by the amazing
generosity of the writers who have contributed to it, and I must
start with a huge thank-you to each and every one of you. This is
the first charity anthology I have been involved in compiling and
I was thrilled that you all agreed to be part of this project so
readily and without hesitation. You are all busy people   who
constantly work under the pressure of deadlines, yet you added
one more thing to your already long to-do lists and selflessly gave
of your time and talent to produce an incredible array of funny,

poignant, topical and heartfelt pieces for *The Big Book of HOPE* that made me laugh and cry – I enjoyed every one.

A huge thank-you too, to Sarah Webb, whose advice many years ago to 'just keep writing' set me on track when I first put pen to paper. Her expertise and experience have been invaluable on many of the projects I have undertaken, and most particularly on this book. We originally met through a mutual friend when I was organising a fundraiser for the earthquake in Afghanistan, and she has been a good friend and constant support ever since. I'm delighted that I can say an official 'Thank you'!

Thanks must go to Paula Campbell and the team at Poolbeg for their unhesitating support of this project from the moment I got in touch to discuss it. Paula saw our vision for the book from the get-go and both herself and editor Gaye Shortland have put huge work into getting it to you, the reader, in the shortest possible time.

I became involved with *The Big Book of HOPE* one spring day back in 2009 when Hazel Larkin telephoned me with an idea for an anthology and a brilliant title. She had been in regular contact with Inkwell and the Inkwell community through the monthly newsletter and knew that to make the idea work the book needed writers – and a publisher. She wondered if I could help.

A writer and journalist whose two beautiful girls are half Indian, Hazel lived and worked in Asia for many years and is passionate about the work of HOPE. Her enthusiasm is infectious and I didn't hesitate to agree! Discussing the project, we realised that we wanted to produce a book that reflected HOPE's varied work, the many different types of people – old and young – that the HOPE Foundation helps; and that we wanted it to be as inspirational for you, the reader, as HOPE is to the children it touches. After one conversation *The Big Book of HOPE*, as you hold it today, was already taking shape. Hazel has put huge work into drawing this collection together and taking it from an idea to a finished manuscript. She is a fantastic ambassador for HOPE.

Preface

Bringing together fiction and non-fiction from some of Ireland's top writers and media personalities, we hope that there is something for everyone in this collection, that it will be a book that you can enjoy yourself or give as a gift, that you will dip into it regularly, finding something new every time. Most importantly, when you buy this book, you will be directly helping the street children of Kolkata. On their behalf, thank you.

Vanessa O'Loughlin
www.writing.ie
www.inkwellwriters.ie

Introduction

The Beginnings of HOPE

A Sister from the Medical Missionaries of Mary, who came to my school when I was fifteen, sowed the seeds that were later to blossom into The HOPE Foundation. I was inspired by her and her stories of children and communities living in places I would have been hard set to find on a map. The idea that one person could make such a huge difference to so many really captured my imagination – and I was convinced that I could be such a person.

As a result of this Sister's visit to my school, I applied immediately to an NGO (Non Governmental Organisation) called Viatores Christi, stating my desire to work with them as a volunteer. Needless to say, my application was gently rejected, but this desire to help was never far from the surface. I believed, even then, that the opportunity to help others was both a duty and a privilege. That belief is still with me.

The early years of my involvement in development work were spent fundraising here in Ireland. I must confess that it went into overdrive when I decided to support my sister Ber, who spent a year in Ethiopia with GOAL in the mid-1980s. At that time my children – Robin, Louise and Ricky – were still at school – and there was no way I was going to abandon them to travel overseas as a volunteer!

In the late 1980s, my husband Dick and I were lucky enough to have been in a position to holiday in South Africa and Swaziland.

While we were there, we went to visit refugee centres run by GOAL on the borders of Mozambique, where we witnessed firsthand the appalling horrors the Mozambican civil war visited upon that country's citizens. I knew, after that visit, that I was definitely prepared to make a life-long commitment to helping the world's poor. It was now time to start figuring out how exactly to go about making that intention a reality.

My first stop was University College Cork, where I enrolled as a mature student and earned a Diploma in Development Studies. I knew that a desire to do good wasn't enough and I needed to gain more knowledge about development work.

Once I had a broad understanding of the issues surrounding the area, I felt more prepared to roll up my sleeves and get started. Additionally, my own children had – very considerately – grown up and were old enough to be able to survive for a while without me! My first overseas volunteer assignment was with GOAL in war-torn Somalia in the early 1990s, where I worked in a feeding centre with 2,000 children. Gunfire, shootings, starvation and death were part of daily life there. In the feeding centre, two other Irish volunteers and I narrowly escaped being shot in the middle of a raid on food just outside the centre. That experience was terrifying – and gave me some insight into the sufferings that the people in Somalia had grown to expect in their everyday lives.

I loved feeling that I was making a difference in Somalia, but I always had a sense that I was – that we were – not making enough of a difference. Still, I reminded myself on a daily basis that 'you can only do what you can do'. I still believe that. If I had managed to save or change only one life, my efforts would have been worthwhile. Every person, every life, is precious. At the same time, my work in Somalia was tinged with great sadness at the loss of so many lives due to war and the famine caused, in part, by that war. Holding a bony, fragile little baby who is dying of starvation is heartbreaking beyond words. Looking into the eyes of children dying of starvation is a terrible thing – children whose energy is so depleted that they do not swat at the flies swarming around, and who do not cry simply because their bodies are no longer capable of producing tears. Hunger does not wait for tomorrow, when people need food today.

Two years after my time in Somalia, I went to work in a refugee camp in Goma in the Congo, just over the border from Rwanda. The camp I worked in had 350,000 refugees who were seeking sanctuary, fleeing Rwanda and the worst genocide since World War II. A million people were brutally slaughtered – most of them hacked to death with machetes. The suffering of the people was unbearable and the stories of what happened to their loved ones are almost too painful to recall, even now. The mass graves where we went to pray will always remain etched in my mind. As will the image of a bulldozer just dumping the bodies of men, women and children into a pit – on top of the decomposing bodies that were already buried there.

It was a visit to Kolkata – formerly known as Calcutta – in India that proved to be the life-changing experience that led me to the work I am involved in today. I met the late Mother Teresa on that visit in 1993, and she had a huge impact on me.

It was on my return visit to Kolkata, accompanied by my daughter Louise, in 1999, that I decided to spearhead the setting up of a new organisation. Of course, there is no way that you can judge the suffering of one group of people as 'more' than the suffering of another; nor can you decide that a certain group of people 'deserve' your help more than another group, but there was something about Kolkata – and the fate of the thousands of street children there – that grabbed my heartstrings and pulled.

Nearly a quarter of a million street children in Kolkata try to survive against all odds in putrid squalor, sifting through mountains of refuse in the rubbish dumps in order to eke out a living for themselves and their families. These children exist in total abject poverty. To see this, relentlessly, every day of my six weeks there was utterly heartbreaking. More heartbreaking was the knowledge that, though I was free to leave, these children – like their parents before them – had no such freedom. They had no choice. They had no hope.

Instinctively, I knew that I could help make a real, positive difference by concentrating my efforts on this one city and her hundreds of thousands of street children. Instinctively, I knew that I could give these children the hope they needed – the hope they deserved.

Obviously, the first thing homeless children need is a home. So, when I got back to Cork from that second trip, I set about raising funds for the first HOPE home. The target figure was £40,000 – the running costs of a home for twelve months. This initial funding was raised by holding an auction in Cork and by approaching friends, family and local businesses, asking for their help.

Of course, my experience and my education in the area meant I was aware that there was only so much I could engineer in Ireland. I needed an Indian partner, and I found one in the form of Geeta Venkadakrishnan. Geeta was invaluable – before The HOPE Foundation came into being, she had worked for another NGO. This meant that she was an old hand, so to speak, and knew the ins and outs of setting up such an organisation in India. She introduced me to a lawyer and other wonderful, helpful people who were instrumental in helping to get The HOPE Foundation up and running.

Although I am, perhaps, the 'face' of HOPE, I must stress that I didn't set the foundation up on my own. I couldn't possibly have. It took vision and passion and hard work on behalf of many people to set the foundation up – and to keep it going. None of the great work of The HOPE Foundation could have been achieved without the hard-working and dedicated HOPE team of staff and volunteers in Ireland, India, the UK and Germany and of course the phenomenal generosity of the people of Ireland who have built HOPE into what it is today.

Since its establishment, The HOPE Foundation's battle against child labour and child trafficking has highlighted the unbearable suffering that the children of Kolkata have to endure. The organisation has successfully rescued thousands of children from a life of misery. HOPE now also operates as a registered charity in the UK and Germany, and has two offices in Kolkata. Together with our local Indian partner groups, and thanks to the support of the public and the Irish government, HOPE now funds and operates over 60 projects in Kolkata, working with street and slum children, their families and communities.

Projects range across the areas of shelter, healthcare, education, vocational training, child protection, anti-trafficking, anti-child-labour and child rights advocacy. The projects include eight child-protection homes, a children's hospital, an HIV/AIDS hospice and a drug-rehabilitation centre for children and teenagers. Other services, such as HOPE's primary healthcare programme's mobile clinics and Night Watch emergency-rescue project, extend across vast areas of the city and reach out to thousands who have no access to state services.

On my visit to India in 1993, I had worked in the southern state of Maharashtra, where an earthquake destroyed a huge area and many thousands of people were killed. In more recent years, when two great disasters hit India, an earthquake in Gujarat in 2001 and the 2004 tsunami which hit Tamil Nadu, HOPE was involved in the emergency responses. Initially, HOPE took care of the immediate needs of the victims of these disasters and, in the longer term, helped to rebuild people's homes and restore their livelihoods.

One of my most positive memories of Tamil Nadu is of handing over fishing boats to local fishermen: boats which had been bought by funds raised in Ireland. Naturally, there was some trepidation on the part of these fishermen at the thoughts of returning to sea. To encourage them, my sister Jenny (who is HOPE's Overseas Director) and I went with them on that first post-tsunami fishing trip. It was truly an inspiring day, and the joy of these fishermen when they first went back to sea in their new boats is forever etched in my heart.

For me, this work is a labour of love, so I work on a voluntary basis – depending on my long-suffering husband, Dick, for support. I regard my life as privileged and I feel very honoured to have been given an opportunity to serve the poorest of the poor in the developing world, most especially the children. I'm afraid I abandon Dick, my children, my beloved grandchildren and my home in East Cork every year for four months to work on HOPE's projects in Kolkata. It is my second home and the children are part of my extended family. I have seen the older girls Shoba, Parveen, Mongola and Babali grow up into beautiful, educated young ladies making their way in the world.

When I am in Kolkata I like to stay in the Panditya home, one of the HOPE girls' protection homes. I love spending time with the children that I adore, and watching them all grow up to be well-adjusted adults – though I must admit that sharing a bathroom with twenty girls every morning can be quite a challenge!

The responsibility of ensuring the smooth running of The HOPE Foundation is sometimes overwhelming. When the end of the financial year comes, I give a big sigh of relief that we have met all our commitments and I brace myself as we start all over again with the fundraising for the following year. Most of my adult life has been dedicated to caring and sharing with others. Of course, to my mind, this is a normal way of living – I am, after all, one of twelve children. My journey with HOPE is hugely rewarding, as so many lives have been saved and thousands of children are being educated and I know that they will have a secure future.

The greatest heartbreak but also the greatest joy in my work with the poorest of the poor has been among the street children of Kolkata – I know that I can never abandon them. While there are 250,000 street children in Kolkata, The HOPE Foundation will have 250,000 reasons to exist.

I think that this quotation from George Bernard Shaw sums up my attitude to my life:

'I am of the opinion that my life belongs to the whole community and as long as I live, it is my privilege to do for it whatever I can. I want to be thoroughly used up when I die, for the harder I work the more I live. I rejoice in life for its own sake. Life is no brief candle to me. It is a sort of splendid torch which I've got to hold up for the moment and I want it to burn as brightly as possible before handing it on to future generations.'

Introduction

I want to sincerely thank each and every one of you for your support, it could not have happened without you. HOPE is ours; we share its journey, its joys and its sorrows and we stand together to witness the changes in our society.

The book that you are holding in your hands is a reflection of huge generosity: the generosity of those who have cared enough to buy it, and the generosity of those who contributed to it. Well-known, talented people from all walks of life – politicians, journalists, novelists, broadcasters, artists and businesspeople – generously and selflessly gave of their time and talents to each write a piece for this book. They did so because they, too, were touched by the plight of the babies who are born on the pavements and in the slums of Kolkata. They did so because they wanted to contribute to the housing, feeding, education, protection and health of thousands of innocent children in the teeming city of Kolkata. Each piece in this book holds 'Hope' as its central theme, and is a wonderful testament to the power of hope. It is hope, after all, that keeps us all going.

Maureen Forrest
Honorary Director, The HOPE Foundation

A Life in the Day

Mariam Laskar, sex worker

*Mariam Laskar, 42, a sex worker in Kalighat,
the poorest red-light district in Calcutta*

I wake up around 5am so I can use the latrine early, while it's still quiet. I share it with nine other households. Each has one room about 8ft square. Although Kalighat is a red-light district, families live here too, street vendors and stall workers, but most prostitutes live alone like me.

My room doesn't smell so good because it's next to rotting rubbish and the latrine, but it is away from the street.

I go back to sleep until 8. My bed is a thin mattress on a board lifted off the ground by red bricks at each corner. Under the bed are the pots I use for cooking and washing.

My saris and underclothes are strung on a wire across the small window. I have electricity, a light bulb, a fan, a black-and-white television and a suitcase.

If I'm on my own, as I mostly am, I make tea, heating the water on a kerosene stove in my doorway. If my babu – he's like a special client, a temporary husband, you could say – is with me, I give him naan bread and sweets. Calcutta is famous for its sweets: all colours and varieties you can buy here.

Then I go to the vegetable stalls outside and buy ladies' fingers, brinjal, potatoes, tomatoes and garlic to cook later.

I put on eyeliner, a bindi on my forehead, my jewelled earrings and gold bangles, and I am working the street by 10am. There are three of us who mostly go together – Arati, my best friend, and I watch for each other. I work a little strip just outside the slum beside the Mohambagam football club.

There is a disused pitch and that's where I go with my clients. Mostly they are strangers, rickshaw drivers or hawkers.

Kalighat is the cheapest red-light district, but I have to work here because I'm old now. I need to make 250 rupees a day [about £3.50]; my rent is 45 rupees a day and I am paying off a loan to my landlord for hospital treatment. My clients don't have much money – maybe I get 50 rupees a time. I try to make them wear a condom but mostly they don't. I have been very lucky: I don't think I have any sexual diseases. There is a clinic in Kalighat run by The HOPE Foundation for us. I go a few times each year.

When I was young I worked on a jetty on the Ganges – they call it Babughat. I would go with men on boats they rent. Then I would have 10 or 12 clients a day easily, shopkeepers or truck drivers, and each would pay me 250 rupees.

My own family in Bangladesh has no idea if I am alive or dead. I grew up in a small village with three older brothers and a baby sister.

I was trafficked here when I was 14 by a man who married me. His real wife and children were here in Calcutta, and he brought me here. He sold me to a brothel. I was terrified, but he was my husband and I thought I had to do what he said. I did not have the guts to tell my family what had happened to me, so I never contacted them again.

If I'm lucky I finish around 9.30. There is a lot of waiting around now, so we drink Bangla liquor, a strong illegal drink they sell on the streets. I drink it quite a lot – it helps. If I have made enough money I go home with Arati, and maybe we go to my room or her room and share some food. But if business is slow I stay out all night.

Even if I finish early, I can't sleep until 2 in the morning. I worry about so many things. I have had six pregnancies, but I only have one child, Sheila Khatoon. She's 14 now and she lives in a girls' home run by The HOPE Foundation. I visit her on the last Saturday of every month. I tell her I sweep in a hospital, and I wish I did, but no one would employ me now. She lived with me until she was seven.

She didn't go to school and I couldn't really look after her, but I didn't bring men back to the room with her there. Then The HOPE Foundation found her on the street. I wanted them to take her. If my daughter was to take up this trade, I would want to die. No mother can imagine such a thing as this. But she would have had no choice if she'd stayed here.

At night I think of my parents and my daughter. I think of what would happen to her if I died suddenly. I worry about how I got myself into this situation and what will happen to me in the future when I cannot make money any more. Around 2am I fall asleep, and then I don't dream.

Interview: Andrea Catherwood

Andrea Catherwood is the UK ambassador for
The HOPE Foundation
(First published in *The Sunday Times*, May 17, 2009)

Ivy Bannister

Ivy Bannister is the author of *Magician*, *Blunt Trauma* and *Vinegar and Spit*. Her plays have been produced on stage and radio in Ireland, the UK and Germany, including *The Wilde Circus Show*. Her radio credits include fifty contributions to RTÉ's *Sunday Miscellany*. She has won the Hennessy Award, the Francis MacManus Award and the OZ Whitehead Award, among others. Ivy lives in Dublin and New York.

Love *

Ivy Bannister

Fintan and I are on the floor. Around us is a sea of legs, the round, plump legs of children playing the violin. I am holding Fintan from behind, gripping him tightly with both arms and knees, to prevent his limbs from flailing out. His head twitches. The children with their violins pay us no mind. They are accustomed to Fintan and me. Besides, they are absorbed by their music, the remarkable music. It's a concerto by Vivaldi, and they are playing it on their half-sized violins. Their bright eyes watch the teacher. Their fingers fly, and their bows move in confident unison.

Inside my grip, Fintan grunts and thrashes. My torso sways, rocking in time to the Vivaldi. I hum softly in his ear. Bit by bit, he loosens up and grows still.

The children end the concerto with a flourish. The other mothers applaud from their chairs along the walls. The teacher smiles. The children tuck their violins into rest position, and bow. The lesson is over.

I am still on the floor with Fintan, but my knees and arms have gone slack. The little episode has worked its way through, and Fintan is himself again. He claps his hands slowly and deliberately, copying the adults. He beams, sunny as a baby, forever my first-born.

In a couple of weeks, he will be sixteen.

Where love is deep, much will be accomplished. These words are always in my head. They are the words of Dr Suzuki, the gifted

Japanese *sensei* – or teacher – who believed that all children have music within them. If they are taught with love, Dr Suzuki said, they will learn to play; and these splendid young violinists are the proof of the *sensei*'s method.

We come to this violin course every summer, my children and I. We descend upon Kilteen, a backwater in County Limerick, where children arrive from all over Ireland to play music together for a week. We do not make this pilgrimage for Fintan's sake because, of course, he does not play the violin. No, we come for the twins – my daughters, Fintan's sisters. Rachel and Rebecca are eleven years old and the mirror image of one another. They are accomplished players both, on intimate terms with the works of Dvořák and Boccherini and Handel.

I could leave Fintan at home in Dublin, sharing him out between my mother and the rota of carers, who help us when the need arises. My husband, too, is willing to take the time off work if necessary. But I refuse to leave Fintan behind.

My husband says, 'You don't trust us. You don't believe that anyone else can look after Fintan as well as you can.'

'That's not it,' I say, shaking my head, although it's true that no one understands Fintan as well as I do. 'It's the music,' I say. 'Fintan wants to be surrounded by music.'

'Mummy loves Fintan most,' Rachel says, with a petulant jut to her chin. 'He is her favourite.'

'Yeah,' Rebecca says.

'Don't be silly,' I laugh. 'You are all three my favourites.' And that's true too . . . in a way.

For I don't doubt that I love my children equally. However I know – deep down inside myself – that Fintan alone has been the momentous event of my life. Most women can count a string of significant happenings in their lives: the meeting of a partner; the birth of each child; the advent of one professional opportunity or another. But my life has been defined mostly by the fluke of an extra chromosome. For me there was life before Fintan, and there is life with Fintan. Nothing has changed the texture of my days like this one thing, a chromosome too small to be visible to the eye.

During the break, we sit in the corridor, Fintan and I. Bursting with energy, Rachel and Rebecca drop their violins at our feet and take off. They run, skip and jump up and down the narrow length. It's as if they can't bear to be still, as if their every muscle must be moved. I see how the other mothers watch them. The fact is that my girls are dazzling to watch. Partly it's their hair, which is a particular shade of blond, so light as to be almost white. And partly it's because there are the two of them. Either one would be a picture on her own, but to have the pair of them together is pure magic, the ideal of childhood with its freshness and potential.

They look so beautiful in their white shorts and pale green tunics that my eyes fill with tears.

'Swallow,' I say abruptly to Fintan. 'Wipe your face with your handkerchief.'

Obligingly, Fintan mops at his chin, which gleams with dribble.

The fact is that sometimes I almost hate my twins. They are too perfect. They are too lithe, too well made, too pretty. They are so perfect that it breaks my heart. If only they could be less, and Fintan more. If it were in my power, I would coarsen their features, muddy their hair, diminish their talents to make Fintan better. I would choose three ordinary children, three children the equals of one another. I'm sure I would.

Would I?

Someone has given Fintan a name-tag, just as if he too were enrolled in the course. He fingers it proudly. 'Fintan,' he says out loud, tracing his finger around its plastic edge. 'Fintan.'

The children who travel to Kilteen are special. The music seems to ennoble them, make them more sensitive. There's no mockery here, no graphic imitations of Fintan's waddling walk or slow speech, none of the ignorant stuff that we get at home, that cuts me to the quick.

Fintan himself never registers the cruelties of others. He is too good. In fact, he is the best of children. He doesn't drink, shoplift or experiment with drugs. There is never any difficulty with him at all, except for his little turns, his seizures. What's more, I always know where Fintan is, which is more than any of my friends can boast about their teenaged sons.

Fintan follows me into the next class obediently. He holds my hand.

The teacher is working on a piece by Bach, part of a double concerto, which the twins adore.

'My turn,' the teacher says, then plays an intricate phrase on her violin. 'Your turn,' she says, and the children echo it competently.

The music sweeps me up and dazzles me. Four hundred years, I marvel. People have been playing these notes for four hundred years. I share this information with Fintan, whispering it into his ear.

'What?' he says.

'Four hundred years,' I repeat softly, squeezing his hand.

He squeezes mine back. Then his hand strays dangerously towards his lower parts.

Quickly, I hand him the scrap of cloth that I always carry in my bag.

He latches onto it eagerly. It's part of an old, silky tie of his father's, and Fintan loves it. He weaves it between his fingers, pulling it through them, again and again. It keeps him happily occupied for hours.

I listen to the music and I watch him. I love his gentle face and his stubby hands. I love the round moons of his nails, and his fat, soft lips. I love his flat nose and his almond-shaped eyes. I know what there is to know about this boy. I can catalogue the litany of his likes and his dislikes better than I can my own. I know that he likes ducks and teals and snow geese and cormorants, and all the birds that live near the water. I understand that robins leave him cold and that chickens frighten him. I remember the infinite hours we've passed together near ponds, rivers and the sea. Once upon a time, the girls came willingly with us. Later I had to bribe them with the promise of chips. Now they dig in their heels and stay at home. Now it's just Fintan and me, hand in hand, looking for ducks.

And I love it. For I have learned to watch with him, to marvel at the sheen of a feather, to wonder at the whirr of wings.

Fintan's head is bent towards the music. Can it be that he's tugging the tie through his fingers in time to the Bach? I am right about the music, I know I am. It settles him. He will have no more fits today, no more turns.

Perhaps I watch Fintan too closely. Perhaps I love him too much, understand him too well. Who knows? But what else can I do?

At lunch the children sit at one table, and the mothers at another, only Fintan sits beside me. The air is filled with talk: the cacophony of children; the banter of lively women. I nod and smile, to all intents part of the happy, gossipy crowd.

Only Fintan alone says nothing. He is absorbed by the business of eating his sausages. He is proud of how well he manages knife and fork, how exactly he cuts the sausages. But as I nod and smile and natter, my mind strays to a dark place. For just as I know that there was life before Fintan and life with Fintan, I understand that nothing stays the same. I realise that sooner or later, there must be life after Fintan; and it's a thought that fills me with terror.

In the afternoon, there is a concert. A tot with glasses plays a creditable minuet; she couldn't be more than six years of age. The twins are next. They tackle the Bach double concerto with panache. It's their party piece, the joke being that they keep switching parts. Everyone laughs, and the applause is enthusiastic.

'You must be very proud of your girls,' the woman sitting next to me says.

And I am. When they grow up, the world will open its arms to receive my daughters. No matter what they choose to do, their future looks good. But I am proud of my son as well. And what can the future hold for him?

I see him, my son Fintan, sitting on his own in the corridor, dragging the silky tie back and forth through his fingers. The tot comes along, the one with the glasses who played the minuet. 'Why are you always playing with that rag?' she says.

He looks away, avoiding eye contact.

11

But she grabs the tie. She hands him her violin instead. 'Take it,' she says.

'No.'

'Yes.' Gently, as if he were a big doll, the small child arranges the violin on my son's shoulder. She moves his chin into place and places the tiny bow into his hand.

My heart flutters.

'My turn,' the child says, then tugs at his arm so that the bow shudders down the string.

'Good boy,' she says. 'Now your turn.'

Fintan looks around desperately. But he can't see me, concealed as I am in a doorway.

'Play,' the child says.

Fintan bites his lip. Suddenly, he pulls at the bow. It jerks and groans down the string, a definite sound. Fintan's face stretches into a slow smile. Then he tries it again.

'Good boy,' the child says, and scampers away.

Love, I think. *Where love is deep, much will be accomplished.*

Alex Barclay

Alex Barclay is the author of three bestselling crime novels, *Darkhouse*, *The Caller* and *Blood Runs Cold* which won the Ireland AM Crime Fiction Award in 2009. Her fourth novel, *Time of Death* was published in August, 2010. Her work has been translated into eighteen languages.

Calloway Hart and the Town of Sable Forge *

Alex Barclay

You did not live in the town of Sable Forge, you fell victim to it. It had staggered through the last of the Montana mining boom and lay heaving for breath ever since, cobbled together from its broken parts, an off-centre axis to vast and lonely ranches.

The people of Sable Forge were all mismatched body parts, hair going the wrong way to strange places and minds going no further than they had to. Main Street had all the stores it needed and the corner bar where I first saw Calloway Hart. It was summer 1949. He was twenty-seven years old, a giant on a bar stool. He had umber skin and green eyes, hair that was once fair, but had darkened. He wore a blue denim work shirt and canvas pants, battered steel-capped boots and a gold signet ring. It was two in the morning and he was telling the story of his life's dead end. Calloway Hart had chosen the tree he would swing from. 'In the prettiest corner of Sable Forge,' he said. 'A strong tree . . . able to take the weight of me.'

The silence that followed was of men weary of Calloway Hart and his plangent youth. They leaned against the bar with their bottled beer and whiskey, their faces lined by harder stories than his. Calloway Hart put down his glass and walked past me through the door, trailing the smell of dead fires. He was a smokejumper, a man who earned his living parachuting into wildfires, fighting back flames.

Every Friday night in this bar, in this new town I had come to, I would watch him start his evening quietly hunched over his drink. He

15

would look out from under his brow and, like a fly, his eyes would settle on you until you felt them. Then they would be back on his bourbon: hot water and grain, no less than fifty-one per cent corn.

As the night stretched on, Calloway Hart would unfold his pain as he unfolded his body, eventually sitting up straight and proud, only to tell us again how he wanted to die. '*And* you can leave me there, and who would give a good goddamn, anyway?' he would finish, his eyes swimming.

Calloway Hart had a dry mother and a drinking father – all his life, his home lay between the height of a pure blue sky and the blind depths of a raging fire. At eighteen, he left Sable Forge, a tragic consequence of his parents' ruptured spirits. He laboured on ranches across the mid-West before he went to war in Europe to battle his enemies and his past. He returned to Sable Forge at the war's end and before he had walked the length of Main Street, he was bereft of the comfort of turmoil. Within days, he hitched a ride to a smokejumper base in Missoula that was trading conscientious objectors for veterans.

The second time I saw Calloway Hart, he staggered toward me in a dance hall. He grabbed my wrist and jerked me close. He moved his hands to my waist, raising me off the floor and drawing circles with me around the room.

'You're like a doll,' he said, as he knocked me against the other dancers and we stumbled and he caught me just as I was about to fall. I stood before him, my head spinning, then walked away, leaving him red and sweating. Later and drunker, he tried to apologise and I tried to accept it. When I passed him on the street the next day, he kept his head down.

Oh, handsome Calloway Hart with looks to hide your fears, then drink to drown them in.

The following Friday night, he retreated into his bourbon and his pity-turned-inward. After weeks of listening to him, 'Why haven't you just done it?' I said. It would have stayed under my breath if my breath wasn't laced with gin. Calloway Hart turned my way.

'You have the right job,' I said. 'You could steer that parachute a couple feet closer . . .' The quieter he stayed, the more I wanted to talk. 'Or is it the tree?' I said. 'Is it a special tree, the one you talk about?' I could feel my eyes alight.

'If I don't like the way I live, why would I want to die that way?' he said.

Not long after, a wildfire raged across a forest of lodge pole pines fifty miles west of Sable Forge, and Calloway Hart was gone. The bar was a quieter place that Friday. I wondered if somewhere in a damp, smoking forest, Calloway Hart lay dead. And by the end of the night and the last of my gin, wondering had turned to fearing. So when the doors of the bar closed behind me, I walked one mile by moonlight to Calloway Hart's ranch. I saw his mailbox, white letters on green. I made my way up the long, dusty drive. The house was simple, timber-framed, as unvarnished as its owner. A breeze rushed through the trees and wrapped my cotton skirt around my thighs, whipping my hair into the wind, bringing me a little closer to my senses. Somewhere out back, a horse whinnied. I turned and walked home, wondering what the town tale-tellers would say of the woman who provoked Calloway Hart to his death.

I saw him the next morning in the doorway of the grocery store with a length of laid rope coiled and hanging from his shoulder. I watched as he slung it into the back of his pick-up.

The following week, a stranger moved in beside Calloway Hart at the bar, a man from Alaska who had never known the heat of a Montana night. And the barman said Calloway Hart jumps right into flames and could he imagine from his home in the ice and the snow what that would feel like and the stranger said no he could not and the barman said to ask Calloway Hart. In an instant, the heat we all felt was the heat of Calloway Hart's anger. But the stranger did not know him like we did and he turned to him.

'In the middle of all that destruction, is there anything good to be found?' he said.

Calloway Hart was still. And when we thought that no answer would come, he looked at the man. 'When I am falling, the sky and the earth are revolving all around me and I am engulfed. Not by the flames, but by the beauty. Green and blue beauty.'

Then I saw Calloway Hart smile – an extraordinary, beautiful, salvaged smile. And I was gone; with him, wherever he was.

'It's a brave job for any young man,' said the Alaskan.

'It's not brave,' said Calloway Hart.

'Oh, I don't know–' said the man.

'Yeah,' said Calloway Hart. 'You don't.'

Silence throbbed in the bar-room.

'Well, to you, maybe it's a vocation,' said the man.

'A vacation?' said Calloway Hart. 'A vacation?'

'I said vocation, sir.'

Calloway Hart had already risen to his feet when he was tripped up by a word. But a word couldn't hold him back. He lunged for this stranger, pushing his chest, sending him staggering backwards against the pool table, snapping his head off the lampshade that overhung it. Yellow light rocked back and forth across the tense faces at the bar, coming to rest on Calloway Hart, one leg forward, one fist back. The man, smaller by a foot, moved toward him and hit him clean on the jaw, sending him down so quickly he did not have a chance to make a sound. Then he was on him again, dragging Calloway Hart up by the throat, raining down blows, using the drunk man's leaden weight against him.

Calloway Hart waited until the man had gone before he stood up to order another bourbon. And more. And soon we heard again about the rope he would buy and the knot he would tie. When he left, the old men shook their heads. It was as far as they would go to acknowledge his young, damaged spirit.

'What happened to him?' I said.

And I was met with silence. Until one of the men from the bar followed me to the door and told me to stay away from Calloway Hart and told me why.

Later that night, I stood at my kitchen window in the childhood home of Calloway Hart, looking through the cracked windowpane where his father had slammed his mother's head over and over until the glass turned red. I could see into the darkness where Calloway Hart, nine years old, had jumped barefoot from the swing, leaving it dancing, empty and wild, behind him as he ran to her side. I imagined the motion of the ropes dying slowly along with her.

When another Friday night came, I watched the man who gambled with fire and, against all reason, I hoped for his smile. But I did not see one before he left. And I left soon after. I pulled the door of the bar behind me and stepped into a man's ashen shadow. I breathed dead fires. And on dark, dry Main Street, Sable Forge, I was dissolved by hot water, grain and no less than fifty-one per cent corn as Calloway Hart kissed me everywhere without his mouth ever leaving my lips.

Later on his wrought-iron bed, he undressed me; huge hands on tiny buttons. With his eyes closed, he called me beautiful.

'I understand why you do what you do,' I said afterwards. 'And why.'

'Do you?' he said.

'Yes.'

He turned his back to me. 'You think too much.'

In the morning, he looked at me, fighting back flames.

Oh, callow heart.

Two weeks later, drunk and lost, Calloway Hart stopped me on the street and told me that he loved me, that I was the only person who could save him. One week later, he told me that he should love me

19

but he did not. And then, that he loved someone else, someone who didn't look at him so close.

Oh, Calloway Hart, you can no more capture your thoughts than the shore can capture the waves.

One more wildfire took Calloway Hart away. He was burnt over – out-run by the flames. He fought, they said. He fought hard.

For months afterwards, I stood at my kitchen window, tracing the darkest verge of the cornfield, drawn to the shadows cast by a rutted trunk and its rope-scored boughs, following them back to the disturbed ground underneath. Until, finally, Calloway Hart dissolved into the earth and the breathing roots of his chosen tree.

Each spring, its flying seeds carry more of him away, planting him all across Sable Forge. And when the rain falls, torrents of silted earth spread his pain, and mine, still further.

∽ ∾

Senator Ivana Bacik

Ivana Bacik is an Irish politician, practising barrister and academic. She has been Reid Professor of Criminal Law at Trinity College Dublin (a position previously held by Presidents Robinson and McAleese) since 1996. As a writer, Ivana contributes regularly to both *The Irish Times* and *The Irish Independent*. She has also written and contributed to leading Irish criminological texts and has quite a high media profile, often being asked to contribute to radio and television programmes on pertinent issues of the day.

The XX-Factor **

Senator Ivana Bacik

When Barack Obama was elected as President of the US, a defining aspect of his campaign was the focus upon the theme of 'hope'. At a bleak economic time, his candidacy represented hope for the many thousands of voters who put their trust and faith in him as their leader.

Here in Ireland, we too are facing a bleak economic future, with more pay cuts and job losses looming across both private and public sectors. Everywhere, people are looking for answers. How can politics be changed to achieve greater hope for us all?

There is one key change that I believe could create a more hopeful type of politics. That is, an increase in the numbers of women active in our political system. At present, Ireland has an appalling record on women's political participation. Women account for more than half of the Irish population, yet the proportion of women TDs has never exceeded 14 per cent. In fact, over recent years, Ireland's rate of women's political representation has actually worsened. In 1990, Ireland was in 37th position in the world classification of women's representation in national parliaments. However, by October 2009 Ireland had fallen to 84th position, with only 23 women TDs out of 166 (13.8%).

This means that our democracy is not truly representative, and there is widespread public support for changing the status quo. Since my election as a Senator in 2007, one of my key campaign priorities has been to try and increase the numbers of women in politics.

With this in mind, in December 2008 I organised an event in Leinster House to commemorate the 90th anniversary of Constance Markievicz's election in the 1918 general election, the first in which women had the right to vote. I invited all living former and current women members of the Oireachtas, 80 in total, to take up seats in the Dáil chamber; a powerful way of celebrating the women elected, but also of showing how few women have ever been elected in our nation's history. The photograph, displayed on the Oireachtas website, represents the only time that the Dáil chamber has ever been half full of women!

The 'Oireachtas Women 1918–2008' event was a day of great hope, joy and celebration. I am very happy to say that among the former women Oireachtas members who gathered that day was Nuala Fennell, who very sadly died subsequently.

Other women present on the day included former Clann na Poblachta TD Kathleen O'Connor (now Fitzgerald), who won her Kerry North seat in a 1956 by-election; former TD Eileen Lemass, the daughter-in-law of Sean Lemass, who was first elected in 1977; and Máire Geoghegan-Quinn, who became in 1979 the first woman Cabinet Minister since Constance Markievicz.

Following the success of this event, in April 2009 I got the agreement of the Joint Oireachtas Justice Committee, of which I am a member, to establish a Sub-Committee on Women's Participation in Politics. As Rapporteur to the Sub-Committee, I drafted a report which was adopted by the Joint Committee, with overwhelming cross-party support. The report was launched on 5 November 2009, and its recommendations were debated in the Seanad in April and May 2010. I am hopeful that they will ultimately be adopted by the government.

The first task of the report was to examine the challenges facing women on entry into politics; we summarised these under five headings (the 'five C's'):

- Childcare
- Cash
- Confidence
- Culture
- Candidate selection procedures

The report makes a series of recommendations aimed at addressing each of these challenges. First, under the 'childcare' heading, we found that the 'long hours' culture in politics discourages women from being more politically active. We recommended that family caring responsibilities should be accommodated, both for men and women in politics.

Under the 'cash' heading, we found lack of resources to be another major factor inhibiting women's progress. We recommended, among other things, the establishment of a national fundraising campaign to finance women's electoral campaigns; and the provision of additional funds by political parties to support women candidates.

The third heading was that of 'confidence'. Women tend to lack sufficient self-belief to participate actively in political life, so we recommended that political parties should introduce recruitment drives to 'head-hunt' women in local areas; and that mentoring and leadership training programmes should be provided for aspiring candidates.

Under the 'culture' heading, we found that the 'overall masculine image of politics' remains as a powerful barrier for women. We recommended that specific steps be taken to encourage more girls and women into politics through civic education programmes, and the creation of a national data bank of potential women candidates.

Finally, the issue of candidate selection procedures within political parties has been identified as the single most important obstacle to women's political participation. The question is how best to reform these procedures to achieve increased numbers of women politicians.

Experience elsewhere in Europe, especially in Belgium and Spain, shows that legislative electoral quotas are the most effective models for change. Thus, we recommended that candidate quota legislation be adopted, to oblige each political party to impose a maximum limit on the proportion of candidates of any one gender selected to run in elections at local, national and European levels. Such legislation should be introduced on a temporary basis only, to provide that no party could have more than two-thirds of their candidates of one gender in the next general election.

Largely due to the economic recession, politics in Ireland has a very negative image currently. Changing our political system to make it more representative, and to give more women prominent roles in national governance, could only help in improving levels of hope for the future.

There is widespread concern about the low levels of women in Irish politics. Unless legislation is introduced to address this, Ireland will continue to languish at the bottom of the international league tables for women's representation, and our democracy will remain 'unfinished' – in a hopeless state. Indeed, I believe that there is no hope for achieving real change in Irish politics unless we act decisively to address the glaring democratic deficiency in our system of political representation: the lack of women.

Maeve Binchy

Maeve Binchy lives in Dalkey, Co. Dublin. She was a schoolteacher and journalist in *The Irish Times* and since 1983 has written novels, short stories and stage plays. Many of her books have been adapted as films. She is married to the writer and broadcaster Gordon Snell.

Hope *

Maeve Binchy

Brian was looking forward to his eighth birthday.

He thought he was going to get a bicycle.

'You'll never get a bicycle,' his friend, Milo, from next door said. 'They'd never let you have a bike.'

Brian was stung in defence of his mother and father.

'Yes, they would, they're mad about me,' he said.

'It's *because* they're mad about you they'll be afraid you'll break your neck or ride out under the wheels of a bus.' Milo was nine and he knew everything.

'I bet I *will* get a bike.' Brian was mutinous about it.

'Don't put too much hope in it. Hope is for losers,' Milo said and went off whistling.

Brian couldn't whistle properly, which annoyed him. But maybe when he was eight it would come to him naturally. When he was eight he might get picked for the team too. And by the time he was ten he could even be Man of the Match.

He noticed that his father was clearing out the garage, getting old, useless things like broken spades and hoes that had rusted all in a heap which he was going to take to the dump.

If *that* wasn't a sign that a bicycle was expected, then what was?

Indoors his mother had a little book about *Safety on the Roads*. Another hint.

She asked him questions about zebra crossings, and traffic

lights, simple things that he knew but obviously she was preparing herself for the day he set off on his own on his new bike.

'You know, Brian, the thing about life is everything changes, nothing stays the same,' she said.

'That's right,' said Brian. She was right. Of course things *would* change when he had a bike and would put on his helmet and cycle to school.

His father said unexpectedly in the garden to him, 'You do know, Brian, that whatever sort of a mess we made out of everything, the one thing we got right was you.'

Brian hadn't an idea what he meant.

'In what sort of way exactly?' he asked

'You're so good-tempered, so full of hope – you always have been.' His father seemed to have got a cold then as he started blowing his nose very loudly indeed.

'But isn't hope for losers?' Brian asked. That's what Milo had said.

Dad's cold had got worse.

'No, it's for winners,' he said eventually through the barks and the coughs.

Brian decided to check with his mother.

She was clearing out the food cupboard and marking things on labels with a felt pen.

Obvious things like *Flour* and *Sugar*, and *Sultanas*. Things you'd need to be mad not to know what they were.

'Why are you doing that, Mam?' he asked.

'Because you never know,' she said.

'Never know what, Mam?'

'Never know who might be opening up this place. You'd want them to be able to find things. Especially if they were foreign.' It was a mystery.

'Is hope for losers or for winners, Mam?' Brian asked, hoping for some insight.

'Depends,' his mother said. 'If you get what you hope for, then I suppose it's for winners. If you don't get what you hope for, then it's definitely for losers.'

No help there then.

There was going to be no party at home for Brian's birthday; it would be a visit to the cinema and then to get a burger. The burger place did ice-cream birthday cakes as well.

'Will there be any grown-ups?' Brian asked.

'Apart from me, no,' Mam said.

'And Dad of course.'

'No, your Dad is busy that day,' she said.

This was puzzling. Brian's birthday was on a Saturday.

'Is it true, Dad, that you're busy on my birthday?' he asked.

'Is that what she told you? That I was busy?'

'I think that's what she said but I'm not sure – she was talking about labelling everything in the food cupboard for foreigners as well, so maybe I got it wrong.'

Dad looked very grim.

'And what other pearls of wisdom had she got for you?'

'Nothing more.'

Brian didn't want to tell Dad that he had checked out with his mother about hope being for winners or losers.

'You took it up all wrong, Brian. It's not that I'm busy, it's just that we decided we'd do your birthday every second year. Remember last year your mam had to go away to your grandmother and so I took you all to the circus?'

Brian did remember but not clearly.

Anyway that didn't mean that Dad should stay away this year, did it?

Apparently it did.

'I don't know what it's all about,' Brian complained to Milo.

'Your dad has a fancy woman – a foreigner! – that's what it is.'

Milo, being nine, understood the whole world.

'But why would the foreign woman be looking into our kitchen cupboards?' Brian asked fearfully.

'When she comes to stay when she and your dad get custody of you, that's all.'

'What's custardy?' Brian asked.

31

'Don't be an eejit, Brian – they have to divide you from now on. That's what happens.' Milo had lost interest.

This was bad, very bad.

Brian had nobody else to ask.

He tried to remember what they had all said about hope. It was complicated.

Milo had said it was for losers, Dad had said it was for winners, Mam had said it all depended on how things turned out.

And it was impossible to know how things were going to turn out.

Mam went on cleaning things and labelling things, Dad was packing things in boxes.

Brian felt less sure about the bike.

He had thought they would give it to him together, but if they were going to divide him up as Milo said that made it very uncertain when he would get the bike at all.

Brian decided that he must speak about it.

So when they were having one of their silent Saturdays, a week before his birthday, he asked them straight out about what was bothering him.

'Could you tell me what "custardy" means?' he asked.

Normally they loved him to ask a question like that, showing an interest in words.

Not today.

They glared at each other.

'You had to go blabbing about it,' Mam said to Dad.

'You told him and you are a very bad person,' Dad said to Mam.

Brian looked at them wildly.

'Neither of you told me, Milo told me, but I don't know what it is, and I didn't want Milo to know that I didn't understand, so I couldn't ask him,' Brian said.

'Milo knows nothing,' Brian's dad said.

'But he's nine,' Brian said, astounded.

'He still knows nothing,' Mam said.

They sort of half-smiled at each other and that was a bit of an advance.

'There's another thing,' Brian said – bold now since the first question, even if it hadn't been actually answered, had made them more relaxed.

'Fire ahead,' Dad said.

'It's about the bike, next week – you see I was hoping that I could ride it round and round in front of you so that you'd see how good and careful I was and you wouldn't worry about my being under the wheels of a lorry or anything.'

Brian looked from one to the other to see how this was going down.

They were looking at each other properly, like friends.

'And where did you get the idea that you were getting a bike this year?' Mam asked.

'Because Dad was clearing out a space in the garage and you said that everything was going to change, and so I worked out that meant I was going to be riding the bike to and from school. What else could it have meant?'

Neither his mam nor dad said anything. Dad looked as if he was getting a cold again.

Mam looked as if she was going to cry.

Maybe they hadn't thought of a bicycle at all!

Possibly they didn't have the money.

Maybe there was too much going on with dividing Brian between them and custardy and cleaning garages and kitchen presses.

Or maybe it had something to do with hoping.

That had never been properly sorted out.

Brian wondered was he the only person in the whole world who didn't understand whether hope was great or silly.

And how would he ever find out?

'You see, nobody would tell me whether hope was good or bad, so I kept hoping for a bike. But maybe it was silly.'

And then something amazing happened.

They both put out their hands towards him at the same time.

It was like the old days before all this edgy business began.

'You must never give up on hope, Brian,' Mam said.

'Hope is the real winner, son,' Dad said.

And then they planned the delivery of the bike on Friday.

Brian was going to ask them what custardy meant.

But something stopped him.

Whatever it was, it didn't look as if it was something he had to face now.

Much easier to leave things as they were.

Sam Blake

Sam Blake is Vanessa O'Loughlin's pen name. Sam (like Vanessa!) is represented by Sheila Crowley, Curtis Brown, London.

Till Death Do Us Part *

Sam Blake

Katie Granger glanced anxiously over her shoulder, her finger hovering over the mouse. Mark had definitely said he'd be away all weekend, hadn't he? The door was firmly closed, the house locked up, the perimeter alarm activated. She'd checked everything before she came up. And she hadn't dared put the light on, had pulled the curtains tight in case the light from the computer screen was visible from outside. But all her precautions didn't stop fear playing up her spine like the high notes of a clarinet, didn't stop the whisper of his aftershave from setting her nerves on edge. *She shouldn't be here, shouldn't be in his study, shouldn't be checking his email.*

But what else could she do? Not knowing what he was really up to was eating her up. In the last year he'd become so secretive, spending so much time away from home, she just had to know if he was seeing someone else . . .

'I'll be back Monday night.' Mark had hardly looked at her as he'd tossed his black nylon holdall into the boot of his BMW on Friday morning.

'Who is it you're going to see?' Katie could hear the tension in her own voice, tried to hide it, fiddling with her hair, pulling the mahogany strands back, twisting them into an elaborate knot.

'Factory in Belfast. Big job.' Mark's voice was cold, like it was none of Katie's business, like he'd already told her but she hadn't been listening. He slammed the boot closed, came around to the driver's door, his pale blue eyes almost grey in the weak dawn light. Katie took a step back, nodding, hiding her disbelief.

He was paying her back. Every time he went away he was paying her back.

'So why are you staying all weekend?' Now Katie knew she sounded like she was nagging.

'Taking the MD out to dinner after I've had a look at the place. Golf Saturday. Like I said, it's a big job.'

Must be.

'Is Sharon going?'

'Sharon? Why would she?'

'Oh, you know, to take notes, make tea. That's what she does, isn't it?'

Katie pulled up the sleeves of her sweater and crossed her arms tight. Sharon was young, blonde, looked like she'd stepped out of Elite Model Agency right into the offices of All Coat Ltd. Like exterior paint was the place she'd wanted to be in all her life. Like filing was her vocation.

Payback. Big time.

'I've got to go.' Mark paused, the silence gaping like an open wound. 'And Sharon's *not* coming.' He sighed. A blast of irritation, like he was biting his tongue, like he had more to say, like it was obvious. But it was old ground.

Katie moved the mouse, the screen transforming like a door opening into another world. Mark's world. A world she had locked herself out of with one too many glasses of champagne . . .

Clicking to open his email account, Katie could feel her hand shaking. She swallowed, taking a deep breath. *What did she hope to find?* She could feel sweat pricking the back of her neck like a needle. *She had to know if there was someone else.* The business trips, all the secrecy, had started before Venice had even been thought of, was probably one of the reasons she'd agreed to go, was probably one of the reasons she'd . . . she caught her breath, focused back on the screen.

Inbox first.

The confirmation of this so-called meeting had to be here somewhere, and if it wasn't . . . if it wasn't . . .

Scrolling down, Katie checked each subject heading. Nothing. What would Mark have called it? He hadn't mentioned the name of the factory. Katie mentally kicked herself. *Why hadn't she asked?*

Deleted Items next.

Golf. *Was that it?* He'd said he was playing golf . . . she opened the email.

As agreed. 9.00 Saturday 3rd November.

Today.

No signature. No sender's address. Odd. Katie right-clicked on the message properties. It was forwarded – the path mostly gibberish. The only words she could make out were **Ultimate Solutions.** Was that the company Mark was visiting?

Outside, a sound like a shotgun going off almost lifted her out of her seat.

Dear God, what was that? Katie froze, listened hard, straining her ears over the pounding of her heart. In the silence of the study it had sounded like a bomb, a clatter of metal on metal. Could it have been the outhouse door? It was on a spring, caught everyone out when it slammed. *Was someone out there? Had Mark come back early?* But he'd know about the door banging . . . Thoughts raced around her head like tracer fire. Biting her lip, fighting to control her panic, Katie closed out of the email account, banged the laptop shut, was on her way to the window when the house alarm triggered, the sound reverberating around her head, its scream like a banshee.

The Gardaí swept the grounds, blue strobes cutting through the drizzle, torch beams dancing in the darkness.

'We've had a look around. The gate to the stable yard was open all right, but nothing else seems out of place.'

'I'm sorry, I panicked. That crash . . . the alarm . . . I was sure there was someone . . .'

'It's no problem. We'd rather be called out to a false alarm than something more serious. There's been a spate of aggravated burglaries around here, and this is a big house. Make sure you call again if you're worried.'

Watching the tail lights of the patrol car disappear down the drive, Katie shivered. *She was sure someone had been out there. She'd definitely closed that gate.* The Gardaí must have frightened them off.

Now, safely inside with the alarm reset, Katie strained her eyes across the manicured lawns, scanned the thick woods surrounding the property. Through the trees, a pair of headlights slid along the lane. *Jesus, who was that?*

It wasn't like her to get spooked. But tonight Katie was; well and truly.

Pulling the curtains closed, Katie turned back to the living room, unsure what to do next. *She didn't have the nerve to go back to the study, that was for sure.* She glanced at her watch: 10pm. She needed to relax, to curl up with a stiff drink and a movie.

Minutes later, ice cracking in a glass at her elbow, Katie flicked through the satellite channels looking for Zone Romantica, trying to keep her mind on the TV.

Ultimate Solutions. The name of the company stuck in her head, flashing like a neon sign.

It didn't sound like a factory. More like vermin control.

She flicked again. True Movies. A courtroom scene, a man in the witness box.

'And how much did you pay this man to kill your wife?'

Katie froze. *To kill his wife?*

Surely not. But *Ultimate Solutions?*

What had Mark said the last time they'd rowed? It had been the way he'd looked at her, the way he had lowered his voice that had scared her the most: *'I'm not giving all this up, I'm not giving you up to anyone . . .'* She'd thought it was the drink, but . . . in utter disbelief, Katie joined the dots. *The house, the business*. With her dead, Mark would be able to keep it all. *Surely not*.

9pm. The email had said 9pm. *What time had she heard that noise?* It must have been around nine . . . *Surely not*. Surely he hadn't hired someone to come after her when he was away . . . when he had the perfect alibi . . . Her stomach turned, bile burning the back of her throat. *Surely she must be imagining it*. But the Guard had said there had been a lot of burglaries in the area – if she was found battered to death, the house ransacked, it would look like a burglary. And Mark knew all about the break-ins; she'd heard him telling the stable lads to make sure they locked up properly.

Leaving the TV on, she bolted for the door. *There had to be more emails to Ultimate Solutions*.

Upstairs, Katie trawled Deleted Items again. Finally she found it. Another obliquely titled email, this time nothing more than a mobile number. Stunned, she sat back and looked at the screen.

Was this it? Did Mark really hate her so much he wanted her dead? *Was this the number of the man Mark had contracted to kill her?*

How could she find out? Google?

Nothing on a company called Ultimate Solutions in this country. One in New Jersey, one 'headquartered' in Houston; nothing here. Katie pulled at the roots of her hair. *But, if she was right, a contract killer would hardly have a shop window on the internet, would he?* Should she call the Gardaí again? Katie reached for the study phone, hesitated. *They'd think she was mad, hysterical*. She'd have to come up with more than this to convince them . . .

Perhaps she should call the number herself? *Perhaps she should pretend she wanted to have someone killed?* But what if it all turned around and she was accused of trying to have Mark killed? *That would solve all his problems*. Katie's mind worked fast. To be on the safe side she'd better use a phone that couldn't be traced back to her – one of those pay-as-you-go ones you could get in the supermarket . . .

Next morning, sitting in the breakfast room, her coffee cooling, Katie looked at the phone in her hand. She'd hardly slept, had been up at six heading for the nearby town, a woollen hat pulled over her hair, dark glasses concealing the rings around her eyes.

It was now or never. *And she could be wrong, she could be totally wrong . . .*

The phone was answered after one ring.

'Ultimate Solutions.' A man's voice; distant, strangely distorted.

What the hell should she say? Katie put on an American accent, fear sending her voice up an octave, her body shaking uncontrollably. *At least it didn't sound like her . . .*

'Eh, I was given your number. I have a problem . . .'

'Our business is problem solutions. What sort of problem is it?'

His voice was deep and smooth, and despite the distortion made the hairs stand up on the back of her neck. Katie could feel her cheeks blazing.

'Erm, it's a big one.' She had to work hard at the accent but his voice was calming. Suddenly she wanted to hear him speak again.

'We're very good with big problems.' The pitch was low, smoky like a late-night jazz club, faintly amused. *Was he laughing at her?* For a moment anger peaked her heightened emotions; but it didn't last. Her blush was hot. Red hot. *Thank goodness he couldn't see her.*

'I need . . .' she faltered. 'It's someone I know . . .' Deliberately vague, she paused, waiting for his response.

'A man?'

Oh Jesus . . . she was right, she had to be right. The way this conversation was going, there was no way Ultimate Solutions were contract cleaners.

'Yes, yes . . .'

'It could be expensive.'

The pause was loaded.

'Money's not a problem.' *At least she was sure of that.*

'Good, that's good. Why don't I call you back in an hour, give you time to think about it?'

'Okay, okay, that would be great.'

Phew! Katie put the phone down, her hand trembling, stomach cramping with what? Fear? Terror, more like. *What had she expected?* Not what had just happened, that was for sure. And he was calling back in an hour – what was she going to say then? She'd have to think of something, string him along, see if he'd let something slip. But . . . Katie kicked herself . . . *he was hardly going to implicate himself on the phone.* He was a professional, and she could be anyone. But how could she ask him directly? Then wouldn't *she* be committing the crime, contracting him? He wasn't doing anything wrong until he pulled the trigger.

Until he pulled the trigger. Her blood ran cold. Was Mark really prepared to go that far?

Payback. For one stupid mistake. *Did he hate her that much?* It wasn't like she'd planned it, like *she'd* come up with Venice for their 'teambuilding' event. Katie cringed inwardly. Mark had made it sound like she'd shagged the entire office: 'Teambuilding? Fucking teambuilding? What sort of team was Gary Priest thinking of building with *my wife?*'

Mark had slammed the front door so hard that the plaster had cracked. It was still cracked. A permanent reminder of the cleft in their relationship, of all their hopes and dreams fractured, damaged beyond repair. As if she needed one.

Why had she let it happen?

It had been a huge mistake. Bigger than huge. Katie knew she'd sacrificed her marriage, and to make it worse had landed herself with a prat who was so damned persistent, calling her, sending her flowers, he'd driven her insane. *If he'd left her alone maybe Mark would never have found out.* But the damage was done the moment he'd seen them together in that crappy hotel. Mark couldn't believe that she'd been telling Gary to back off, trying to make it clear that it had been all one-sided, a drunken fumble she'd been too far gone to resist – that she was happily married.

Happily married; before.

How could she have been so stupid? Katie knew damn well that Mark didn't do betrayal. Of any sort. At any level. *No matter what the circumstances.*

In his book loyalty came in one colour: the green of his service beret. One colour. Not in shades like blood, or the sky. One colour.

Mark had always said that, after the Falklands, meeting her and building the business were the only things that had kept him sane. But now that their marriage was over – had he finally gone over the edge?

Well, two could play at that game . . .

'Decided?'

'Yes, definitely. I need my problems solved, once and for all.'

The man from Ultimate Solutions chuckled, that same persistent distortion making it sound sinister. For a moment Katie was sure she was going to vomit.

'So you need an ultimate solution?'

'Yes . . .' She almost forgot to fake the accent.

'I'll need some information from you. A photo, address, mobile number, the subject's regular movements.'

'Right . . .'

'The quicker the better – once you've decided.' The man paused, 'You have a wonderful voice – how old are you?'

Stunned, she tried to steady her breathing. *Why did he want to know that?*

'I don't think . . .' She stopped herself – even with the accent she knew she sounded prissy, *and he wasn't someone she wanted to piss off.* 'Thirty-four.'

'Dark hair?'

'You're very intuitive.'

'Have to be.'

She could almost hear his mind clicking, information slotting into place.

'Five eight or nine, size twelve?'

Her stomach knotted: how the hell did he know that?

He was watching her.

Moving to the window, Katie scanned the tree line. *Was he out there now?* Watching, waiting? Bile rose in the back of her throat, but before she could respond, the man spoke again, his voice rich with innuendo.

'And I reckon you're into yoga.'

She drew a breath. *He was flirting with her.* No question.

Jesus, now she knew how a fox felt when it was cornered. It took her a moment to answer . . . she had to say something, didn't want to rile him by sounding awkward, but if she told him the truth . . . *He was watching her* . . . Maybe he already knew.

'Pilates actually . . .' *Could he hear the tremor in her voice, sense her fear?*

If anyone had told Katie Granger that she was going to spend the rest of the weekend talking on the phone to a man she suspected of being a contract killer, or indeed, how those conversations were to change the direction of her life, she wouldn't have believed them. She was the one who was always top of the class, bright, sassy, with heaps of common sense. *But the instinct of self-preservation overruled common sense every time.*

'So what are you doing now?'

'Riding.'

Sunday afternoon, the air sharp, mist swirling across the fields.

'Boots, crop, the whole lot?'

'That's about it.' Breathless from her ride, it was a struggle to keep up the accent.

'It's time we met . . .' he paused . . . the silence . . . was it her imagination . . . suggestive, rich with innuendo . . . 'got things moving.'

Already? A shiver shot up Katie's spine.

Unaware of her hesitation the man continued, business-like, 'Do you know the Ritz Carlton Hotel in Wicklow? It's in Enniskerry.'

She'd been there with Mark . . . a wonderful weekend wrapped in a bubble of luxury . . .

'I know it.' It came out more of a squeak than a statement. Katie cleared her throat self-consciously.

'Meet me in the reception hall. 7pm. Sit down. Wear a red headscarf.' *A headscarf? No one wore headscarves.* 'Don't want to mix you up with anyone else.'

'How will I know you?'

'Don't worry, I'll find you.'

6.50pm. Katie touched her head self-consciously. She'd cut up a T-shirt to make the headscarf, had wasted precious moments deciding what to wear. She'd gone for a black top, jeans and stiletto-heeled black boots. *Mark had always loved this top.* She knew she looked good, her hair loose under the scarf, but it didn't stop her stomach tangling into a knot of fear . . . and . . . and hope. Hope that she was wrong; *hope that if she wasn't wrong that she could turn this around.* Hope this man from Ultimate Solutions wouldn't blow her away the moment he stepped through the door. *What would she say?* He was expecting her to pour out her problems but, right now, *he* was her biggest problem. Well and truly.

In Katie's stomach, a great black moth flapped its wings. *When the hell had this been a good idea?* Jesus, she was playing with fire . . . had she done enough not to get burnt? *They always said it was harder to kill someone you knew than a total stranger.* Dear God . . . and she still didn't even know what he looked like. In her head she'd conjured up a picture – a mixture of James Bond and . . . the realisation hit her hard.

Mark.

In her head, she'd imagined he must look a bit like Mark.

Was she going mad? The pain was like someone twisting a knife in her heart. Mark had made it absolutely clear that their marriage was over, despite her tears, despite her telling him how much she loved him. Over. Finished. And *he* was the one who had contacted this man . . . Katie drew a shaky breath, fighting the tears. *So now it was time to move on . . . and maybe it was time to redress the balance.*

'Hello.'

The voice behind her made her jump.

Standing up, spinning around, her hand flew to her mouth, eyes widening in shock. But she didn't get a chance to speak. Reaching out for her, grasping her roughly by the wrist, the man from Ultimate Solutions pulled her to him, his mouth covering hers, rough, insistent, needy; awakening emotions she had long buried.

At last he released her, breathless, her heart pounding.

'Red suits you, Mrs Granger.'

Struggling for words, the questions tumbling over themselves, she was suddenly weak; but he was ready, his arm around her, cradling her weight.

'What's going on . . .?

He pulled her close, nestled his face in her hair, his lips fluttering over her neck, making her heart beat even faster.

'Long story. Too much competition in exterior paint . . . and I needed a new challenge. This pays way better.'

'But . . .'

Mark didn't let her finish. 'So who's the problem in your life?'

She paused for a heartbeat. 'A guy called Priest, Gary Priest . . .'

❦ ❦

Brian Crowley MEP

Brian Crowley MEP has topped the poll in Munster in every election he has contested. Such consistency makes him one of the most successful public representatives in Irish electoral history. Born in 1964, he is a wheelchair user owing to an accident when he was sixteen. His career as a public representative began back in 1993, when the then Taoiseach appointed him to the Senate 'to be a voice for all those who have no voice'. Brian Crowley is now the longest-serving Irish MEP in Europe and has also served on President Mary McAleese's Council of State.

Making a Difference **

Brian Crowley MEP

There's an old Greek legend about a woman named Pandora that sheds an interesting light on hope. Zeus, king of the gods, gave her husband a large jar full of afflictions – things like sickness and heavy toil. Pandora, out of sheer curiosity, took the lid off the jar. Before she knew it, the evils had rushed out of the vessel, spreading over the earth. But the jar also contained one thing that was not an affliction, and this stayed behind: hope. The crucial thing about Pandora's 'box' (as the jar came to be called) is not what escaped it, but what remained. It is a fact of life – of the human condition – that we cannot prevent illnesses and accidents and other sources of misery. But it is also a fact that hope lies buried in our souls. As long as we have life, we have hope.

Hope has as many hues as the colours of the rainbow, itself a resonant symbol of hope. There is the resolute hope of the hospital visitor, determined to bring good cheer and solace with a smile and conversation. There is the dreamy hope of the child imagining what Santa Claus might bring her at Christmas. There is the quiet hope of the parent sending her child off to a new school. There is the nerve-jangling hope of towns, cities and countries, as their representatives compete in sporting events – when Ireland won the Grand Slam in 2009, beating Wales in the Millennium Stadium, every Irish pass, tackle and kick carried the hopes of the nation. And then there is the profound hope that exists deep down inside us – the sort of hope that sustained Nelson Mandela during his imprisonment on Robben Island.

Hope is the antidote to despair (which literally means 'away from hope'). It is the medicine, the cure. Martin Luther King said that if you lose hope, 'somehow you lose the vitality that keeps life moving, you lose that courage to be, that quality that helps you go on in spite of it all'. More recently, his fellow American, Barack Obama, praised hope as the quality that has made his country what it is – a crucible of aspirations: 'Hope is what led a band of colonists to rise up against an empire; what led the greatest of generations to free a continent and heal a nation; what led young women and young men to sit at lunch counters and brave fire hoses and march through Selma and Montgomery for freedom's cause. Hope is what led me here today – with a father from Kenya, a mother from Kansas . . .' We Irish have known full well the hope that Obama has eloquently described – it is the same hope that has accompanied our migrants to all corners of the globe.

Hope comes easier to some than to others. It is the difference between those who see the glass half full and those who see it as half empty. And it is a quality that can be passed from person to person, like a healthy virus. History is littered with examples of individuals who have kept hope in the face of dismal circumstances, as well as those who have inspired hope in other people. Great religious leaders, such as Jesus Christ and the Buddha, gave profound hope to their followers – especially those who were living at the bottom of society. And the same is true of those inspired souls who have founded charitable organisations such as St Vincent de Paul, the Simon Community and the Peter McVerry Trust, to name but a few – organisations that have continued to kindle the spirit of voluntarism in Ireland and abroad.

The Gospels, of course, abound in examples of hope. There is the story of the woman who suffered from excessive bleeding for twelve years. She had spent all her money on seeing an array of doctors. But she had got worse, not better. When the medical profession cannot help your condition it is easy to fall into despair. But hope had lingered in her – she believed that if she could just touch a bit of Jesus's clothing she would be healed. She spotted her chance on an occasion when Jesus was surrounded by a crowd of people. She touched his cloak and felt her body heal. Although Jesus was doubtlessly being jostled by the crowd, he was aware that 'power had gone out from him'. He asked who had touched him and the woman came forward, trembling with fear. She knew she had taken a liberty. Jesus told her that her faith had healed her. Whatever we might feel about the miracles in the Gospels, it was hope that had brought the woman to Jesus; hope had told her that her doctors did not represent the end of her journey; hope had given her the courage to touch Jesus's cloak. Faith did the rest.

Jesus inspired people to do things they did not think were possible. His 'volunteers', or disciples, spread his teaching of love and compassion through the Roman Empire. He showed that one person can release the innate goodness in others – the whole ethos of voluntary work is based on this simple fact. And it is voluntary work that is the engine of our charity organisations. Ireland has a proud record of volunteering, from the local GAA club to international charities. One of the best known of the many charities that make a real difference to our country is the Society of St Vincent de Paul. It has flourished here for more than 150 years and now has nearly 10,000 volunteers – ordinary people who offer their time and energy to help the socially excluded.

We are so used to charities like St Vincent de Paul that it is easy to forget that they have not always existed among us and that they were the result of one person's vision and perseverance. The individual behind the Society was a young French student named Frédéric Ozanam. Born in 1813, he lived at a time when the Church was on the retreat after the convulsions of the French Revolution. Yet he and a group of his friends believed strongly that compassion and direct action based on Christian values could help the poor and suffering of the slums of Paris. Frédéric and his group named their new society after St Vincent de Paul, a 17th-century French priest who had devoted his life to helping the poor. And they were helped in getting off the ground by Sister Rosalie Rendu, a member of the Daughters of Charity, which was also operating in Paris at that time.

Frédéric did not want a quick fix to poverty. It was not simply a case of a soup kitchen and a friendly smile. He wanted to change attitudes, particularly those of the well-off towards the destitute – he talked about there being 'a violent clash between opulence and poverty'. The rich had to change their world view: 'The poor person is a unique person of God's fashioning with an inalienable right to respect.' And he urged his fellow society members not to tide 'the poor over the poverty crisis'. They should, instead, 'study their condition and the injustices which brought about such poverty, with the aim of a long term improvement'.

By the end of Frédéric's life in 1853 some 2,000 volunteers had joined his society. It now thrives in more than 130 countries with nearly a million volunteers. Out of acorns come mighty oaks.

As mentioned before, one person can free the innate goodness locked inside others. That is what happened in Dublin in 1969 when a man named Anton Wallich-Clifford gave a talk to students from Trinity and UCD. He spoke about homelessness, in particular the homelessness of the Irish in Britain.

Wallich-Clifford knew a lot about homelessness. He was a probation officer and had to deal with a large number of ex-offenders. Many of them had failed to find permanent homes after their discharge from prison, and, more than that, many needed something beyond a bed for a temporary duration in a hostel. What Wallich-Clifford felt they lacked was a basic respect, kindness and being listened to in 'an atmosphere as different as possible from the dismal disinfected corridors of doss-houses'. In 1963 he founded the Simon Community, with the aim of giving practical help and, crucially, emotional support to those struggling to fend for themselves. The community spread to various parts of

Britain. Then in 1969 it crossed the waters to Dublin, when the students took up the baton and, three nights a week, began to distribute soup and sandwiches to those sleeping rough in the city. Like inspired like: over the following years new Simon Communities were founded in Cork, Dundalk, Galway and other parts of the country. Nowadays there are some 800 Simon volunteers working in the country. They provide accommodation, campaign at a political level on housing issues, organise detox programmes, and man charity shops to raise money. All this came from a probation officer who recognised the need to respect a person's humanity no matter who they were and what they had done.

Wallich-Clifford was inspired to take action on behalf of the homeless from his direct experience with working with ex-offenders. Others who have felt impelled to help the needy on the basis of experiencing life at the bottom of the heap have included the Irish entrepreneur Niall Mellon and the Jesuit Fr Peter McVerry. In 1974 McVerry took up residence in a tenement building in Dublin's northside. There he saw life in the raw – drug addicts, alcoholics, crumbling rat-infested buildings, and children who had left school early with little education and no jobs to go to.

In 1979 McVerry opened a hostel for young teenagers; four years later he founded a society, now called the Peter McVerry Trust, to look after and give shelter to boys between the ages of 15 and 18. Over the years, the society has grown, providing more flats and houses for homeless boys. Like the founder of Simon, McVerry emphasised that people need more than material help – no one should be stigmatised for being poor – and he has tirelessly campaigned on behalf of the young homeless.

Niall Mellon's road to Damascus came during a visit to South Africa. While visiting a township near Cape Town he was moved by the poverty he witnessed there. In 2002 he founded a charity, the Niall Mellon Township Trust, to provide houses for the poor in South Africa's townships. Every year, volunteers from Ireland go over to South Africa to take part in week-long 'building blitzes' – in 2008 some 2,000 volunteers constructed more than 250 homes. And apart from putting up houses, volunteer workers also help to train South Africans to learn the skills of the building trade. It is another impressive story of how one person, inspiring others to volunteer, can instil hope among the poor.

Perhaps the most potent symbol of hope is the candle. And one of the best-known logos of any charity is the candle crossed by barbed wire: Amnesty International provides hope to political prisoners as it campaigns to safeguard human rights. Seán MacBride began the Irish branch of it in 1962, a year after it had been founded by Peter Benenson, a British lawyer of Jewish extraction whose mother's family had escaped from Russia during the revolution. The Irish section of Amnesty now has 20,000 members with some 40 local groups.

The spark that turned Benenson into a campaigner occurred in 1961 while he was taking the Tube to work in London. He was reading a newspaper article about two Portuguese students who had been drinking in a Lisbon café. Fatefully, they raised their glasses to toast 'freedom' – at a time when Portugal's government was autocratic. The two students were arrested, tried and sentenced to seven years in jail.

Now, most of us reading a newspaper report like that would have tut-tutted and moved on to the sports pages. But something deep down moved Benenson. His immediate impulse was to get off the train at Trafalgar Square and register his anger at the Portuguese Embassy. Instead he hatched a more thoughtful plan which was to bear extraordinary fruit. On 28 May 1961, he published a long article in *The Observer* newspaper entitled 'The Forgotten Prisoners'. It made an appeal to governments all over the world to empty their jails of political prisoners or to give them a fair trial. The article struck a chord with thousands of people, and letters came pouring in, offering support.

Benenson's article was reprinted in newspapers worldwide and the response was again huge. What started out as a one-year campaign to raise awareness turned into a permanent organisation. Within a year, Amnesty International had taken root in half a dozen countries, including Ireland. Now it operates out of more than 150 countries, with some 1.8 million members.

After Benenson's death in 2005, Irene Khan, Amnesty's current Secretary General, said of him that he 'brought light into the darkness of prisons, the horror of torture chambers and tragedy of death camps around the world'. And that light originated from a single moment on a Tube train.

Khan also said of Benenson that he 'believed in the power of ordinary people to bring about extraordinary change'. This is important. If we go on through life thinking that it is only the genius, the inspired or the hero who effects change we may miss our own opportunities to make a difference to others. Although Ozanam, Wallich-Clifford, McVerry, Mellon and Benenson have achieved truly remarkable results, they were not superhumans, just ordinary people who could not bear to sit idle in the face of suffering. Perhaps their greatest gift was, yes, hope. The sense of hopefulness in themselves to make something work. And the sense that they could create hope in others.

Having their sort of hope does not have to result in global organisations with millions of members. It can result in small-scale actions at a local level. In 1974, for example, a group of parents in Bantry got together to discuss how they could improve the lives of children with learning disabilities. From these discussions arose CoAction, a group that has now formed branches in other parts of West Cork, namely Castletownbere, Clonakilty, Dunmanway and Skibbereen.

CoAction's motto, 'A Local Service for Local Needs', sums up its ethic: it places emphasis on the involvement of people from communities in the region, rather than relying on some centralised organisation in Dublin or elsewhere. CoAction began with purely volunteer workers, but now it includes professional specialists as well. They provide pre-school groups and home support, as well as a range of services such as physiotherapy, occupational therapy and speech and language therapy. Perhaps more than anything else, they provide a model of how communities can help themselves at a local level.

Empowerment is a state of mind – the realisation that you do not have to wait for others to act on your behalf. Change starts with a thought, a conversation and then a phone call.

∽ ∾

Declan Burke

Declan Burke writes regularly for *The Sunday Times, The Irish Independent* and other leading national newspapers. The author of *Eight Ball Boogie, The Big O* and *Crime Always Pays*, he lives with his wife and daughter in Co. Wicklow. Declan is the creator of the enormously popular Crime Always Pays blog, which shares the latest news, reviews, gossip and slander about the dicks, dames and desperadoes of (mostly) Irish crime fiction with his dedicated readership.

Blowback *

Declan Burke

Lauren was quiet on the drive over. Carl didn't push it. He was always nervous meeting new people too. So he said: 'We should probably get some munchies.'

'Oh yeah? Yeah. Okay.'

He pulled in onto the brightly lit forecourt of the petrol station and parked up beside the shop. He said: 'So what do you like for munchies?'

Lauren thought about it. 'I don't know,' she said. 'I'll come in with you.'

He got a six-pack of Coke, a family-size bag of marshmallows. She got a couple of Twix and a two-litre bottle of Diet 7-Up. He threw some Mars bars in on the deal and when everything was totted up he asked for a packet of extra-large Rizlas. The surly kid behind the till gave him the eye but Carl just stared back, handing over the money.

Back in the car Lauren unscrewed the cap from the bottle and glugged a couple of mouthfuls. She handed it across, wiping her mouth. She hiccupped and giggled. He resisted the urge to wipe the mouth of the bottle and took a swig. She arched a severe eyebrow and said: '*Giant* skins?'

Carl handed her the bottle and put the car in gear and shrugged.

Cathy was coming downstairs just as Richard was opening the door so the introductions were made in the cramped hall. In the kitchen Cathy put the kettle on to boil and said: 'Well, what do you think?'

Richard lined the mugs up on the counter. He shrugged. 'Lauren's a nice name,' he said.

Cathy shook her head. 'She isn't his type,' she said.

'I've seen him with blondes before.'

'I'm not talking about her *hair*,' Cathy said. She spooned coffee and sugar into the mugs. She poured the milk. She stirred. Richard thought that the grating of the spoon sounded like a helicopter crashing in slow-mo. 'She's not even a real blonde,' she said.

'Doesn't seem to bother Carl,' Richard said.

'She's too young for him,' Cathy said. 'She must be ten years younger than him. I don't mind *young*er, but ten years?'

Her husband nodded and folded the top of the milk carton and put it back in the fridge.

Richard put the tray down on the coffee table and then pulled the coffee table closer to the couch.

'Two sugars, Lauren? Is that what you said?'

'That's lovely, Richard. Thanks.'

'Instant's okay?'

'That's fine. I prefer instant, actually.'

'How's the job going, Carl?' Cathy asked.

'Yeah, grand. Same shit, different day.' Carl roached the joint and twisted the other end into a little spiral. 'How're the kids?'

'Not a loss on them.'

'Yeah?'

'Yeah.'

'Good, good.' He sparked the jay, drew deep and exhaled.

'So how's the new gig?' he asked Richard.

'Yeah, grand. Getting used to it.'

'Yeah?'

Richard shrugged. 'It's not that different to McNulty's.'

'Except now he's home by six every evening,' Cathy said. 'So he gets to see more of the kids.'

'Nice one,' Carl said. He handed the joint to Cathy.

'Last night,' Cathy said, before taking a drag, 'Emily bumped her forehead against the banisters.'

'Oh yeah?' Carl said.

'Yeah. She was *baw*ling.' Cathy looked at Lauren. 'So what do you suppose Ciara does while I'm trying to fix Emily up?'

Lauren shrugged. 'I don't know,' she said. She half-smiled.

'*She* banged her head off the banisters too. In sympathy, like.' Cathy took a drag and shook her head, half-smiling. 'Both of them screaming their lungs out. Banshees.'

'Kids can be so cute,' Lauren said.

Richard picked up the remote control and flicked through the channels with the sound muted.

'You have no idea,' Cathy told her. 'I could write a book,' she said.

'Then there was the time', Cathy said, 'when Carl dived into the ditch.'

Carl snorted, looked at Lauren, rolling his eyes. She smiled back.

Cathy held up the joint. 'Who gets this next?' she said.

'Carl,' Richard said.

Cathy passed the joint on to Carl. 'Where were we?' she asked Richard.

'Where were we when?' Richard said.

'The time Carl dived into the ditch,' Cathy said.

'Derry,' Richard said.

'Derry,' Cathy said. 'That's right. We'd just come through the roadblock –'

'Checkpoint,' Richard said.

'What?' Cathy said.

'It was a checkpoint, not a roadblock.'

'Well, whatever.' Cathy stared at Richard for a moment and then looked back at Lauren. 'Anyway the car started to conk out. So we pulled in to see what was wrong and the boys couldn't figure it out. Me and whatshername were in fits.' She looked at Carl. 'What was her name, Carl? The American girl?'

'Cody.'

'That's right. Cody.' Cathy winked at Lauren. Lauren smiled softly. 'Then they couldn't get it started again.'

'Someone,' Richard said, 'had a habit of leaving the lights on when they turned off the engine.'

'Anyway,' Cathy said, 'the next thing Cody and me know, we have to get out and push. We have to bump-start the engine.'

'Jump-start,' Richard said.

'That's what I said,' Cathy said. 'Jump-start. So we're all pushing and the car's starting to roll and suddenly it back-fires.' She slapped her hands smartly. Lauren started. Cathy grinned. 'And the next thing you know, Carl's diving over the ditch. He thought it was the soldiers from the roadblock firing at us.' She cackled. 'All I could see was Carl's arse disappearing over the ditch.'

Lauren grinned at Carl.

Carl shook his head. 'What *happ*ened,' Carl said, 'was –'

'He fell *back* over the ditch,' Richard said. 'When the car jerked forward, he lost his balance. And fell *back* over the ditch.'

Cathy frowned. 'No way,' she said. 'I *saw* him do it. He dived. Head first.' She looked at Lauren. 'Like a swimmer,' she giggled.

Lauren smiled and then looked at Carl again. He shrugged. She smiled, tut-tutting.

'You *could*n't have seen it,' Richard said. 'You were doing the steering. You'd have had to be looking in the rear-view and side-view mirrors at the same *time* to see him dive over the ditch.'

'*I* wasn't steering,' Cathy said. 'I was *push*ing, from behind. Me and Cody and Carl. *You* were the one doing the steering.'

'I was *push*ing,' Richard said. 'I was pushing beside *Carl*. And he lost his balance and fell back over the ditch when the car kick-started.'

'What are you *talk*ing about?' Cathy said. '*I* was pushing beside Carl. Me and Cody.'

'How would that look?' Richard said. 'Me steering and you two girls out pushing. How would that look?'

'I don't know how it *look*ed,' Cathy said. 'But that's the way it was. And I saw Carl dive out across the ditch.'

'How long ago was this?' Lauren said.

Richard looked at Carl. 'It was what – about eight years ago?'

Carl nodded. 'About that, yeah.'

'It must've been pretty funny,' Lauren said. Carl passed her the joint. She giggled and then looked at Carl again. 'Did you get any points for degree of difficulty?' she asked.

Carl just grinned. Richard shook his head, remembering.

'Some fucking hero you'd have made,' he said. 'The Brits open up and you're into the ditch.'

'Cody never blinked,' Cathy told Lauren. 'She must have been used to shooting. Being American, like. All those drug dealers.' She looked at Carl. 'Where was she from, Carl? I mean, where was she from in America?'

'Florida,' Carl said. 'I think it was Florida.'

'She was really pretty,' Cathy told Lauren. 'And her skin was just *flaw*less'.

Lauren handed the joint to Richard. 'Really?'

'She was very young, though,' Cathy said. 'She must've been five or six years younger than Carl. What age was she, Carl?'

Carl shrugged. 'I don't know. 'Twenty-one? Twenty-two?'

'You like them young, huh?' Lauren said to Carl. Then she winked at Cathy. 'Young and impressionable.'

'As long as they're fluent in yes,' Carl said, 'age isn't a factor.'

Richard stubbed the joint. He scrabbled among the detritus on the coffee table and groaned. He said: 'Shit. We're out of skins.'

'You're kidding,' Cathy said. Then she said: 'Didn't you get skins when you went to the shop that time?'

Richard shook his head. 'I thought we had plenty,' he said.

Lauren looked at Carl. Carl said, 'Fuck, that's a pisser. I was getting nicely toasted, too.'

Lauren was quiet on the drive home. Carl said: 'So what'd you think?'

'They're nice people,' Lauren said. She hummed along with the stereo. She reached across and squeezed his knee and then left her hand on his thigh. She yawned. 'I liked Richard,' she said. 'He seems sound.'

'A gent,' Carl said.

'You used to work together, right?'

'Yeah. But we were mates before that.'

'Okay.' She hummed some more. 'Hey,' she said. There was a tease in her voice. 'What was all that about you diving over the ditch?'

Carl shrugged. 'Fucked if I know,' he said. 'My wrist was in a cast, broken. I was the one doing the steering.'

Lauren thought about that.

'*You* were the one doing the steering?'

'Yeah,' he said. They were coming up on the petrol station. The forecourt was brightly lit. 'Hey,' he said, 'the shop's still open. Want to try for some more munchies?'

∽ ∾

Claudia Carroll

Claudia Carroll was born in Dublin where she still lives. For many years she played the part of Nicola Prendergast on *Fair City*, a character she describes as 'the horrible old cow that everybody loves to hate'. She left the show in 2006 to pursue a full-time writing career, the only job she reckons where you can wear pyjamas, look out the window all day and still get paid. Since then, she's published seven novels, all bestsellers, two of which, *I Never Fancied Him Anyway* and *If This Is Paradise, I Want My Money Back*, have been optioned for movies.

She is currently working on her eighth novel.

Prejudice and Pride *

Claudia Carroll

The one advantage of having your birthday on Valentine's Day is that, if you are in a relationship, boy oh boy do you get to see how that guy really feels about you at this doubly romantic time.

Like I did tonight.

When he stood me up.

Your basic worst nightmare, in our 'special' restaurant, where I was left sitting all alone at a table for two, in my 'serial result' little black dress, waiting for excruciating minute after minute, with all the other couples staring at me, almost with thought-balloons coming out of their heads, thinking, 'God love her, sitting alone at a table for two, glancing at her mobile every ten seconds, do you think maybe she's escaped from some kind of institution and is now double checking her phone to make sure that they're not coming after her?'

Every few minutes or so, my overactive imagination threw up some new catastrophe that might have delayed him. He got the date wrong (no, says the logical part of my brain, how could he have? It's Valentine's Day, for God's sake, kind of unavoidable in the calendar; just about every Hallmark shop in the country has been shouting about it from the rooftops since, like, Christmas).

Or that he's been in a horrific car accident and can't ring me on account of being in a coma (humm . . . probably unlikely, but sure as hell beats being stood up). Or . . . ooohhh, now I have it, maybe he was mugged on his way to the restaurant and they took his phone, and somehow the police got it all wrong and arrested him by accident and now he's in a police station somewhere, thumping on a table saying, 'But I can't possibly take part in a police line-up, my girlfriend is sitting waiting for me, right this minute, my *girlfriend*, I tell you!' Then, tomorrow morning there'll be a huge banner headline about this terrible miscarriage of justice and he'll be on the news saying, 'The worst part was that I couldn't get a message through to my beloved girlfriend . . .'

Okay, I suppose it would explain why his phone is switched off but . . . well . . . wouldn't he just have used his one phone call to ring the restaurant and explain?

So, after almost a full, excruciating hour of nursing a mineral water and pretending to be getting text messages from him the whole time, eventually I had to admit I'd been beaten.

Right. Nothing for it then. Massive damage limitation required if I was to get out of there with my head held high. Well, high-ish.

My old days in the college drama society came in very handy as I accosted a passing waiter, mentally directing myself to try and sound faux-casual and not like some ham actress in a daytime soap.

'Oh, can you believe this?' I said, having to resist smacking my hand off my cheek in a 'can-you-believe-how-ditsy-I've-been-in-the -manner-of-Teri-Hatcher-from-*Desperate-Housewives*' style. If you're with me.

'Madam?'

Shit, now even the waiter is talking to me in a Special Needs voice.

'Huge misunderstanding,' I say, brightly as I can, 'my fault entirely, my boyfriend's been waiting at home for me all this time, so sorry to hold up a table but do you think I could ring for a taxi?'

Somehow, someway I make it back to my flat, head straight for the answering machine and play back all eight messages that are on it.

None of which is from him.

Okay, now the sobs start. And having done my best to be a

brave little foot-soldier all evening and hold it together in public, now the waterfall of tears that are falling are almost causing me physical pain. I try my best to shove away the numbing thought that this can't be happening – how can it be happening? For God's sake, I live in a flat where the duvet matches the curtains – how can I have just been stood up in a restaurant on my birthday? Surely that's someone else's life, not mine?

But it *did* happen. I just got stood up in the worst, most public way possible with not as much as a message of apology waiting for me when I got home, nothing.

I howl to the four walls and collapse into bed – a big, shivering lump of dumped despondency.

And that's when it happens.

I'm not quite sure how much time has passed, but I'm still lying on the bed, fully dressed, with the pillow like the Shroud of Turin, there's that much make-up cried onto it, when something wakes me up.

Sweet Baby Jesus and the Orphans, am I seeing things?

There, sitting at the edge of the bed is my granny. No, I'm not hallucinating, it really *is* her. My most beloved gran, looking like she's just stepped out of a hair salon and not like she's been dead for the best part of twenty years. I sit bolt upright and rub my eyes in disbelief.

'Oh, did I give you a fright, love? Sorry about that.'

'Granny? Is . . . it really . . . you?'

The part of my brain that's still functioning is telling me, 'It's only a dream, this isn't real, you know this isn't really happening,' but the rest of me is saying, 'Bloody hell, if my subconscious mind is playing tricks on me, it's certainly done its revision.'

She looks like my granny (neat twinset, sensible, flat brogue shoes from Marks & Spencer, Marcel-waved hair that we all used to laugh at and say, 'Are you waiting for that look to come back into fashion or what?'). She sounds like my granny (soft, lyrical Monaghan accent, always gentle and always with 'pet' or 'love' tacked onto the end of every sentence). Bloody hell, she even smells

71

like my granny (Lily of the Valley perfume and boiled aniseed sweets, her favourites).

There's a thousand things I'm dying to ask her, but all my confused, muddled brain can come up with is, 'So what's Heaven like, Gran?'

Anything just to keep her talking. What the hell, even if it is only a dream, it's the nicest one I've had in a long, long time and certainly outclasses the horse's head at the foot of the bed I'd probably be hallucinating about otherwise, given the horrific night I've just had.

'Oh, Heaven is lovely, pet,' she twinkles back at me. 'Just like a big retirement home in the sky. You know, before I got there, I was expecting choirs of angels and harps and for it to be a bit like "Songs of Praise", but it's not at all. We have stair lifts and Thora Hird and the Queen Mother and sherry in the afternoon. And all my old friends are here now, love, except for poor Rose Hobbs – can you believe she's the last one of us to go? Her idea of getting fresh air and exercise is to throw open a window to have a cigarette.'

I cannot believe this. I cannot believe I'm sitting here having this surreal conversation with someone who's been dead for nearly twenty years, about the Queen Mother and stair lifts. I'm looking at her with my jaw somewhere around my collarbone, only waiting on her to start quizzing me about plot updates on *Coronation Street*, when out of nowhere she starts tapping what looks like a tiny earpiece and talking to someone else, a bit like the way the CIA do in espionage thrillers.

'Yes, love, we're on our way. We'll be right there.'

'Granny? Are you okay?'

'Oh yes, pet, it's just we need to get going. Have you a nice warm cardigan? Look at you, out in the middle of February in that skimpy little dress, you'll get your death.'

'It's Calvin Klein,' I say defensively, rooting around in a drawer for a snug fleece and throwing it on. God, whatever's going on with this dream, it's like being a teenager again, except back then

Granny used to give out to me for wearing 'Kids from Fame' stripey legwarmers with matching furry earmuffs. (Hard to believe, but back in the dim, distant 80s, that rubbish was all the go.)

'And I'm sure it'll be lovely when it's finished. Ready, love? Nothing to worry about, just take my hand.'

I do and it's the weirdest sensation because next thing I know, I'm in my boyfriend's apartment. For definite. I'd know the giant boy-toy plasma screen TV anywhere, it's so big and brash, and he's the only person I know with an actual oil painting of a Ferrari hanging over his bookcase.

Then Granny sees me transfixed by something and nods quietly, as if she already knows what I'm about to say.

'My photo was there,' I stammer, 'right there, and now it's gone.'

'Shhhh, come on now, pet, we're nearly done here and then we can be on our way.'

Her eyes look towards the bedroom door as a slow, sickening feeling starts to come over me. He's here, I just know he is and the worst part of it is . . . I don't think he's alone either. Two champagne flutes on the coffee table . . . oh God, a pair of black stiletto heels abandoned just outside the bedroom door . . . and there's music playing softly in the background . . . jazz music, which I know for a fact he only ever plays when he's trying to score. Worked on me, didn't it? Otherwise his CD collection consists of the type of music soccer hooligans listen to whenever they're feeling philosophical.

On mute, stunned autopilot, I manage to get as far as the bedroom door . . . and then I see them, him and her . . . both fast asleep, cuddled up together, clothes strewn everywhere, him snoring like there's a Zeppelin passing overhead, as he does, and just a peep of blonde, curly hair from under the duvet.

Okay, dream or no dream, now I want to be sick.

'He stood me up . . . he left me just sitting there, Gran, and the whole time the bastard was with someone else . . .'

The sobs are uncontrollable now and for a second I'm afraid I'll wake them both up. That's all I need, on top of everything else, to be done for breaking and entering and won't my defence sound just wonderful? 'Sorry, Your Honour, my dead granny made me do it.'

'Oh don't worry, pet,' says Granny, perching on the edge of a sofa, then sinking into it. 'They can't hear us at all, I promise you. Now I'm sorry you had to see that, love, but you will thank me in the long run. You see, I was so worried about you and all this precious time you've been wasting on men that are just beyond useless. You needed your eyes opened, love, and that's why I was sent back down to you. So you'd see for yourself what was going on. Now would you ever give me a hand out of this sofa, there's a good girl? Dreadfully uncomfortable and you know what I'm like with my back.'

I haul her back up, feeling dizzy with all this, and again she seems to read my thoughts.

'You have to ask yourself this, love, and you need to be very honest. When was your last promising relationship?'

'This one,' I sniff.

'And before that?'

'Emmm . . . lemme think . . . Laurence Sullivan.'

'Who . . . ?'

It's as if she already knows the end of the sentence before I even open my mouth.

'Who ran off to Las Vegas and married an air hostess,' I say.

Granny sighs and shakes her head. 'And before that?'

'Tom Sullivan.'

'And what happened with him . . . ?'

'Just stopped calling me after a while, which I put down as a classic case of relationship fizzle.'

'Oh you poor thing, and before that?'

'James Harry.'

'Who turned out to have a wife and kids the whole time – I know, love, I remember.'

'Gran! Do you have CCTV cameras up in Heaven trained down on us the whole time?'

'Not quite, but we have our ways and means. You see, I just want you to be happy, that's all. Because I don't think you are.

You've been alone long enough and now it's time for you to be with someone. Isn't that what you want? To finally get married and maybe make your poor mother a granny herself one day?'

I sniff, and the tears actually physically sting me.

'But I want you to be with a good man, love. The right person. No more messers who think it's all right to treat you like this. Now come on, take my hand. We've a long night ahead of us.'

Dazed, I obediently do as I'm told and next thing I know, the two of us are in a church. Except now it's summertime, it's packed and there's a wedding going on. An invisible choir up in the organ loft are trilling out the 'Ave Maria', and there's an almost over-powering smell of lilies . . . oh no, wait, hang on, that's just Granny's perfume.

Oh shit and double shit. Then I realise just whose wedding it is . . .

'Granny! Get us out of here, quick before we're seen!'

She's sitting very comfortably in a side pew beside me and I'm about to grab her hand in the hope we can just, I dunno, be beamed up or something, when I see . . . no, it can't be . . .

It is. It's me. I'm looking at myself, standing in the pew beside granny, except I'm aged about twenty-five, in a horrible purple, flowery suit, big hair and waaaaay too much blusher.

This is a deeply humbling experience. Not only have I not aged well, but my sense of style back then . . . well, put it this way, the dress I have on could easily double up as a cover for a Hummer, no problem.

'I know,' says Granny, doing her 'reading my thoughts' thing again. I think that's going to be her party piece. 'But just take a look at the altar, pet. That doesn't look like a groom that's deliriously happy to be taking vows today, if you ask me. And don't tell me that I've just been watching too many soap operas, love, because we've no telly up above, you know.'

I can hardly bear to look, mainly because, although this wedding happened almost fifteen years ago, I still remember it so well.

I should explain.

The groom is a very old, very dear friend of mine called Tim

Keating. He was my first love and I was his, and oh God, he was just so lovely, but there was a problem. We were fifteen when we met and we dated till we were about twenty-two. Then . . . well, come on, I mean, twenty-two?

'He wanted to marry you, didn't he, pet?' asks Granny, looking at me keenly.

She's right, he did and I said no. That's the trouble with meeting a true soul mate so early on in life: you think they grow on trees. It took me a lot of years and a lot of loneliness later to realise what a rare diamond I'd let slip through my fingers.

'Come on, Granny, I was twenty-two. I mean, who gets married at that age? Cousins and internet brides, that's who!'

Then I shut up, remembering that she probably doesn't know what the internet is, but then she seems to know an awful lot about pretty much everything else that's been going on in my life.

'Anyway, he's married now and that's all there is to it,' I trail off lamely. I think he may even have kids too . . . did I hear something about twin girls?

Hard to know. Tim and I sort of lost touch after he got married, the way you do. Although to be brutally honest I suspect his brand-new wife wasn't a big fan of having his ex-girlfriend as such a close pal and really, would you blame her?

'Take my hand,' says Granny firmly and before I know what's happening, we're off again.

Oh God, this just keeps getting weirder and weirder.

Now we're both standing in the front garden of a perfectly normal suburban house. I glance around anxiously, half-expecting a baby grand piano to fall on my head, like in a Laurel and Hardy movie, but nothing . . .

'Be patient,' is all Granny says, wandering over to where some stargazer lilies are neatly potted (her favourites), and bending down to smell them.

And that's when I see it.

A jeep comes gliding down the road and pulls right up outside. The doors open and out clamber two gorgeous little girls, of maybe eight years old. I dunno, hard to tell when you're a non-parent. They're very alike: same height, same long, fair, swishy hair. Then just as the driver's door opens . . . it hits me.

'Gran! It's him! It's Tim and his twins! Quick, run or they'll see us!'

'No one can see us,' she replies calmly, resolutely not budging from where she's standing over by the lilies. 'Just watch and learn, love.'

I do and I can barely believe what I'm seeing.

It's Tim, my lovely Tim, slamming the car door shut with an expensive clunk and striding in that long-legged way he has towards the front door. He looks tired, grey, washed out and my heart goes out to him.

Then the front door opens.

'Oh my God, Granny, it's her . . . it's the wife!'

'Ex-wife, I think you'll find, love.'

I can't believe it. There's Tim, calmly handing over his daughters and there's what's-her-name, in a Juicy Couture tracksuit with gel nails, coolly making arrangements for Tim to pick up the twins for a movie night during the week. There's a guy in the background, just in the hall behind her, hovering proprietorially. They don't even ask poor Tim inside. I can't tell you how weird this all is; like watching a soap opera unfold before my eyes, except somehow it's all real.

'Is she with someone else now?' I ask Granny in a half-whisper. 'That guy beside her?'

'Shhhhhhh!'

The door is closed, practically in his face, and Tim slowly trudges back to his car. God love him, he looks crushed, there's no other word for it.

'So they're separated then?'

'Yes, love. For quite some time now. He's living on his own in some awful shoebox of an apartment in town and he only gets to see those lovely daughters of his twice a week. Heartbreaking for him. And that's her new fancy-man, who had no problem just moving lock, stock and barrel into a house that poor Tim is still paying the mortgage on. Shocking carry-on.'

Oh no, no, no. This is just all so wrong. Tim was always such a family-oriented person; to be a separated dad must just be killing him.

'Do you know,' says Granny, looking at me with a twinkle, 'I think it's high time you called him, love. Get in contact again. Maybe arrange to meet up for a nice lunch or something. You're lonely, he's lonely and I'll tell you this: there's not a day goes by that he doesn't think about you.'

'Oh Gran, I couldn't, it would just feel so . . . awkward. I mean, after all these years, suddenly I just contact him out of the blue? Wouldn't I just look like a complete saddo?'

Okay, so I'm explaining myself very badly, but what I mean is: come on. Even desperadoes like me have to draw the line somewhere.

Granny just sighs. 'And you wonder why you're all alone?'

I don't even have time to answer. She takes my hand and, whaddya know, we're off again.

Oh no, no, no, no, no, no, no, no!

This is the worst yet.

Now we're back in my apartment, and I'm looking at myself, sitting all alone and drinking a glass of wine in front of the TV. I'm a lot older, maybe sixty-ish, and the funny thing is I look the spitting image of Granny now. There's a mangy-looking fake glitter Christmas tree hanging sadly in the corner and on TV I'm watching . . .

Prince Charles? Can that be right? I gasp as it dawns on me. He's King Charles now and he's giving his televised Christmas Day speech, which can only mean . . .

'Granny? Why am I all by myself on Christmas Day?'

'Because this is the life that you've chosen, pet. Doesn't exactly look like a lot of fun, now does it?'

She's absolutely right, I look pathetic and sad and lonely. Suddenly, I'm hating this. I mean, I know it's only a dream, but I will myself to wake up and snap out of it.

I mean, for God's sake, what is this? Has my granny suddenly turned into the Ghost of Relationships Past, Present and Future or something?

'I will *never* end up all alone on Christmas Day!' I snap. 'For starters, I'd be with Mum and Dad.'

'Your parents have long since passed on, love. And your brother and all his family are off skiing.'

'What about my friends?'

'All with their own children and grandchildren today, pet. They've invited you over for Stephen's Day, of course, but Christmas is a time for family and you chose not to have one, remember? This is the life you created for yourself.'

Now she's looking at me keenly again.

'All that went wrong in your life, pet, is that you met your soul mate *young*. And now he's alone and you're alone and you won't get in touch with him again. Don't let pride lead you to this,' she says, pointing to the sixty-year-old me in the armchair.

Suddenly, for about the tenth time tonight, I start to sob.

'No,' I sniff, 'I don't want to end up like this. It's not too late, is it? I can still change my fate, can't I?'

But Granny's gone and now I'm back on my own bed, shivering and crying.

It's a no-brainer.

Next morning, I take matters into my own hands. I call Tim's mother, we have a lovely chat and she tells me about his marriage break-up and how upset they all were, but how Tim is now slowly starting to rebuild his life again. She gives me his number and I have to brace myself.

Come on, come on, we all have a road not taken, here's a rare chance to do something about mine . . .

In a strange way, this just feels right, so I go for it.

And do you know what the weirdest thing of all is?

As I pick up the phone with trembling hands to dial Tim's mobile, I'd almost swear I can get the smell of lilies.

∽ ∾

First published in *Prima* magazine

Bill Cullen

Bill Cullen was born in the inner-city tenements of Dublin. One of fourteen children whose mother, Mary Darcy, was a fruit seller, Bill was selling on the streets from the age of six. Bill set up his own motor business and in 1986 he took over the troubled Renault car distribution franchise from Waterford Crystal. His turnaround of that company is a business success story, well chronicled in his memoirs *It's A Long Way from Penny Apples*, which hit the No. 1 slot in Ireland and the UK. Bill is President of the Irish Youth Foundation, which raises 1.5 million a year for youth projects in Ireland, giving opportunities for achievement to kids like himself. He is also well known today as 'The Boss' of TV's *The Apprentice*.

Mary Beats off the Eviction Bowsies **

Extract from *It's a Long Way from Penny Apples* (MERCIER PRESS)

Bill Cullen

'Avicshun! Avicshun! The Corpo are here for Missus Walsh! It's an Avicshun!'

Mary Darcy opened her eyes and sat up listening. 'Did I hear "Avicshun"?' she asked slowly.

Rita nodded just as the roar went up again: 'Avicshun! Avicshun! It's the Corpo for Missus Walsh.' With that, there was a loud bang of a door hitting the wall, and the tramp of hobnailed boots on the stone hall.

Mary's face flushed red and she stood up, with anger in her eyes. 'Give me that poker, Rita,' she said, 'and Liam, you get that sweeping brush and come with me. You girls mind the little ones.' There was a pause as she retied her white apron around her swollen tummy and then took the poker and waved for Liam to follow her.

'I don't believe this,' she said. 'It can't be an Avicshun in this day and age, in this kip of a house.' She opened the door and then leaned back to dip her fingers in the holy-water font and blessed herself and sprinkled some water on her son. There were roars and screams coming up the stairs from Missus Walsh's room at the back of the hall. 'Let's go,' she said and down the stairs she went, with Liam behind her.

The Corporation had taken over the tenements years before from the profiteering landlords who had evicted tenants left, right and centre for not paying their rent. But the Corpo had a more charitable outlook and evictions were now seldom seen. Only one had happened in the last twelve months: that had been at the top end of Summerhill, and the ould fella was moving on anyway. It was still a fearful sight to see the Corpo men throw every piece of his belongings out onto the footpath and leave him sitting there in the rain while they boarded up the doors and windows of the room. His brother arrived later that night with a horse and cart. They loaded up his bits and bobs and off they went, never to be heard of again.

When Mary turned the corner of the stairs, she saw three Corpo lads in the hall, with Missus Walsh's table and chairs already being handed out from man to man. Some children were standing barefoot in the hall crying and she could hear Missus Walsh's voice from the room pleading tearfully: 'No, no, don't throw us out.'

Mary let out a roar – 'What's going on here, ya bowsies!' – and she smashed the poker on the banisters with a loud crash that brought the men to a halt.

'Who's in charge here?' she shouted, and out from the room came a big, red-faced man, followed by Mister Sutton the rent collector.

'I'm in charge here, missus,' said the big man, in a country accent, 'now you just buzz off and mind your business. This is an official Corporation eviction, and you'll be in the clink if you're not careful.'

Mary gave the banister another bang with the poker. 'Well, aren't you the big brave culchie now, threatening women and children, sneaking in here when our men are out working to pay your rent? If it's trouble you want, you've come to the right place and I'm telling ya to leave Missus Walsh's things alone or you'll have me to deal with,' she shouted without taking a breath.

'And as for you, Mister Sutton, come out from hiding behind that culchie and speak up for yourself. Don't you know Mister Walsh was in hospital for a few months with the kidney stones? And he's back working now and they'll clear off the arrears. Don't ya know all that and why are ya here with these latchicos doing your dirty work?'

Mister Sutton just blinked behind his glasses as the big man did the answering. 'Listen, woman, it's none of your business. He's had plenty of warnings. When any tenant falls behind by more than six months' rent, it's out. That's the policy and there's no discussion.'

Turning to his men, he said, 'Right, me lads, let's get on with the job,' but before they could move Mary smashed the banister again with the poker.

'So that's the policy is it, now? Let's throw the sick man and his family out on the street is the policy, because they owe the Corpo a few lousy pounds. Let's get a big brave culchie up from Cork with his pals to dump them on the road. Sure they're well used to this job. Didn't some of ya help the English landlords during the famine days? Turncoats and informers ya are, who take on only the women and children. We'll leave the room there empty and put Missus Walsh out in the rain. Well, that's the policy we had when the Brits were here, and many's the brave Irishman's blood was spilt to get them out and change that policy. Is this what Michael Collins fought for? Of course, he was a great man from Cork and he was shot in the back by one of his own. The like of you. Let me tell you this, me boyo – the first man that moves a stick of furniture out of this hall will get my poker over his head.'

What a tirade. The big Cork man was kicking the wall, saying 'Feck ya! Feck ya! Feck ya!' Mary Darcy stood halfway up the stairs in her white apron, heavily pregnant, waving the poker, her face flushed with anger. Her young son stood beside her, with a sweeping brush held across his chest.

Mary came down the stairs into the hall and took a chair from one of the men, without resistance. 'Now, Mister Sutton,' she said, 'why don't you get these men out of here and let's see how we can clear off Missus Walsh's arrears. Sure I've two pounds here in me pocket. Wouldn't that be a better thing to do than have some of these culchies in hospital.'

The big man was livid with temper at the insults that had been heaped on him. He would have killed any man who used those words to him, but he was helpless and frustrated when faced with a pregnant woman.

The rent collector broke the tension. 'Well, are you saying, Missus Cullen, that we can have the arrears paid?' he asked.

'Of course I'm saying the arrears will be paid, Mister Sutton,' she replied. 'Get rid of these boyos and we'll sit down on these chairs and work everything out.'

'Right then,' said Mister Sutton, turning to the big man. 'You go on back to the office, Shamus, and I'll sort this out.'

The big man kicked the wall in frustration. 'Bejaysus, I'll go back to no feckin' office,' he said. 'I'll go down to Conway's pub and you'll meet us there to pay us for our day's work, so you will.' And down the hall he went, with the sparks flying from his hobnailed boots. The other men put down the furniture and trailed out after him.

'Bring that stuff in now, Liam,' said the Ma, 'and why don't you put the teapot on, Missus Walsh. I'm sure Mister Sutton could do with a cuppa tea while we talk business.'

Twenty minutes later, Mister Sutton left, with the promise of six shillings a week payment off the arrears as well as the rent from next week on. Missus Walsh didn't know where she'd get the extra money from.

'Don't worry about that, Missus Walsh. We've won the haggle today, and we can win it again if need be,' said Mary, as she left to go back upstairs.

Vera and Rita had been watching the commotion from the landing. When Mary arrived back, it was to a steaming mug of tea and a slice of toast ready for her on the table. She smiled at them all and sat down. 'Isn't it a great bunch I have here now. The girls looking after the house and this young fella standing in for his da,' she said, ruffling Liam's curly black hair. 'You can put this poker and that brush of yours away now, son,' she said.

But as she sipped her tea, she grimaced and said, 'Liam, run down and tell Mother Darcy to come up here quick, and Vera, will you put that big pot of water on the stove.'

That evening, Carmel was born in the tenement room. The children had all been hooshed down to stay in Molly's. When they trooped back for bed, Mary was sitting up with the new baby and Billy was there beside her. Mother Darcy was having a mug of shell cocoa; she had a proud look on her face and her sleeves were still rolled up.

'Mother Darcy brought the new baby up from the chapel in her shopping bag,' was the story Rita gave.

The Da was back in Brooks Thomas, but only part-time. He got the odd few days' work with his brother Jack in Granby Pork Products. Granby were up in Granby Lane at the back of Dominick Street Church, beside the rear of Walden Ford Dealers. At other times, he worked as an usher in the picture houses: the Plaza in Granby Row and the Rotunda Cinema at the Parnell Monument. His military training was great for keeping the queues of children under control, and he was meticulous in his cleanliness for the butcher's. But he'd no work coming up to the Christmas, and the markets had a lean spell for Mary, who was still nursing her new baby, Carmel. The rain was seeping in around the tenement windows and Billy had used up bundles of *Herald*s plugging the cracks to keep the draughts out.

One day his old army pal Johnny Coleman had dropped in with six army greatcoats. 'You have to keep these children of yours warm in bed, Mary,' he said, 'and these are just the job.' The coats went over the thin blankets and were a godsend for the kids.

'Snug as a bug in a rug you are now,' said Mary.

'Don't mention bugs, Mary,' Billy said. 'I've spent the last week fighting the clocks and spiders coming in these damp walls. The powder I got down in Con Foley's Medical Hall seems to be working. It's certainly done the job on the oul' mattresses, because I haven't seen a hopper since I doused them.'

Mary was quiet as she rocked the baby's cot. 'We'll have to get out of here, Billy, before this bloody place takes another of our babies. Have you heard anything from the Corpo? Mick Mullen put in a word for us and he told me that with seven kids now, we should be getting an offer of a place soon.'

Billy looked at her and said, 'No, I haven't seen Mick, but I'll go and find him in Liberty Hall tomorrow. And I've to see Alfie Byrne next Tuesday.'

Mary didn't respond. She just kept rocking the baby's cot.

'Jack has promised me some corned beef and pigs' feet for Christmas,' Billy continued. 'It'll make a fine dinner for the kids. They love the trotters.'

It was no use. She was away somewhere else. So he just undressed and went to bed. Hours later, he woke. Mary was at the table darning some of the children's gansies, singing her song in a low voice as she rocked the cot with her foot:

Somewhere over the rainbow, skies are blue,
And the dreams that you dare to dream, really do come true.

Norah Casey

Norah Casey is CEO (and owner) of Harmonia, Ireland's largest magazine company printing over four million magazines annually for the Irish, British and US markets. Harmonia's stable includes strong women's brands: *Irish Tatler, U, Woman's Way* and **www.ivenus.com**; and specialist titles like *Food&Wine, Auto Ireland* and *Ireland of the Welcomes* (aimed at the Irish diaspora with over 80,000 US-based subscribers). Norah was awarded the Veuve Clicquot Business Woman of the Year Award for 2007/8 and has won the Publisher of the Year Award for three years running.

The KNOCK *

Norah Casey

Now here's a good story about hope, love and Destiny . . .

Life was not like a coffee ad. This much he knew.

For weeks now he had drawn up plans. First he thought he would just go up there and knock on the door. And when she opened it he would . . .

What? What would he do?

That was the stumbling block. He thought he could casually say something about needing sugar. But he never had sugar in his flat and if things went to plan she would end up living with him and would discover that he hated sugar. She would know he had duped her and then she would fly at him in a rage and throw all her clothes in a suitcase and march straight out the door.

He could see it all happening and found himself choked with tears at the thought of it.

So, back to the knock on the door.

In his hopeful moments she would answer with a smile which widened at the sight of him and she would say, 'Why, Johnny, I thought you'd never knock on the door! Come in, come in, I was just baking chocolate cake in the hope that you'd arrive.'

Some mornings, as he listened to her putting on the radio and running the shower – his sense of hearing being preternaturally keen in her regard – this particular scenario would play out all the way to their first-born son.

After the chocolate cake was finished they would talk and talk and talk. And when sleepiness overtook them she would ask him to stay and they would lie in each other's arms and in the morning make mad passionate love. He knew all the details but you, lovely reader, have to use your imagination – because Johnny was a deeply private man and I am only giving you a glimpse of his anguish and fantasies.

So, back to the knock on the door.

In his worst 'three o'clock in the morning, blackest hour', he imagined the following.

Every step – all 59 of them – from his door up to her apartment is measured out and he matches his steps, breath for breath, with his heartbeat. *Thump. Thump. Thump.* He gets to the door. He feels his breathing can be heard in Outer Mongolia so he calms himself, waits for his heart to stop thumping, fixes his tie and prepares to knock.

Then the door flings open and she's there laughing and shrieking and behind her a naked man is chasing her and laughing, laughing, laughing and gouging a hole in his heart that will never heal. He sobs. His vivid mind won't let him rest and he follows the story all the way to *their* first-born son and he a witness to their happiness and love.

At these moments he knows he will never knock on that door.

Then morning would come and life would take over for a while.

Johnny has a good job. Not the most exciting job but it's not the worst job either. He's a financial adviser. But Johnny isn't boring. His friends would say that he is sensible – a sound man – willing to lend an ear or a fiver if you needed one or the other. And he is faithful to his friends. He remembers birthdays and anniversaries. So he isn't boring but, if truth be told, he isn't the most exciting either.

That's why what happened to Johnny was all the more remarkable – a rollercoaster in an otherwise settled life.

So, back to the KNOCK.

I knew I would start using capital letters eventually because the KNOCK became the biggest thing in Johnny's life.

It had started soon after she moved in, in January – around a nanosecond after he saw her humping a suitcase up the stairs. In his mind he rushed to her aid and manfully took the case and lifted it up to her floor.

What really happened was this.

He came out his door to go to work and saw this woman. Large brown coat, long brown hair, jeans, boots, suitcase – all in a flash frame – like in the ads. He was about to turn away to walk out the door to go to work.

And then she turned.

'Hi, there! Just moving in. If I can ever get this blasted case up the stairs.'

He stood frozen.

What he saw was this woman. Beautiful big smile, flushed face, beautiful big brown eyes, sparkling, shining, shimmering – oh, those eyes! He was mesmerized. And nothing would come out of his mouth. In his head a whole heap of stuff was crashing in, trying to push to the surface.

He was sorting through all the possibilities of what he might say.

He looked down for a moment to gather his thoughts and courage, and began the most important sentence of his life. 'Can I . . . ?'

And she was gone. *Thump, thump, thump,* the suitcase followed her up the stairs. How could a normal working day in the middle of a miserable January begin with such hope, only to crush him with despair?

That was before he even left his building.

He feared he would not be able to concentrate on the mortgage applications and the pension reviews. But he did. That's our Johnny. Solid and dependable.

But not for long.

So began the period I like to call 'THE KNOCK TIME'.

Johnny came home that evening fuelled with a passion for his little flat which heretofore he had never possessed. It was just a flat. But now it wasn't just a flat. It was the home of his angel, the woman he was going to marry and he rushed towards it with excitement. When he got to the front door he took an age to enter the building.

He stood in the foyer looking at the empty post-box for Number 2. Pretending it was jammed with letters when in fact he was putting back in and taking out the telephone bill he had picked up that morning. But there was no audience for his theatrics (albeit a little low-key on the dramatic front). Then he walked down the corridor to his ground-floor flat: Number 2.

He fiddled with his keys. He stalled after he heard the click. But there was no repeat performance of that morning's thrilling escapade. *Thump, thump, thump,* went his heart. But otherwise it was silent – eerily silent they would say in the horror movies. But then they had never come home to a flat in Ringsend at 6 pm on a wet Thursday in January. There was nothing eerie about that silence – it was just an absence of noise.

Especially noise from the stairwell. Sadly.

Johnny made some tea and he thought and he thought and he thought. There was a purpose to his evening. How to find a way to get the woman upstairs to talk to him. Because the rest would be easy. He knew in his heart, his head, his other places, that they would fall in love and Destiny would take over. But there was this big challenge first. How to get to her in a way that didn't make her feel he was desperate.

He liked the word 'nonchalance' and that was his ambition. A 'nonchalant' encounter that would develop and grow and escalate and take them over. Then Destiny.

So he decided that the only thing to do would be to knock on the door. At this stage there was no need to capitalize the 'knock'. It was such a small thing to do.

So he thought, 'I will go out the door of Number 2 and go up the stairs and walk to her door and knock on it . . .'

He stopped and pondered. 'And then I will ask her for a . . . what? What does she ask for in that coffee ad? Sugar . . .' Yes, that's what he'd do.

Now, dear reader, you already know the dilemma about the sugar so we'll say no more.

Then he had it. 'Coffee.' He hardly drinks it but every now and again he likes a cup so it is plausible that he might not have it in his cupboard. And how they will laugh in years to come about them meeting over his simple need for a coffee on a dreary Thursday in January!

So he opened the cupboard and discovered a jar of coffee. Not a bother. He poured the granules down the drain and worried about all that caffeine going into the water system. But only for a second. Then, jar in the bin, he headed for the door. Then he stopped and thought that an empty jar would add 'authenticity' to his request so he headed back to the bin.

By now the empty coffee jar was nestling among the tea bags and soggy toast and orange peel – the detritus of breakfast – and he had to put his hand in to retrieve it. He did it like they do on that TV show – *I'm a Celebrity Get Me Out of Here*. He closed his eyes and imagined spiders and locusts and slimy things and he bravely wrestled the empty jar and got another meal for his camp mates. (Look – if you haven't watched the show you won't understand but Johnny does and so do I.)

So there he was with the worst-looking coffee jar in Ringsend. So he headed for the sink to wash it off. And ran it under the hot tap and discovered the error of his ways when the label began to slide off effortlessly.

And that was the real bitch about it. If he was trying to get that label off he knew it would stick to the jar and only budge in small centimetre pieces so that forever you would be picking bits of white gluey bits off it and you would never get the pristine glass that he was now staring at. He dried the jar. Now what the hell was he going to do?

Okay. 'Regroup,' he thought.

There must be something else.

So he thought about tea. But that would be no good because he has a slight addiction to tea and would never run out and that would be obvious when they got together.

How about milk? Yes. Yes. Yes. Milk would be the perfect thing. Very easy to run out of milk and in order to have his tea (which he can't live without) he had to have milk. So he went to the fridge. And of course there was a two-litre carton with a sell-by date well into the following week but he knew how to fix that. Over to the sink and his milk joined the coffee granules into the Ringsend water supply. He bypassed the bin. All systems go. He had the empty milk carton and he was heading for the door.

His thoughts turned to the knock. She would answer (same smile) and he would say: 'Hi. I saw you this morning moving in and I . . .'

That's when it hit him.

How could he go upstairs and ask her for milk when she had just moved in? How crass was that? He would have to be the most insensitive man on the planet to proposition a woman on the first day in her new flat with a request for milk. He should be bringing her milk, and tea, and coffee.

He stopped mid-stride and headed back to the cupboard.

By now he had no coffee and no milk, which left him with tea bags. He couldn't go upstairs and give her tea bags. The path to true love was never more crooked. He listened to the rain battering the window and put on his coat. Off to the local supermarket for the essentials and then he would be well equipped for the trip upstairs.

A proper welcome.

He would buy cake as well and then he wouldn't be embarrassed, when over some family dinner in years to come, she'd tell the tale of her gallant husband's attempt at wooing her. And to think she might have said: 'Can you believe it? He came up to borrow some milk and me surrounded by empty packing cases!' He suspected that she would never say that because he would never have stood a chance and Destiny would have had something else in store for him.

Anyway all was right again and he was off to buy the perfect moving-in offerings. He forgot a plastic bag and had to splash out on buying one at the till – 'This is how much she means to me,' he thought.

So he was heading back home. The rain was pelting him, his coat was getting heavier and heavier and he could feel the wet seeping into his shirt so that it was sticking to his shoulders.

He didn't feel very romantic when he turned into his street. Even less so when he saw her. Brown coat, brown hair, jeans, boots – getting into a bloody taxi!

Apart from anything else, where did she manage to get a taxi on a miserable Thursday evening in January – in Ringsend? He stood in despair as the taxi whisked her away to . . .

Okay, he didn't want to let his mind wander down that road.

He gave himself a good talking-to all the way back to Number 2. He didn't even know her name, she could be engaged, married, on the run. He would go into his nice, cosy, dry flat and watch some TV.

But of course he didn't.

He began to think about the knock. Because tomorrow it might be too late to say 'Welcome to your new flat' and his humble offering would be inappropriate. He worried over this. Then he thought about whether he could give her flowers. Would that be better? But did it strike the right note of 'nonchalance'? He didn't think so.

And in any case he hadn't really contemplated what would happen once she opened the door.

That's when the real horror began.

That's when the knock became the KNOCK and assumed capital letters.

What would happen if she answered the door with a man? What would happen if she looked at him, perplexed, and said: 'Why would you do such a thing? I don't even know you!'? What would happen if she answered the door and spoke to him in Russian and he didn't know what she was saying? What would happen if she answered the door and laughed in his face at the absurdity of his meagre gift? Horror of horrors! What would happen if she answered the door with her arms locked around another woman?

Okay, dear reader, you get the idea. Poor Johnny, who was never prone to a vivid imagination, was suddenly struck with the wildest and most creative scenarios that would happen after the KNOCK.

So weeks passed.

He discovered her name was Ruby. He loved her name. She left in a taxi every evening at 7 pm. Exactly. He was left with one hour from arriving home until the time of Ruby leaving to contemplate the perfect moment for the KNOCK. She arrived home at 1.10 am. Too late for him to affect an air of 'nonchalance'.

His friends began to worry. Johnny missed a birthday in week two and was too distracted to listen to poor Martha's tales of woe about her parents' divorce in week three. He stopped going out and for three weeks he stayed in the flat hoping that was the evening she would come home early.

Now, just as an aside, I need to put Johnny's suffering in context lest you think I am exaggerating. Johnny had had girlfriends before. While he was not a man of the world by any means, a nice solid boy from Athlone would always attract willing companions. So he had a fair share of dates and previous romances. Quite why he was so struck by Ruby he had no idea. He just knew when he locked eyes with her that they would be together. Ask anyone who finds their one true soul mate and they will tell a similar story, you cynical reader.

He was in love.

So back to the KNOCK which has taken on biblical proportions in Johnny's life.

And then it comes to pass that one evening he hears the taxi pull up outside. He hears her phone ringing to let her know of its arrival. He hears her open her door. And by the way it's the same ritual every evening so he has heard it all before. He hears her clattering down the stairs and before he even knows he is doing it he is out the door and at the foot of the stairs just as she reaches the third step from the bottom.

Step 48 of the 59 steps from her door to the door of Number 2.

She looks at him and he looks at her. Big brown coat, brown hair, jeans, boots, beautiful big smile, brown eyes sparkling, shining – and he smiles back.

She says: 'I wondered if we would ever meet again.'

And he says: 'So did I.'

She would never know how much there was to tell about those three words 'So did I.'

She goes to pass him by and he moves to one side with nothing in his head or his mouth to hold her.

She turns. Laughs and says: 'I was hoping you'd knock on the door but when you didn't . . .' At this she pauses.

And he says: 'Could I knock on your door when I get home tomorrow?'

And she says that would be great. 'I nurse a very frail woman and I do the twilight shift and she always sends a taxi so anytime other than then would be good. I'm Ruby, by the way.'

'And I'm Johnny,' he says.

And his heart is filled with hope.

And what happens next, dear reader, is a matter for Destiny.

∽ ∾

Don Conroy

Don Conroy is a man of many talents – a writer, a television presenter, a naturalist, an environmentalist and a working artist who has had many exhibitions. He studied life drawings and culture at the National College of Art, and worked as a designer and illustrator for advertising agencies as well as acting professionally in the theatre. Perhaps best known to the young people of Ireland as Uncle Don on RTÉ's *The Den*, Don has also had TV series of his own – *Paint for Fun* and *The Art of Don*. Don is also the author of many books for children and young adults.

Little Wing's Vision *

Don Conroy

The forest was silent except for an icy wind that moaned through the branches of the pines. Beyond the forest, the land was shrouded with a heavy snowfall. Winter had truly taken its grip on the land. Some of the snowdrifts had banked up the tree trunks. The river was frozen and mostly covered by the heavy snow that had been falling for several days. Some distance from the forest, a few scattered tepees could be seen. But no sign of life. Even the dogs were gone. The few mustang ponies were being used by the remaining braves to hunt for food for their families. Although game was very scarce, they had refused to go to Fort William like most of their tribe. Giving up one's freedom for a meagre supply of food and shelter, living in stables like a beast of burden. This did not suit the last of the Lakota people. Even their friends, the Cheyenne, had been placed in reservations far from their home.

In one of the tepees, where the old chief, Red Hawk, slept, a young boy stirred under his star blanket. With a deerskin to lie upon and the woollen blanket made for him by his grandmother, he kept warm on those very cold nights. Looking up through the opening in the roof of the tepee, he could see the bright light of the morning.

Peeping over the blanket, his eyes scanned the tepee to see if his father, Skin Walker, had returned. There was no sign of him. His grandfather, Red Hawk, sat upright with his back against a lodge pole. Almost completely covered in a buffalo-skin pelt, his eyes were closed but his arms seemed to be held in a ritualistic position. Little Wing's big, bright, brown eyes began to really study the old man. His face was so lined, like a cobweb, Little Wing thought. His arms and legs were bony and his skin was like rippled leather.

Little Wing sat up, scrambled over to the entrance and lifted back the flap to look out.

'Close that,' the frail voice of Red Hawk commanded. 'We don't want to lose the heat.'

'Sorry, Grandfather,' said the boy. 'I was just looking to see if my father was coming.'

'Throw some sticks on the fire.'

The boy gathered the last few faggots and placed them carefully on the dying embers of the fire.

'Your father is a good man,' said Red Hawk. 'He'll find us something to eat, you'll see.'

Then the old man gave a rattling cough. The boy wished his grandfather hadn't mentioned food for, as soon as he did, he could feel the hunger pangs. It was as if the old man sensed it. He pulled out a small piece of dried fish from a bag. The boy bit into the salty, smoked fish and chewed it slowly, savouring every morsel. Then he suddenly remembered that his grandfather had said yesterday that the piece of fish was the last of the food.

'Grandfather, what about you?'

'Oh, I'm not hungry,' he smiled.

Each day was filled with amazing stories. His grandfather seemed to be full of them. He would tell of the great days when the land was full of game. The buffalo, the bighorn, the mule deer, the prairie fowl and the grayling. It was the time of the great warriors; Red Cloud, Sitting Bull and the bravest of all, Chief Crazy Horse.

'How did Chief Crazy Horse get his name?' asked Little Wing.

'Well, when he was born, a wild horse ran through the village,' said Red Hawk. 'Do you know why you're called Little Wing?'

'Tell me.'

'Well, the night you came to us from the spirit world was a

beautiful, warm, starry night. I remember it well. My first and only grandson. When your father heard your cry of arrival, he hurried towards the tepee and saw an elf owl perched on one of the lodge poles. It flew away as he approached. When your mother asked, "What shall his name be?" your father answered, "Little Wing," and told your mother about the owl.'

The old man's cough seemed to be getting worse. The boy offered the old man some river water from a leather pouch. The cough seemed to ease after taking a drink.

'Tell me about the buffaloes, Grandfather,' the boy asked eagerly, as he had never seen a live one. He had touched the old, brown skin that his grandfather kept wrapped around his thin body. There was a buffalo helmet hanging from a lodge pole that the medicine man wore in times of great ceremonies. He too was gone, along with Little Wing's mother and grandmother, from the fever that had entered the village four moons ago.

'The buffalo has always been a great friend to our people and other tribes. It fed us, its coat kept us warm in wintertime and we made ropes from its hide and pouches. We never hunted it more than we needed to, always thanking the animals for giving up their life for us and asking them to return again from the spirit world to the grassy plains. But when the white man arrived with his iron horse, travelling on ribbons of steel, across our lands, he brought the hunters from across the sea, with their deadly smoking guns. They destroyed the great herds and left the carcasses rotting on the sacred grounds.'

The old man began to cough and cough. Then he lay back, breathing heavily.

Little Wing decided that his grandfather needed help and food and if his father hadn't returned by nightfall, he would travel at first light to try and find his father and bring back some food.

To his amazement, he heard the sound of a horse neighing and snorting. Had his father finally returned? He hurried outside. There was his father's horse, Swift, but no sign of his father. He called out but there was no answer. Two hares were tied around the horse's neck.

The boy got dressed and ran over to another tepee where Grey Crow and her daughter lived. He explained what had happened. The old woman said she and her daughter would take care of Red Hawk and cook a warm meal with the hares, to feed him and the others. Little Wing thanked them, then returned to his tepee to quickly get his bow and arrows, blanket and rope. He brought the horse over to a log and stepped up on the log and onto the horse's back.

'I'm sorry I've no food to give you,' he whispered in the horse's ear, 'but help me find my father, and I promise to get you sweet grass to eat.'

The women could be seen shuffling through the snow, across to the old chief's tepee.

The boy gave a sigh of relief for he knew his grandfather would be in good hands and soon have a warm meal. The boy said a prayer to Wakan Tanka, the Great Spirit, to help him find his father. Then he headed out across the blanket of snow, hoping Swift would find a way. The horse moved slowly but sure-footedly, head down, through the heavy snowdrifts. Then on through the lonely forest.

Hours passed with no sign of his father or any other form of life. On out through the forest onto the wide plains. He felt colder and colder. A myriad of snowflakes began to drift down from the sky, but he continued on. The day wore on, then the sign of night began to close in. He stopped near some boulders and trees. Pulling down some small branches, he made a dig-out in the snow beside the rocks and laid some branches down, then covered them with his blanket. He gently urged Swift down on the ground beside him and lay against the horse for warmth. The horse was a great comfort to him as the darkness closed in. He had known the horse since he was a small boy. Swift was a strong and gentle creature. Little Wing settled to sleep, making the most of the situation.

He had the strangest dreams. A white buffalo appeared to him. He could feel its warm breath on his face. Although the creature was massive in size, Little Wing felt no fear. Then he had visions of his father and grandfather talking and laughing together. Then his mother and grandmother appeared from behind the white buffalo and smiled, telling him not to be afraid. They reached towards him.

His beautiful dream was shattered by the piercing howl of a wolf. Little Wing leaped to his feet, pulling his knife from its leather sheath and anxiously looking around. The night was clear and cold. The full moon bathed the world in its silvery light. He knew the wolves must be hungry. Then a large alpha male appeared above him on a boulder and stared down directly at him. Little Wing's heart was pounding in his chest. He turned around. There were at least seven wolves surrounding them. Swift was standing alert, snorting. The wolves stood, stock still, staring at them, then slowly padded away. The night became silent again but Little Wing lay wide awake for the rest of the night.

The early morning brought a pale sun which hung like a lantern in the sky. The boy set off again on his mission to find his father. He encountered the wolves some distance away. They had found a dead moose and were feeding on its carcass.

Swift passed slowly by the wolves and turned eastward. The boy sensed that Swift seemed to know where he was going so he let the horse lead him on. Then, to his astonishment, he saw what looked like a white buffalo up ahead, just like in his dream. He turned the horse in the direction of the buffalo but as he approached the area, it seemed to vanish. All that could be seen were great snow mounds.

Swift came to a standstill. The boy tried to coax him on but the horse would not move. The boy's hands were numb with the cold and he knew the horse must be exhausted and hungry but there was nothing he could do only keep moving, otherwise they would freeze to death.

But Swift refused to move. The boy tried everything but to no avail. Finally, he dismounted and pulled at the reins. 'Come on, Swift! Good boy! We have to keep going.'

Swift pulled his head back. The boy decided the horse needed a rest. He would let him have a short rest after which Swift would hopefully obey and move on.

Little Wing blew on his hands. The horse neighed.

A strange sound could be heard, slightly muffled by the snow. The boy listened intently. He could hear the sound of a wooden flute. Little Wing walked towards where the sound was coming from. The horse came behind and nudged him. Snow began to collapse, revealing a ravine. Little Wing carefully inched over and looked down. He could see a dead elk, partly covered by snow, lying in the ravine. Then his father peeped out from under a ledge. He couldn't believe his eyes when he saw his son peering down at him.

'Father, are you all right?'

'Most of me,' he smiled broadly. 'I'm afraid I've broken my leg.'

'Don't worry, Father, I'll get you up.'

The boy was so relieved to see his father, he forgot all about his fear, hunger and coldness. Backing Swift to the edge of the ravine, he tied the rope around the horse's shoulders and threw the other end over the ledge.

His father edged his way over to the elk and tied the rope around its body. If Swift manages to haul the elk up, then the tribe will have some food, he thought.

'Pull away, Little Wing!' he shouted.

The boy pulled the horse forward. It was a fierce struggle, Swift slipping once in the snow. Little Wing was shocked to see the elk rather than his father appearing over the edge. Little Wing quickly untied the rope and was about to throw it down to his father, when he noticed the rope hide was slightly frayed from the sharp rocks. He called down to his father, explaining that the rope was torn.

'Son, listen to me. Try and get the elk onto Swift's back. He will kneel down at your command. Go back to the village with the food. The elk will sustain the families for several days. Do it now, hurry, my son!'

'No,' said Little Wing. 'I won't leave you!'

'You must,' said his father. 'The tribe is more important – go now!'

Tears streamed down Little Wing's face. 'There must be another way.'

He prayed to Wakan Tanka again, to save his father's life.

Swift neighed and looked westward. The horse nudged Little Wing who was still sobbing and praying. The boy turned and saw four horses with riders upon them. They moved slowly towards him. Were they ghosts of his ancestors coming to take his father to the spirit world?

As the riders approached, one called his name, 'Little Wing!'

The boy shrieked with joy for it was the other braves from their tribe. They could not believe their eyes. There was Little Wing with a large elk and his father's horse. They had left the village together to get food. After a long search without any luck, they agreed to separate and journey in different directions to hunt, agreeing to meet at Buffalo Rock after two moons. The boy urged them to hurry and rescue his father who was in the ravine and badly hurt. One, Red Wolf, climbed down on a rope and put a splint on Skin Walker's leg. The other men gently hauled him up to safety. Little Wing's father was so happy and relieved to see his band of brothers that he gave out a cry of joy.

'Keep your strength,' smiled Red Wolf.

They pulled some branches from a nearby tree and made an A-shaped frame with the branches and some rope. The travois was put on Swift and a blanket and rug were placed on the stretcher. They journeyed slowly back to the village, Little Wing on Swift, pulling his father on the stretcher. Another carrying the elk.

There were great celebrations when the braves returned. Little Wing's grandfather seemed much stronger. He hugged his son and grandson, giving the boy an eagle's feather for his bravery. They had a great feast in the chief's tepee. Many stories were told that evening. Then Little Wing was asked how he managed to find his father. He told them that he followed the White Buffalo. The old chief was amazed.

'This is big medicine,' he exclaimed.

Then they heard what sounded like thunder. The people looked at each other and went outside the tepee. Across the river was a large herd of buffalo. The old chief shrieked with joy and began to dance. The men carried Skin Walker out to witness the wonderful sight.

'So that's what buffaloes look like,' said Little Wing.

His grandfather laughed loudly.

Little Wing noticed a circular green patch, below the pine trees. There, Swift was nibbling on fresh green shoots. The boy looked at the sky and thanked Wakan Tanka.

Evelyn Cusack

Deputy Head of Forecasting at Met Éireann, Evelyn Cusack is one of Ireland's best-loved weather forecasters. A regular on RTÉ TV and radio, she is passionate about making science accessible for all. She has one daughter, Fleur, who is ten. Evelyn has recently been to both Nepal and Cuba, walking to raise funds for MS Ireland, a charity very close to her heart.

What Hope Is There for Planet Earth? **

Evelyn Cusack

Let's start at the very beginning of our known Universe – the Big Bang, estimated to have occurred 13,700 million years ago (mya: million years ago). Maybe there were other Big Bangs and other universes and maybe there are other Big Bangs going on in other dimensions even as you read this but, hey, let's just deal with the facts as we understand them now in 2010. By a series of fantastic physical processes our galaxy, the Milky Way, was formed about 10,000–11,000 mya and then along came our planet Earth, 4,600 mya, and a little later our moon was formed. And so our amazing journey began.

It is estimated that there are 10 billion trillion planets in our Universe. Are we the only living beings in existence? Certainly we are very lucky to be here at all, although millions of suffering children would surely question that. We are just the right distance from our sun (just 5% closer and we would burn up and about 15% further we would freeze). We have a molten interior whose magnetic field shields us from deadly cosmic radiation. Tectonic plates renew the surface and volcanoes feed our atmosphere. Also our moon provides a steady gravitational influence without which we would wobble erratically and have a wildly fluctuating climate unable to sustain our type of life.

In fact, the moon is drifting away from Earth by about 4 cm a year, so in about 2,000 million years its benign caretaking will be gone. If that doesn't get us then we will definitely be wiped out when the Sun reaches white dwarf status and dies – that's in about 5 or 6 billion years from now. So we are really in our middle years as a planet but we may plummet to disaster long before our natural end. And the cause of this is mankind itself.

The earliest evidence for life on Earth comes from hydrocarbon residues from aquatic bacteria in metamorphosed sedimentary rocks in Greenland (*phew!*) which are dated at about 3,800 mya. About 2,700 mya, primitive photosynthesising micro-organisms released increasing volumes of oxygen into the early atmosphere. The next major step was the formation of the ozone layer which filtered out the ultraviolet light which is so harmful to DNA.

All the time, as life was developing, the Earth's continents were shifting and the composition of the atmosphere was changing. Thus all these processes were intrinsically linked. About 220 mya there was a supercontinent, Pangaea, which stretched from pole to pole. It was a very warm Earth and carbon dioxide was five times the present level. The dinosaurs ruled from 230 to 65 mya. At their extinction the little mammals took over and a mere 4 million years ago Ardi, the earliest known hominid, walked the great plains of Africa.

We now look to when the continents took up their modern position. About 20 mya India crashed into Asia, forming the great Himalaya range and later the Isthmus of Panama formed as South America joined North America. The Pacific Ocean was thus cut off from the Atlantic Ocean and our Gulf Stream was born.

And so at last, as recently as 1.8 million years ago, we reach our modern era of climate and humans. It is therefore in this time span that we must examine our current effect on weather and climate.

A series of ice ages followed at regular intervals due to the orbit, wobble and inclination of the Earth relative to the Sun. The earliest known *Homo sapiens* have been dated in Africa at 200,000 years old. Our last ice age ended about 10,000 years ago and it's only since then that human civilisation as we know it really took off. We exist solely thanks to this benign period of weather. From astronomical calculations another ice age isn't too far off, maybe in about 30,000 years' time. But of course that doesn't take into account man's interference with the atmosphere.

Our first known input was when rice was begun to be grown extensively in China about a thousand years ago but it wasn't until the beginning of the industrial era in the mid-1800s that we really began to have a measurable effect. Carbon dioxide levels have risen from their pre-industrial levels of 288 ppm (parts per million) to 388 ppm this year. We know this because of rigorous scientific studies of ice-cores from Greenland and the Antarctic which sample the atmospheric composition as far back as 800,000 years ago.

We have been merrily burning away huge quantities of coal, oil and gas laid down in the Devonian period, 400 mya, as well as destroying our rain forests. Thus we are pumping vast quantities of carbon dioxide into the atmosphere. We are also releasing lots of methane due to our huge consumption of meat. These so-called Greenhouse Gases, first described by the great Irish scientist John Tyndall in 1859, are resulting in a rise in global temperatures.

Dean Jonathan Swift wryly remarked many years ago: *''Tis very warm weather when one's in bed.'* Think of yourself lying down and going to sleep. You lose heat. It is blocked and kept in by your duvet (if you are one of the lucky citizens of Earth). On a winter's night you would get very cold if your duvet fell off and equally you would nearly melt if a dozen duvets were piled on top of you. In effect, the Greenhouse Gases are like piling up a load of duvets over the Earth.

It is a scientific fact that the atmosphere is warming up, proved beyond reasonable doubt. It is incredible that special-interest groups and anti-scientists who are denying this are given an influential platform in the world's media as in 'I don't believe.' Well, global warming is not a matter of faith; it is a matter of physics! This warming is linked to anthropogenic (man-made) emissions. If our emissions are not curtailed or stopped ASAP, they could lead to incalculable changes in our climate which could destroy whole cultures and cause widespread extinctions. Possible effects include drastic sea-level rises, droughts in some areas and deluges in others.

Homo sapiens translated from Latin means 'wise human'. We managed to save our ozone layer, so vital to life, by banning CFCs. Let us hope we can do it again and that we live up to our name and save our beautiful planet Earth which we are so lucky to inhabit among the vast expanse of our amazing Universe.

∽ ∾

Evelyn Cosgrave

Evelyn Cosgrave lives and works in Limerick. Her poetry has been widely published in national journals and in 2000 she was selected for Poetry Ireland's Introductions series. Evelyn was shortlisted for the Strokestown Poetry Prize. She was a finalist in the Rattlebag/Dublin Writers Week Competition in 2002. Her first novel, *Desperately Seeking*, was published in 2008 and her second, *Can I Tell You a Secret?*, in 2009. Evelyn is currently working on her third novel.

Vegetable Soup and Chicken Lasagne *

Evelyn Cosgrave

I think of that summer as my summer of waiting. I was waiting for my Leaving Cert results; I was waiting for my mother to stop fighting with my father; and I was waiting for *him* to look at me and say something meaningful that would change my life forever.

The Leaving Cert wasn't really a big deal. I was leaving home anyway no matter what results I got. I didn't really care where or what course as long as it got me away from my parents. So I couldn't pretend I was worried or anything, but I was still waiting. I was still curious to know whether it would be Arts in Dublin, or Cork, or Galway, or Maynooth, or Social Science in Dublin, or Cork, or Galway, or Maynooth, or Psychology in Dublin, or Cork, or Galway, or Maynooth. The most important thing was that I would be getting out of school (which I had convinced myself I had outgrown by the end of fifth year) and I would be starting a new life in a flat somewhere that was at the very least a two-hour drive (once you factored in the traffic and getting across town) from home. It was simple really; I was just waiting for the word to go.

My mother fighting with my father was a little more complex. It had been going on for longer than the Leaving Cert for a start. I *could* remember a time when they weren't fighting but it was distant and hazy and I wasn't sure if I trusted what I was remembering. It was easier to just assume they'd always been fighting because what difference did it make now anyway? It wasn't as if they were suddenly going to realise they didn't like fighting any more and go back to how they had been in the time I can hardly remember. When I said I was waiting for them to stop fighting what I meant was that I was waiting for one of them to move out. My mother probably, seeing as Dad had the business (was married to the business as my mother always said) and she had pretty much hated the business all her life. Yet, bad and all as the fighting got sometimes, neither of them ever said anything about leaving or getting a divorce even though it seemed to me to be the most natural thing for them to do. My mother regularly screamed at my father that he was an impossible man to live with but she never followed one of these outbursts by charging upstairs to pack a bag and he never suggested that that's what she should do. I think that's the thing that frustrated me most about my parents – they couldn't even argue properly. It was like they were going at it from opposite sides of a brick wall. A very thick, high, wide, impenetrable brick wall. It was as if neither could hear exactly what the other one was saying, or see the effect of what they were saying on the other's face. My mother fired off volley after volley of pointy missiles hoping for the best and my father just dodged them and went back to whatever he was doing.

The business had always been a problem. It had been in my father's family for generations and he was very attached to it. It was just a building really – an old Georgian three-storey in the older, not very fashionable part of town – and its use had changed with each generation. It had been a post office around the turn of the century and right through to the formation of the new state, run by my great-great-aunts, one of whom passed it on to my grandfather, who got rid of the post office (he thought being in charge of a post office was a fussy, girly thing to be doing) and turned it instead into a general grocery store. The shop was hugely successful because it offered everything a housewife of the time could possibly need, in personable surroundings, all delivered to her door (if she so desired) at an affordable price. By the time my father took it over, Dunnes Stores had invaded the city with a vengeance, followed shortly by Quinnsworth, so Dad closed the grocery and opened a café. Well, a restaurant initially but he was smart enough to realise that there was more money and less hassle in a café that did solid, medium-priced home-cooked food for breakfast, dinner and tea.

And that's where I was, literally. Up to my elbows in vegetable soup and chicken lasagne, staring across the floor, wishing, willing him to look up and see me and realise that I existed.

I suppose he was no one special, really. He was just this guy who'd been coming into the café more or less regularly all summer. I didn't know where he worked, I didn't know what his name was, I didn't know what age he was, but I had theories about all of these things. It was likely he either worked for the Tax Office (Sarsfield House was just around the corner and all the tax people ate with us from time to time) or that he was an accountant or a solicitor (there were big firms of both in the building across the road). He didn't strike me as the solicitor type however – he wasn't quite hard-edged enough – or at least his suit wasn't quite sharp enough, which meant that he was either a tax person or an accountant person, neither of which should have made him the least bit interesting to me.

Yet he was; devastatingly so.

He wasn't all that good-looking. If it wasn't for the walking stick I probably wouldn't have noticed him in the first place. He had brownish hair cut kind of badly so it was neither a clean, short style nor one of those trendy baby-rock-star looks. His face was nice but I couldn't ever say exactly what it looked like because when he was in the café I couldn't allow myself to look at him, even a normal amount, in case I ended up staring at him. When I was serving his food or taking his money (the café is a self-service carvery type – Dad has always maintained that table service is a shocking waste of resources), I used to try and catch the colour of his eyes but the glare on his glasses dazzled me. As for his body, it wasn't exceptional. I mean in the conventional sense it wasn't exceptional; to me, he had the most fabulous physique imaginable. I suppose because it was exactly that – imaginable. There are so many places your mind can go with a slim frame under an oversized suit. To be honest he could have been any of those boy accountants or trainee civil servants that I'd been looking at and completely ignoring since I was fourteen and first started working in the café.

Yet, there was something about the way he moved that made him seem more present than everybody else. Because he walked so slowly he necessarily inhabited space for a much longer time and the whole room was heavy with anticipation from the moment he first started out to the moment he reached his destination. It was as if anything might happen in that time: the wind could change direction, the world could stop spinning and I, somehow, could become something, anyone, else.

Of course he *had* spoken to me. He had said things like:

'So what do I owe you?' and

'What's in this one?' and

'Is that a curry?' and

'I'll have a brownie as well.'

Obviously these weren't the sorts of things I was waiting for him to say. I didn't know exactly what it was I wanted to hear; I just knew I'd know it when I heard it. He didn't seem to talk much to anyone. Most days he came in on his own before the big lunch rush and he sat at a small table for two with his back to the door. That's why he nearly always had his face to the counter but he rarely looked up from his dinner or from the newspaper (*The Sun*) that he often brought with him. (Naturally I would have preferred if he had been reading *The Irish Times* but I liked to think that I was liberal enough not to judge a man by the paper he read.)

On the odd occasion when he wasn't alone he was with one or other of two quite geeky boys, but never with both of them. They didn't talk much; I couldn't hear them but it looked like they were saying quite dull things like:

'This isn't bad,' or

'I had that yesterday,' or

'This could do with being a bit hotter.'

So I had him pegged as a loner type who found normal everyday interaction with the rest of the world difficult. He wouldn't be one to waste his words pontificating on what Man United did last night or what Arsenal were going to do tomorrow. When he opened his mouth to say something (other than to comment on his food) it would be worth hearing.

As for the walking stick, I had my ideas on that too. If you broke your leg you'd use crutches, wouldn't you, so clearly he hadn't just broken his leg. I decided that it must be some childhood injury like getting his leg crushed so badly under an articulated lorry that his bones never fully recovered. Or perhaps a childhood illness like polio (my grandfather had suffered from polio as a child and had a slight limp ever after) but then I remembered that polio was one of the diseases you get vaccinated against now. Anyway, I imagined it was something like that. Something he would initially find difficult to talk about, but by and by he'd open up and share his trauma and maybe find healing through describing the horror that still gave him nightmares. I would be the person who listened and helped him come out of his shell and face the rest of the world as a complete human being.

Then it happened.

It was the start of August and he hadn't been in for a week. I remember because it had been a particularly bad week. My mother – who spent every week waiting for the weekend (though I didn't know why it should matter to her what day it was, seeing as the work she did looking after the books for the café could be done any time) and spent most of the weekend, except maybe Saturday afternoon when she went shopping, dreading the start of the next week – was in foul form on the Monday morning, claiming she hadn't had a wink of sleep all night because of my father's snoring. He just reminded her about the bed in the spare room and went back to making his Guinness Beef Stew. She wouldn't leave him alone, though; all morning she kept coming into the kitchen to complain about something new. The carpet in the living room was in shreds (it had been in shreds for years); the boiler needed servicing (it was the start of a fairly warm August); the ESB bill hadn't been paid (she was in charge of paying the bills). I was beginning to think that I wouldn't bother to wait the week and a half for my results and go right then, anywhere, just so long as it was far away from the two of them.

It was actually the Tuesday before it dawned on me that he hadn't been in. So I was waiting like crazy for him to arrive but half twelve came and went and no sign. He'd never once come at a time other than half twelve so I knew that was it for the day. And it was the same on the Wednesday, the Thursday and the Friday. I felt like half my life had been taken away from me. The good half; the only half that mattered. I worked like a zombie all that Saturday and on the Sunday I stayed in bed most of the day. By the following Monday morning I was thinking I might never be fully awake again.

But then he came back.

Or at least most of him did. He wasn't using his walking stick and he didn't even appear to be limping very much. He just walked into the café like a normal person and took up a tray and asked for the Shepherd's Pie. Then he took his tray back to his two-seater table and sat down to eat.

This time I did stare. I stared at him while he took up his knife and fork and put it back down. I stared at him while he shook salt over his dinner and then took up his knife and fork again. I stared at him while he ate his first mouthful, then his second, then his third. I kept staring at him until he ate his last mouthful and finally placed his knife and fork side by side on the plate.

Then I wiped my hands on my apron and went over to his table.

'Hi!' I said to him as if he was just anyone.

'Hi!' he said back as if I was just his waitress.

'I hope you don't mind me asking,' I said quickly, knowing that if I thought about what I was going to say I would lose my nerve and not say any of it, 'but I see you don't have your walking stick anymore?'

'Yeah, thanks be to fuck!' he said, looking me right in the eye and smiling like an idiot. 'I'm finally done with the lot of it. Crutches, sticks, splints, the lot.'

'Oh,' I said. 'So you broke your leg?'

124

'Playing tag rugby. And I wouldn't mind but I'm a GAA man myself, I was only filling in for one of the lads.'

'Oh.'

'Yeah, it really pissed me off 'cos it meant I missed most of the season. But I'll be back training soon.'

'Oh.'

'Yeah, so that'll be it for nice lunches in here for me. I'll be back to grabbing a sandwich and going for a run.'

'Right. Well, it's good that your leg healed. Was the Shepherd's Pie okay?'

'Lovely. Lovely job.'

And that was it. As I became aware of the sound of his chair scraping against the tiles, I realised I was still standing there. He was already across the room with his hand on the door. All that was left of him was his empty plate and a crumpled-up serviette.

Suddenly, inexplicably, I felt very cold. It was as if a draught of freezing air had gushed through the door, but the door was closed and besides, outside it was warm and balmy. But something had passed over me and was lingering still. Something that prevented me from gathering up the remains of his meal and going back to my station at the hot food counter.

It wasn't about him, of course. It had never been about him. It appeared to be more about me and the fact that I hadn't a clue where I was going or what I was doing and that for the first time in my life I didn't want to be alone.

So I picked up the plate and serviette and brought them back into the kitchen where my father was mixing the fillings for his tea-time quiches.

'Dad?' I said to him. 'What about a holiday before I go off to college? You, me and Mum. What do you think?'

'I think that's a great idea,' he said. 'I'll get your mother onto it straight away.'

⌘ ⌘

125

Tracy Culleton

Tracy Culleton is from Dublin but is now living in Cloughjordan in Co. Tipperary, location of The Village, Ireland's first eco-village. She's married to Peter and is just getting over the shock of their son becoming a teenager, a grunting, spotty, hoody-wearing, slouching, taller-than-she youth that appeared from nowhere. Her novels include *Looking Good* (which won the RTÉ/Poolbeg 'Write A Bestseller' Competition), *Loving Lucy* and *More Than Friends*. She has a website full of advice for writers at *www.fiction-writers-mentor.com*.

The Half-Written Story *

Tracy Culleton

Laura Mulhearne sat in her car. All around her people passed, from their cars and returning to them, talking animatedly. Occasionally a larger group passed, disgorged from a tour bus, speaking in foreign accents, in foreign languages.

These people would remember this day, Laura thought, for the rest of their lives. And the memory wouldn't be solely because of the stunning views over the wild Atlantic and the exhilaration of the fresh air and wheeling birds. She was sorry about that; sorry she'd spoil their day and their memories. But she had no choice. There was no other way.

She'd be on the evening news too, she supposed. The neutral measured voice of the newsreader would share her fate with the nation. People eating their dinner might – if she was lucky – pause and pass a thought for her, a thought of pity.

A man passed, reading out of a guidebook to his companions. '*Rising to over 700 feet, the Cliffs of Moher . . .*' Laura heard him say before he passed out of her earshot.

A few people, as they passed, cast a half-curious glance at her as she sat still in the car. Just sitting. It looked odd, she conceded. And being on her own, whereas everybody else was surrounded by laughing companions. That looked odd too. *It is odd,* she thought.

In every instant she experienced the impetus to get out of the car, to do what she had come to do, to get it over with. But still she hesitated. She was scared.

Of course she was. Like all living creatures, she acknowledged, she had a strong desire for life. But that was a reaction, a biological blip. That wasn't her reasoned choice.

But the fear was strong. What would it be like? It would be quick, of that she had no doubt. That quickness and certainty was the reason for choosing this location. But quick isn't instant. There should be no pain, no time to feel pain. But there would be terror as she fell. And indeed, terror now as she contemplated it.

The coward dies a thousand deaths; the hero only one, she reminded herself.

And there was terror too in the alternative. In continuing down a dark and dismal path. Days and weeks and months and years and decades of living death. What was the point in that? None. No point at all.

Hadn't she decided this – realised it – in all those months of debate? This wasn't the time to rehash it all. She had gone over it, again and again and again. She had worried at it, pulling at it and manipulating it, over and over. Each time the conclusion had been the same.

Okay. It's time. With a deep breath and a rapidly thumping heart, she opened the car door and swung out, moving decisively, forcing herself to do it. The will is stronger than instinct, she reminded herself.

The April air, here on the Atlantic edge of this northern island, was crisp and fresh. It was energising, almost sparkling. A pale heat caressed her head and back.

She strode briskly up the shallow steps of the path to the Visitors' Centre, overtaking the ambling and relaxed tourists.

I must act normally, she reminded herself. *I don't want the staff to suspect anything.* She was not the first to do this here and it wouldn't surprise her if they had training in what to look for, and had some way of thwarting her. She didn't know, of course, and it was hardly the sort of thing you could ring and ask. But she must take no chances.

So she put a carefully judged half-smile on her face. As she reached the pay desk she took out her mobile phone and pretended to be on a call. 'You've gone ahead?' she said into the receiver. 'Grand. I'm just paying in now, so I'll see you in a few minutes.' She closed the phone and smiled at the young man at the counter. 'One adult, please,' she said.

The cost was reasonable. Less than ten euro to erase all that pain. Literally the bargain of a lifetime.

She strode through the building without glancing at any of its attractions, and through the doors to the outside. The brisk air caressed her again.

She made her way along the path which led a short way along the cliff top, towards a tower. Halfway there she stopped and looked around her.

She thought of a Native American saying: *Today's a good day to die.* Fresh and bright, with a weak sun doing its best to bathe this little corner of the world.

The waves weren't gentle, though, as they pounded their incessant assault against the cliffs. Heaving and twisting and spewing forth a deceptively pretty white froth, they hurled themselves against the cliffs. The cliffs, in their turn, stood impervious, in their arrogance believing that they were stronger than the waves. The waves continued their pounding, smugly knowing that given enough time, they would prevail.

Laura gazed down at the waves, absorbing the awareness that soon she would be engrossed in their tumultuous embrace, joining them in the assault against the rock, her body twisting and flailing. It wasn't a pretty thought. But she wouldn't know. It would be okay. It would be over by then.

'It's beautiful, isn't it?' a voice came from beside her.

She looked around. A woman stood there. A woman maybe ten years older than herself. She had short hair, brown with flecks of grey, with a sharp and elegant cut. She wore wire-rimmed round glasses and her smile was soft and kind. She had on a beige corduroy calf-length skirt under which were brown flat boots, and above which was a burnt-orange soft-wool jumper. This was all covered by a brown leather jacket. She looked as soft and mellow as a perfect autumn day.

'Yes. Yes, it's beautiful,' Laura answered for politeness. And with sincerity too.

It *was* beautiful: wild and natural and empty and – crashing waves notwithstanding – peaceful in a poignant kind of way. But even as she said it, she turned back, away from the woman, indicating clearly that that was the extent of the interaction. It was a passing pleasantry, not a conversation.

But the autumn woman didn't take the hint. 'It's so peaceful here. I come here once a year. As a kind of . . . pilgrimage.'

She left a pause after the word 'pilgrimage', obviously waiting for Laura to ask what her pilgrimage was about.

But Laura wasn't going to do that, no matter how much the woman desired it. She no longer needed to meet others' expectations. That time was gone, and there was a freedom in that.

The pause stretched awkwardly until the autumn woman, clearly not to be deterred, continued. 'Yes, a pilgrimage,' she said, just as if Laura had questioned it. She moved forward a little, nearer the edge, nearer to Laura, and joined her in gazing out at the abyss.

'That pilgrimage . . .' She took a deep breath and said, 'This day eight years ago, I came here to these cliffs, to kill myself.'

Despite herself Laura reacted to that. She turned to look at the woman. 'Really?' she asked, interest peppering the coolness in her tone.

'Yes. Really.'

'Why?'

'All other options seemed closed off to me. It was as if my life was a narrowing funnel, and at the end there was only this.'

'Oh yes!' Laura breathed again. This autumn woman was speaking all her truths, all the truths she couldn't articulate to herself.

The woman looked at her intently. 'It sounds as if you understand what I mean.'

'I do.'

'Tell me,' the woman said softly.

Laura opened her mouth to speak, and closed it again, not knowing how to begin.

'Let's walk,' the woman said then, 'while you tell me.' She turned and began to drift towards the path, and along it towards the tower. Laura followed her, and the two women fell into step together.

'So, you were going to tell me . . .' the autumn woman prompted.

'That narrowing funnel you said – I've experienced that too.'

'Hmm?' the woman said, encouraging her.

'My parents died in a car accident six months ago.'

'Ahhh. I'm sorry to hear that.'

'I loved them very much. I miss them every day. I was an only child, so no support from siblings.'

'Not easy.'

'No. But I carried on. I had a lot to live for even so. My husband and I had been trying for a baby for nearly a year, and I was newly pregnant, about seven weeks.'

'Was?' The woman looked at Laura's trim belly.

'Yes. I lost the baby. An ectopic pregnancy. So I lost a tube too.'

'But you have one tube left?'

'Yes. But knowing how long it had taken me to conceive even with two tubes, and I'm not getting any younger . . . It was all academic anyway. Because my husband left me then. He said it was because I had changed, that I was obsessed about the baby, and grieving too much for my parents.'

The autumn woman gave a whistled intake of breath: sympathy for Laura and disapproval of her husband's callousness all at once.

'You'd think that's bad,' Laura said bitterly, 'but it turns out that was all lies. All excuses. He left me for another woman. A woman, I learned, he'd been having an affair with already, for the past year or so. And guess what – she was pregnant too! But much more pregnant than me. She's had the baby since, I hear. And he's a doting father.'

The bitterness spilled from her lips, the pain and anguish of it all.

133

The autumn woman cast her a supportive and sympathetic sideways glance.

'And there's more!' Laura said, in a mockery of those shopping channels. She was on a roll now, and there was something hugely cathartic about sharing this all, about letting it spew forth in its bile and acid, especially to such a gentle and supportive listener. 'I lost my business too. With all that was going on I couldn't handle it. I lost it all, and I ended up hugely in debt. It took all my parents' inheritance to clear that, and I still lost my house. I'm on the dole now, in a crappy rented house.'

The autumn woman shook her head in sympathy, and that resonated with Laura more than any platitude, no matter how sincerely meant, could have done.

'Yes,' Laura said sadly. 'Yes, I have. I've lost everything. Everything.'

There was silence for a moment between them, with the echo of the pounding waves and the conversation of passing people creating a cocoon for that silence.

Then Laura said, the words forced out, strangled and squeaky, 'And you know, I look into the future and all I see is a black chasm. A nothingness. Nothing to look forward to. No hope. There's nothing to live for any more,' she whispered.

The autumn woman left a respectful silence and then said, 'It's such a coincidence that we've met.'

'It is?'

'Yes. Because I was in a similar situation. That time eight years ago. It wasn't exactly the same of course. My parents hadn't died. But my husband left me, and while I didn't lose a baby, it meant that I couldn't even try to conceive a baby, which I had wanted to do. And I lost my job, and was in no fit state to find another one. So very similar. It brought me to the end of my tether. Like you are now.'

Laura looked at her, fascinated. This woman looked so poised, so content, so *together*. How could she have experienced such devastation?

'Oh yes,' the woman continued calmly. 'When I look back, I can hardly believe it myself. It doesn't seem like *me* who was so despairing and who felt she had no options. But yet, when I was in that place, I couldn't imagine being any different. It seemed so real. And above all, so permanent. As if things would never change.'

'So what happened?' Laura asked. Deep in the pit of her stomach, something stirred. Something that was a stranger to her: possibility.

'I met an old man. I got into conversation with him, just as you and I have got into conversation now. He seemed to know what was going on with me. I don't know how. Maybe he was an angel. Anyway, he had so much wisdom. He told me that it's wrong to declare the story over, when it isn't even half written. That when we're in the middle of a situation it seems set in stone. We can't imagine any better outcome. But that doesn't mean a better outcome doesn't exist. And we have one secret ingredient which helps us to write the rest of the story.'

'What's that?' Laura asked. A magic ingredient sounded *very* good to her right now.

'Hope,' the autumn woman said calmly. 'Hope is the magic ingredient that keeps us going. It's like the story of Pandora's Box. After all the troubles were let loose into the world, Hope was released to help us. And it does. Things can change in a heartbeat, that man said to me. And he was right.'

'What changed for you?'

'Well, to be honest, nothing immediately. Well, in one way nothing. This is real life, not a fairy tale. So I didn't meet the man of my dreams on the way out of the car park or anything like that. But what *had* changed was *me*. My attitude. I now had Hope. And that made all the difference. And that Hope caused me to be proactive in my life. And *that* made the difference.'

'What happened?'

The autumn woman smiled softly. 'I started by doing what little I could with the resources I had. I'd always wanted to design jewellery, but had never had the time before. So now I began to do that. I went hungry, sometimes, to buy materials, but that was okay. And my jewellery began to sell. I'm not selling into Brown Thomas or anything – again, this is real life, not a fairy tale. But I sell well at craft fairs and through my website. And through that I met a lovely man – a much nicer man, in truth, than my husband. And together we have a baby, my beautiful daughter Iris.'

'That's so *inspiring*', Laura said. 'You can have no idea how much all this means to me.'

The autumn woman smiled. 'Remember Hope. That's always the trick, I find.'

'I will,' Laura promised. 'I will.'

She looked down at the waves again, at the angry, crashing waves, and shuddered at the thought.

'It's okay now, isn't it?' the autumn woman said.

Laura took a deep, shuddering breath. 'Yes,' she said. 'Yes, I think it is. Thank you.'

The two women looked into each other's eyes for a long moment, and after a while the autumn woman nodded, seeming to say, *It's okay. You can go now.*

Laura smiled at her and turned and walked down the path towards the exit, her step almost jaunty. There was a long journey ahead, she knew. That story needed to be written. But now it was possible. Now she had Hope.

∽ ∾

Martina Devlin

Martina Devlin's novels include *Ship of Dreams*, about the Titanic shipwreck and its aftermath – inspired by a family connection with the disaster. Her non-fiction includes *Banksters*, a co-authored book about the Irish banking collapse. She has won a Hennessy Literary Prize and been shortlisted twice for the Irish Book Awards. She writes a weekly column for *The Irish Independent* and the *Sunday World* Magazine, and was 2009 writer in residence at the Princess Grace Irish Library in Monaco. Her website is *www.martinadevlin.com*.

Mothering **

Martina Devlin

Unusually, perhaps, a magazine interview with magician Paul Daniels made me sit up and take note.

In it, he told of using a knife to write 'I love you' on a slice of bread which he toasted, the words staying white as the rest of the bread turned brown. At which point he gave it to his wife Debbie McGee for breakfast.

There are those who would cringe at such an image. I am not among them. Indeed, I thought it worth copying, because I was anxious to let my mother know she was loved.

She was back home after three months in hospital, following a massive stroke. A stroke which left her semi-paralysed and utterly dependent. A stroke which meant she struggled daily to pin down the slippy coils of language, and the even more elusive twists and turns of comprehension. But at least she was in her own house and surrounded by her family.

Sometimes, though, I wondered if she knew who I was; who any of her children were. Childlike, there was only 'now' with her – memories of the past, though jewel-bright when they gleamed through, were fitful; as for the future, well, it seemed uncertain at best.

After the stroke, my mother had no concept of herself as a 70-something woman – we did not show her mirrors at that stage, because her hair had turned silver and this would have distressed her. All her life she had maintained her coiffure in film-star condition. And the onslaught of drugs she was prescribed had piled on the weight. Neither physically nor mentally was she the woman she had once been. We realised that, and at times she suspected it, but don't mention the war. Occasionally I could see bewilderment flare in her eyes when my older brothers addressed her as 'Mammy'. No need for mind-reading skills to interpret her thoughts. Why were these middle-aged men calling her 'Mammy'?

She seemed convinced she was twenty-nine. And who can blame her? I wouldn't mind fixing on that age for myself. But if she was twenty-nine, I had not yet been born, her older children were babies – and these people looking after her, while vaguely familiar and really rather pleasant, could not possibly be her offspring.

Our Ulster accents probably sounded wrong to her, too. She had been born and raised in Munster, at the opposite end of the country, and since the stroke her speech, while sometimes jumbled or composed of non-sequiturs, had blossomed into the brogue which nine years working in London and subsequent decades in Tyrone had suppressed. 'Toasht,' she'd order, with a lip-smacking flourish. 'Not bourr-nt.' In her old age, my mother sounded like Granny. I liked it.

Except she had not been able to taste toast since before the stroke. She asked for it now and then, but hesitated upon examining it – the prospect of crumbs was daunting. Her diet was restricted to soft food.

Eating toast seemed a mountain to climb. Until the morning when I toasted a slice of wholemeal bread with a capital B for Bridie (her name) scored into its centre, surrounded by a heart. Taking my cue from Paul Daniels. She clapped her hands and gobbled it down, crumbs and all: it was a triumph. If she could manage that, then she could move on from those infantile custards and mashed potato dishes.

Once again, my mother was confounding the medical profession. Doctors had predicted she would never eat again, after she lost her swallow as a result of the stroke. We had tubefed her for more than a year. It was not ideal – her poor body see-sawed between diarrhoea and constipation, as we attempted in vain to get the mixture right for her. The carers who came in to assist us said this was often the way. It seemed to be regarded as a necessary evil if a patient was tube-fed.

But it was profoundly unsatisfactory: distressing for her, and humiliating as well as painful. I was sure she could eat if we took it gradually.

What convinced me was that she was often hungry – the tube feed, while nutritionally sound, did not satisfy her. She missed food: its taste, the pleasure it gives, the way meals act as bridges to take us through the day.

Medics warned me over and over that she would asphyxiate if I gave her food. Headstrong, I decided to take that risk. To me, her life was so bare of pleasure that it seemed worth some danger to introduce colour into it. Little by little, I started giving her food, the way you would wean a baby. It was tentative at first: milky tea, yoghurt, then a little coffee (which she slapped her lips over, proclaiming it utterly delicious even when her lips missed the cup and none went down), followed by ice cream, soup and porridge. I held my breath with each spoonful, one hand hovering between her shoulder blades, ready to give her an almighty thump.

Cake was a huge hit. We chanced her on a slice when a brother had a birthday, and I bought one to surprise him when he dropped by. As I rummaged in the drawer for some candles, surfing through the usual tide of dog-eared envelopes and leaky pens, I hoped it might activate some memories for her. If nothing else, she was bound to enjoy watching the candles blown out and hearing 'Happy Birthday' sung.

Enjoy? That was an understatement. She ruthlessly annexed the birthday and announced it was her own. Presents, please. Oh yes, the birthday gateau had acted as a trigger all right. In the process, she discovered a passion for cake – one that must have been suppressed throughout most of her adult life, because she watched her weight scrupulously. Caution was now thrown to the winds and she insisted on a daily slice of cake, preferably chocolate.

But for me, the toast experiment – B for Bridie and a heart – was a landmark. Not only was it a new source of nutrition, but it was an advance on mushy food: she had to bite and chew it. The decoration scored into the bread's surface won her over, and toast was back on the menu.

Afterwards, she wiped her lips with a paper napkin, gave me a gummy smile – and demanded chocolate cake as a reward for finishing it all. When I demurred, she burst into tears. Heart-broken, abandoned, tragedy-dogged tears. Nothing was ever done by halves. Who can easily ignore a mother's tears? Even when they know they are being controlled? Her sulks I can ignore, but even today her tears break my heart. I would cry in her position, too – I would cry a lot more often than she does. Back then, however, her tears used to panic me. I capitulated immediately, and she crowed with laughter, too childlike to hide her scheming. Cake it was.

I retreated to the fridge, cut a meanish slice, put it on a small plate in the hopes of fooling her, and carried it through to her customised bedroom-come-sitting room. It was 9 am. Only one and a half hours into the day. She was happy, I was exhausted; I needed to go and lie down. Dream on.

Looking after my post-stroke mum was like managing a small child: a manipulative, lovable, sulky, charming, naughty, winsome toddler. The mother–daughter roles had been inverted – with a vengeance.

Sometimes I suspect that all her life, Bridie has been waiting to become an eccentric old lady. This is her true vocation. All those other roles – schoolgirl, nanny, wife, mother, grandmother – were trial runs. She relishes the role with a glee that is as undisguised as it is unconditional. Let her take her pleasure where she can, I say. She is some woman to adapt to this diminished version of life.

The altered version of my mother is at once recognisable and a little askew. Some facets of her personality remain the same, while others are unfamiliar – though I can't help wondering if she was simply waiting for the opportunity to give free rein to them.

There is nothing novel about her devotion to her appearance. Such was always her habit. She feels underdressed without being drenched in her favourite scent, and with her fingernails painted scarlet – preferably Christian Dior polish. The stroke has frozen one of her hands into a claw, but she continues to insist on a manicure. Naturally, her toenails must be painted red, too. Not that she can see her feet – her condition has left her paralysed down her left side, which is particularly unfortunate because she is left-handed. But her standards have not slipped. A stroke is no excuse for a sloppy appearance in Bridie's world view.

She can no longer squeeze into her polar-bear faux-fur jacket – too bulky in the wheelchair – but it has been replaced with pashminas. A cupboard full of them, each more eye-catching than the last. She is convinced they all came from Brown Thomas, even the ones with Marks & Spencer on the label, because it is the source of all glamour to her. Sometimes I borrow one when I run out on a message, and I can smell her perfume on the cloth. It is as if she is on the errand with me.

She tuts disapprovingly whenever I am too tired to wash my hair after looking after her, warning of the dangers of letting myself go. 'You're turning into a Raggedy Ann. A lady should always look groomed,' she instructs. Behind her back, I roll my eyes and feel as if I am a gauche thirteen-year-old. All adults revert to the status of children if they spend any longer than a couple of nights under the family roof. Meanwhile, she has home visits from the most select hairdresser in town, who is devoted and calls to no one but her. She accepts it regally, as no less than her due. Lotions and potions and above all fashion – 'shtyle', she calls it, in that County Limerick lilt – remain as fascinating now as ever they were to her. Whenever she appears bored or fretful, I fetch her glasses and a glossy magazine. Holding it up for her to see, together we inspect the appearances of the actresses and socialites between its pages. Evening gowns are a particular favourite, while Oscar night thrills us.

To my amusement, however, Bridie has accessed her inner slapper since the stroke. She has discovered animal prints, which once she would have rejected out of hand. This year for her birthday, she asked for a leopard print throw to cover her knees when out and about in the wheelchair. 'You can't beat a bit of bling now and again,' she announced, with stately certainty. I had to leave the room before I exploded with laughter.

At her birthday party, she accessorised leopard print with a tiara. 'Paste,' she sniffed at the stones in the tiara. But she called for a mirror and rearranged it more becomingly among her silver curls, posing for photographs. Looking at the photographs now, I see we forgot her teeth.

We only put in her dentures for special occasions, because they hurt her mouth. Besides, she accuses me of pulling a fast one whenever she looks at her new set of teeth. She needed them after the stroke, because her mouth changed shape slightly – and because I accidentally binned her old ones, clearing out the house in advance of her homecoming. But she wanted a gold tooth in her new dentures, and I failed to read her mind and pass on her intentions to the dentist. Somehow she has become convinced one gold tooth is the height of sophistication. Lately she has discovered the concept of fake tan and is secretly drawn to it, although she worries whether it is quite ladylike. I am wondering how long before the inner slapper prevails, and she despatches me to the shops to purchase a pair for her. ('Run like the wind, Martina!' She radiates urgency – whatever the errand.)

Furthermore, she has heard some of her carers chat about Magic Knickers, and has taken to insisting I buy her some. She has even made me wheel her into Marks & Spencer to examine them. 'But, Mammy, they'd squeeze your tummy,' I tell her. She pouts, and consents to choose some hand cream instead. The battle may have been won, but the Magic Knickers war is far from over.

Bridie's life, curtailed as it is, has its compensations. She perks up at the *Strictly Come Dancing* theme music, because of the frocks and her crush on judge Len Goodman. She is fond of a trip to O'Brien's for a latte, a muffin and some people-watching, although she prefers the occasional glass of wine in the restaurant opposite. And she remains hopelessly addicted to the British royals. She still shakes her head over Margaret Rose (Princess Margaret to you and me) not being allowed to marry Peter Townsend. 'Just like Margaret Rose,' she said, when she saw her birthday photos in that tiara.

She calls 6 pm the cocktail hour and waits expectantly for her libation, insists on birthday cake, complete with candles, naturally, every fortnight and occasionally writes my sister and me out of history by telling visitors she only has sons. It is a mystery why she does this, but my mother has always been an enigma to me – even in the whole of her health.

Sometimes I look into her eyes and wonder if she realises I am her daughter. Or is it only a word she has heard me use about myself, without any true grasp of its meaning? Words are random objects to her and she pronounces the strangest ones, over and over, for no discernible reason. 'Lilac,' she might say, or 'sneaky'. She struggles to access simple words such as 'dinner' but trots out complicated phrases with aplomb. 'You are cordially invited to a Hallowe'en party.' She kept trying to conceal some paper napkins, neon orange and decorated with pumpkins, under her pillow after that particular bash. 'You can have as many as you like, no need to hide them,' I promised her. But she preferred to squirrel them away. She likes to secrete the odd bank note under her pillow, too, although she cannot differentiate intellectually between what can be bought by a note with 5 on it compared with one with 50 printed on it. It just seems to be a comfort to have some.

Now that she is eighty, I can finally see the bold seven-year-old she must once have been. It makes me laugh – but it also leaves me wondering how my grandmother ever controlled her.

Bridie had only been a widow for six months when she had her stroke, at the age of seventy-six. No harm to my father, but she had rather enjoyed the state of widowhood. It reminded her of her single girl days gallivanting around north London, sashaying off to dances in the Irish clubs in those glamorous 1950s frocks with nipped-in waists and a string of pearls at her throat. She resembled Elizabeth Taylor, and was an unrepentant heartbreaker. I grew up hearing stories about the men she dated, including a salesman called Philip who used to give her nylons. When she was ready to settle down, she returned to Ireland and made her choice: another man who worshipped her. As a teenager and a bit of a Daddy's girl, I used to resent what I regarded as her casual approach to my father's adoration. Now, I realise that beautiful women set their own agenda. Because they can.

After forty-odd years of marriage, widowhood proved to be a reprise of those heady days of youth. She was no longer interested in dating or going dancing, but she loved the freedom to eat or not as she chose, stay up late or not as she chose, spend all her pension on a dress or not as she chose. (Mind you, fancy beaded cardigans are more to her taste now.) Her stroke put paid to that porthole of independence, however.

That massive attack, which should have killed her and would have felled a less determined woman, means Bridie needs 24-hour care. The family supplies it in her home, along with some back-up state help.

There was an offer of a place in a nursing home, but we had a powwow and decided to try and look after her ourselves. There are seven of us to divide the responsibilities, although inevitably they are not shared equally. That is the nature of life and families, but we have not fallen out about it. Bridie is our focus, first and last.

None of us wanted her to end her days in an institution, no matter how bright, cheerful and well run. Patients who enter a home are removed from all that is familiar. They lose autonomy: forced to follow someone else's rota of when to wash, eat, sleep and rise in the morning. The central heating thermostat is set too high and the TV volume too loud. And these homes are generally a repository for illness and death. After admission, there is only one way out.

For some residents, it must be death by despair. Even when the staff are caring. Even when they have photographs on the bedside locker and their own duvet cover on the bed. Even when relatives visit regularly and bring little treats to supplement their diet.

People instinctively want to end their days within their own four walls. It is not only about independence – it is about feeling wanted rather than a burden. Our mother was – is – wanted. Even when a battle of wills ensues about whether or not she can wear Bermuda shorts in December.

I worried that she might not like her loss of independence, with her children making life's important decisions for her, but she accedes with good grace. I suspect her eccentric old lady pose is part of her revenge, all the same. Or maybe it is her reward.

Once or twice she has asked me if she will ever walk again. No, I have to tell her. I lie where it is needed, but I cannot bend the truth on this. 'No, Mammy, I'm sorry. You have worked miracles but this one is beyond you.' I hunt for a palliative. 'But at least there are wheelchairs. And handsome young fellows to push them.' Her smile is blinding: elated she still has men dancing attendance on her. Life has thrown up some cruel barriers around her freedom, but it has not dented her spirit.

She can no longer read but I read aloud to her – teenage stories are her preference – although she pretends to doze off if there is too much description. She quite likes me reading my own novels or newspaper columns aloud, although she prefers a brother to do it because she suspects me of skipping parts. They have to pause every paragraph or so and say 'by Martina Devlin' in BBC World Service tones, and she preens and beams her sweet, gum-shiny smile.

She is ecstatic if I make an occasional TV appearance. One of the brothers is instructed to record it for her, and she watches it on continuous loop, preferably with a glass of Baileys, word perfect not only on my responses but on those of fellow guests. Once I appeared as a panellist on RTÉ's *The View* along with Joe Duffy. At one stage he appeared to cut in on me – I had finished, it was not an interruption – but she believes it was and tut-tuts in annoyance. You can see her gearing up towards indignation just before it happens, every time.

She has lost many things, in the wake of her stroke, but she has not lost her expensive tastes. One Mother's Day we bought her new glasses, and when the optician visited with a selection of frames she unerringly chose the priciest pair.

She has gained some things as well. She is more affectionate than previously, touchingly childlike in her longing to be cuddled, to have her hair stroked, to be admired. When I am on the Mammy Minding Rota, we have a little routine last thing at night. I take her face between my hands kiss her and say, 'Pretty as a picture' – which she is. One evening I forgot, and as I turned away she tugged my sleeve. 'Pretty as a picture,' she prompted.

Bridie's stroke has shown us how the brain works in mysterious ways. When she lost her language in its aftermath, her Irish returned to her before her English. She used to lie in bed counting to ten *as Gaeilge*. Did the sounds reassure her? Or was she a small girl again?

Time is meaningless to her. If I run out to the shops for an hour, she greets me with the relief of someone who believed I was gone for good. But if I spend two weeks away, she nods at me as casually as if I had just stepped away for a minute.

All of Bridie's dreams converge on being a small girl in Oola, the village where she grew up. In them, she is running, tumbling, dancing – moving about, free as a bird, with playmates long dead. In her waking hours, she can no longer move: trapped where we place her, in the bed or on the chair.

'I'm an invalid,' she'll say sometimes.

'No, you're the supervisor,' we tell her. 'You have to sit there and watch that we do this right.'

It might be pegging out the clothes – she can see the garden from her window – or we leave the kitchen door open so she can see us wash the dishes.

Some nights as I am thinking longingly about bed, or maybe a bath with a gin and tonic on the side, she fights sleep. 'I'm lonesome,' she might say, 'entertain me.' And she nudges me to sing 'The Mountains of Mourne' and 'The Black Velvet Band'. She joins in where she can, often remembering the chorus, although she can struggle to recall words like 'elbow' or 'garden'. Or Martina.

Bridie will remain highly dependent for the rest of her life – however long or short it is. Yet her recovery from those bleak early days has been astonishing. Rewarding, too. A priest who used to visit her, before being transferred to another parish, attributed the improvement in her condition to love. Simple as that. Even when she did not know we were her family, she recognised that we offered her love. No need for toast indented with a heart and a B.

But being Bridie, she was partial to the pampering.

∽ ∾

Myles Dungan

Myles Dungan is a broadcaster with RTÉ Radio and the author of a number of books on Irish and US history. These include two books on the Irish experience of World War I, *Irish Voices from the Great War* (1993) and *They Shall Grow Not Old* (1995), and *How the Irish Won the West* (2005). His two most recent books are a biography of Captain William O'Shea, *The Captain and the King* (2009) and *Conspiracy: Irish Political Trials* (2009) for RTÉ and the Royal Irish Academy. He was awarded a Fulbright Scholarship to the University of California, Berkeley in 2007 and is currently working on a PhD in late 19th century Irish media history in Trinity College, Dublin.

Nellie Cashman **

Extract from *How the Irish Won the West* (NEW ISLAND)

Myles Dungan

The most significant Irish-born businesswoman to thrive in the American West was born in Midleton, Co. Cork in October, 1845, just as the Great Famine was beginning to bite. Ellen Cashman, familiarly known as Nellie, would give her place of birth as 'Queenstown' whenever asked and the famous port (now Cobh) was only a few miles away from the Parish of Midleton where her birth was registered. She is important enough in the history of the states of Arizona and Alaska to have merited a full-scale biography (by Don Chaput) published in 1995.

By the time she left Ireland with her recently widowed mother and younger sister (both named Frances) Nellie would have been about six or seven, hardly old enough to have carried very many memories of Cork with her to the USA.

The Cashman family settled first in Boston before moving to San Francisco in 1865. At that time the Western city was becoming increasingly Irish. It elected its first Irish-born Mayor in 1867 (New York got its first in 1880, Boston in 1884) and an Irish political machine as dominant as anything seen in the East was already in the making. In 1870 Nellie's sister Frances met and married another Irish immigrant Thomas J Cunningham, a man who was in the boot business and whose expertise would later become useful to Nellie.

In 1872, Nellie began her association with the mining industry in the town of Pioche, Nevada, where she opened a boarding house. The town was hardly a young girl's dream (but at twenty-seven years of age Nellie was no longer particularly young by Western standards). Pioche was 'violent, dirty and in general an unattractive place . . . [it had] seventy-two saloons and thirty-two brothels . . . only Bodie, California, had the same type of crude, uncaring, random and planned violence . . . Tombstone, Arizona, by contrast, was an oasis of peace and tranquillity.'[1] Within a three-year period Pioche saw forty violent deaths, mostly from gunfights. It had a floating population which rarely exceeded 4,000. Many of those were Irish and much of the violence appears to have been caused by miners with very Irish names.

Whether the violence of the town simply got too much for her, or whether she had already developed the nose for an approaching 'bust' for which she would become celebrated, Nellie left Pioche within two years. The town didn't last much longer as a going concern; by 1876 its ore production had declined to about 15 per cent of the 1872 total. But by then Nellie Cashman had established herself elsewhere.

That was in the Cassiar district of British Columbia, a few miles from the Yukon Territory. News of a gold strike in the region reached Pioche in 1872 and a number of miners from Nevada would eventually move there. But Nellie got there before them, in 1874. She became known to the Cassiar miners as 'Pioche Nellie'. Once again she opened a boarding house and made the bulk of her money from 'bed, board and booze.'[2] She also began to acquire promising claims and to 'grubstake' miners in whom she had some confidence. This involved providing them with supplies (and in some cases with investment money) in the hope of a strike. In the event of a bonanza, Nellie shared in the good fortune, depending on what sort of deal had been done with the impecunious miners.

Nellie left the Cassiar district in November, 1874, before the onset of what would prove to be an unusually harsh winter but she was not gone for long and the circumstances of her return marked the beginnings of her legend.

[1] Don Chaput, *Nellie Cashman and the North American Mining Frontier* (Tucson, Arizona, 1995) p8/9
[2] Ibid. p23

She was in Victoria, British Columbia when she got news that the Cassiar region had been cut off by a fierce storm. Many miners had, ill-advisedly as it now transpired, hung on in the area far longer than was wise in the hope of making a lucky strike. Hundreds of prospectors, some of them friends of Nellie's, were now cut off and trapped. They quickly exhausted their supply of vegetables and the mining camp was hit by an outbreak of scurvy (brought on by a vitamin C deficiency).

Nellie could have sat on her hands or even spent hours each day wringing them in anguish. Instead she organised a rescue expedition and led it herself. She hired six men, got together a consignment of vegetables and lime juice and headed for the Cassiar diggings with 1,500 pounds of supplies. Because the snow was fresh and soft and dogs were useless, each member of the party (including Nellie) had to drag a sled themselves. Progress was slow, sometimes as little as five miles a day and the party spent most of January and February, the coldest months of the year, on the trail.

Sometime around the end of February the small party reached the Cassiar diggings and delivered their life-saving supplies. The epic trip was reported (and misreported) in dozens of newspaper accounts and earned the thirty-one-year-old Irishwoman the nickname of 'The Angel of the Cassiar'.[3]

Mining camps weren't the only boom towns of the Old West. In towns where the construction of the railways coincided with the end of a cattle trail, large amounts of money could be made by those brave enough to risk their capital in the often wild and lawless cow-towns of the West. If the arrival of the railway coincided with the discovery of gold or silver nearby, so much the better. It was to one of the new boom towns of the South West that Nellie Cashman headed next. She arrived in Tucson, Arizona, towards the end of the 1870s. According to her biographer 'Nellie was basically a "boomer", a "stampeder" which meant in the West of the late nineteenth century one who was attracted to and was early

3 Anne Seagraves, *High Spirited Women of the West* (Idaho, 1992) p124

on the scene in new communities.'[4] There she met a man who would play a central part in the events which were to make Tombstone, Arizona notorious: newspaper editor John Clum, owner of the Tucson *Citizen*. Clum wrote of his first meeting with Cashman: 'Nellie was the first of her sex to embark solo in a business enterprise. Her frank manner, her self-reliant spirit, and her emphatic and fascinating Irish brogue impressed me very much, and indicated that she was a woman of strong character and marked individuality.' The strong Irish brogue must have been acquired from years spent in the company of her mother because it would certainly not have survived otherwise.

Within a short period she had abandoned Tucson and headed for what she knew best, a burgeoning mining town. In this case it was Tombstone, seventy-five miles to the southeast, which had just had a silver strike. John Clum followed soon afterwards, establishing the Tombstone *Epitaph* in the town in 1880. Clum may have had an overdeveloped sense of irony but his choice of title couldn't have been more appropriate.

Cashman and Clum weren't the only notable new arrivals in Tombstone. Dave Neagle, the man who had shot Dubliner Jim Levy in Pioche, Nevada, also made his way there and became a lawman. But the great law-enforcing family, the Earps, had also begun to collect in the town. By no means the sainted lawmen of myth (Wyatt, Virgil, Morgan, Warren and James were known in Tombstone as gamblers and pimps as much as they were for their talents as US Marshals or Deputies), the Earps allied themselves with one of the two political factions which dominated the town.

Tombstone was prey to the same post-Civil War tensions as many other Western boom towns. The 'merchant' faction, which was benefiting from mining and commercial riches, was predominantly urban (based in Tombstone itself), Republican (the party of Lincoln and the anti-slavery faction), often Eastern in origin (the Earps were from Illinois), while the 'cowboy' faction was rural (living in Tombstone's outlying districts), Democrat and

4 Chaput, op.cit. p27

Texan (with all that implied). Each side had its own champions – the Earps in the case of the 'merchant' faction, the Clantons and McLaurys in the case of the 'cowboys' – and its own propagandists, Clum's *Epitaph* speaking for the 'merchants' while the *Nugget* represented the views of the 'cowboys'.

Nellie Cashman, based in various businesses within the city limits of Tombstone and a friend of *Epitaph* editor John Clum, might have been expected to ally herself solidly with the 'merchant' faction, but, conscious of not alienating anyone needlessly, she made certain to advertise her Cash Store, her Boot and Shoe Store and later her hotel, boarding house and restaurant in both local papers.

Like Pioche and the Cassiar district, Tombstone had a large Irish-born population (in addition to the first-generation 'Irish' who would have been classified as 'American'). The 1881 Cochise County census (Tombstone was the county seat) shows a population of 5,300 in Tombstone of whom 2,880 were American while 559 had been born in Ireland (the largest foreign born contingent – next were 423 Mexicans and 300 Germans).

This meant that there were many Roman Catholics in the town and it was in Tombstone that Nellie Cashman became involved in one of the activities that were to shape her life and become the basis for her reputation. She led a campaign to build a Roman Catholic church and a County Hospital in the town. It was a highly successful campaign, due in no small part to Cashman's incredible energy. Not only did she run a number of businesses (some with her sister Frances who had arrived in Tombstone with five young children after the death of her husband), she became a highly persuasive fundraiser and still found time to champion the cause of the Irish Land League in Tombstone. (She collected $200 for the Land League in Tombstone in 1881 – Tucson in the same year, despite having twice the Irish population, contributed nothing.)

On 26 October, 1881, came the infamous bloodletting at the OK Corral when three members of the Clanton/McLaury faction were killed by the Earps (with the assistance of Doc Holliday) in the most famous street gunfight in Western history. The Earps were not universally applauded for their actions even within the city limits of Tombstone (the Irish-American Johnny Behan, who had lost his lover to Wyatt Earp, attempted unsuccessfully to arrest them). Cashman's friend John Clum, Mayor of the town as well as editor of the partisan *Epitaph*, sided with the Earps in the murderous struggle that followed but Nellie had other things on her mind. Frances Cunningham became seriously ill in December 1881, and Nellie was forced to sell out their joint business interests while she looked after five children under the age of ten.

After Frances recovered her health Nellie went back into the restaurant business again, opening the grandiosely named American Hotel on Fremont Street, only to suffer a further setback when one of Tombstone's periodic fires, on 25 May, 1882, destroyed much of Tombstone's business district. Both Nellie and Fanny suffered minor personal injuries protecting their hotel. One report claimed that 'the plucky ladies stationed several of their friends with buckets and kept the building thoroughly saturated with water, thereby preventing the flames from communicating'. Financial disaster was averted. The American had only been in business a month at the time of the fire.

With that astute nose for detecting the decline of a boom town before the downturn became obvious, Nellie decided to give up on Tombstone in 1883, at around the time her sister gave up in her battle with tuberculosis. Frances Cunningham died on 3 July, 1883. Nellie had already made arrangements for the five children for whom she was now legal guardian. Places were found for each of the Cunningham children in Catholic boarding schools and their aunt set about finding the means to support them.

Her first venture almost ended in disaster. Attracted by rumours of a gold rush in the Baja California region of Mexico, Nellie and a group of Tombstone miners set off to travel the 1,000 miles from Arizona to the Mission Santa Gertrudis. Because of her experience elsewhere, Nellie appears to have been in effective charge of the operation. Legend has it that the miners were ill equipped for the heat of the Baja (far hotter even than the Arizona desert) and quickly began to run out of water. Nellie is supposed to have volunteered to find the Mission, locate water and return to the rest of the group. All, according to anecdote, was accomplished successfully and the plucky Irishwoman, once again, saved the day.

The truth, according to her biographer Don Chaput, is probably more mundane. Nellie appears to have made one crucial leadership decision when she insisted that she would lead only a small party of Arizona miners to the reported location of the gold. If a strike had indeed been made and if conditions allowed, then the rest of the group would follow. It was, in fact, the reserve group that rescued Nellie and her advance party. By then dozens of other returning miners had brought the bad news that the significance of the find had been greatly exaggerated. If there had been gold, then it was already gone.

The Arizona miners returned to Tombstone empty-handed but the legend of Nellie Cashman continued to grow. The San Diego *Union* of 16 June, 1883, writing about the abortive Baja gold fever, singled the redoubtable Irishwoman out for praise. 'In all the vicissitudes of life she has maintained the highest self-respect, but is as ambitious in her notions as Joan of Arc. In Arizona she could raise a company at any time who would follow her to the death, either in search of gold or Apaches.'[5] The flowery article glossed over the fact that she had very nearly led just such a company to their deaths.

For the next few years Cashman, confidence dented by the narrowly averted disaster in the Baja, contented herself with running the Russ House in Tombstone, and making significant amounts of money on the side by buying and selling prospecting claims (one of which she named the Parnell Mine, in honour of one of the motive forces behind her beloved Irish Land League, the great Charles Stewart Parnell).

Two incidents in 1884 have been cited as further demonstrations of Nellie's entitlement to Western canonisation. In one she is said to have objected strenuously to the erection of a grandstand in

[5] Chaput, op.cit. p63

Tombstone, designed to give local voyeurs a more comfortable vantage point for witnessing the hanging of five convicted murderers. Her sympathy is supposed to have been aroused by the fact that two of the men waiting to be executed were Irish, Daniel 'Mick' Kelly and William 'Billy' Delaney. Taking the law into her own hands, she gathered together a group of like-minded individuals on the eve of the communal execution and destroyed the grandstand. Later she made sure that the bodies of the five men (three of whom she is said to have converted to Catholicism) were not handed over to the nearest medical school for the use of pathology students. Less florid accounts of the affair suggest that local miners tore the bleachers apart when they discovered they were expected to pay a dollar and a half to get a grandstand view of the executions.

She is also said to have thwarted a murder attempt by some of the miners whom she normally championed. Whether as a simple (if courageous) act of humanity or as a way of aligning herself with 'capital' against 'labour' she managed to conceal the Superintendent of the Grand Central Mining Company in her buggy and convey him through the streets of Tombstone to the nearest railway station (Benson) and safety. EB Gage had aroused the animosity of the town's miners by enforcing a fifty cent a day wage cut after a fall in the price of silver. This had led to threats of kidnapping and lynching against him.[6] This story has the imprimatur of John Clum but contemporary accounts contain no reference to the involvement of Gage in what was a brief, but nasty, labour dispute. Still less do they talk of any 'rescue' by Nellie Cashman. Nevertheless, on the basis that 'when the legend becomes truth, print the legend' both stories have added to the angelic aura surrounding Cashman. Don Chaput suggests that both are the work of a covert beatification committee which included her nephew Michael Cunningham, a man who had the ear in the 1920s of John Clum. Neither story is referred to by Nellie herself in numerous newspaper and magazine interviews.

By 1886 Nellie was getting restless again. Her nephews and

[6] Seagraves, op.cit. p126 (Both stories come from what is a colourful but not totally reliable account of Cashman's life)

nieces had either been started in business or otherwise provided for, so her ties to Arizona were loosening. As Don Chaput observed, 'Nellie had little geographical loyalty. Her allegiances were to excitement, to promise, to the optimism and loud noise of a thriving camp, town or city. She was gradually concluding that this was no longer possible in Arizona Territory.'[7] A trip to New Mexico in 1887 brought her no joy and the following year saw her back in Tombstone. For much of the next decade she followed the rushes and the booms around the newly established mining camps of Arizona before she swapped the arid deserts of the southwest for the ice and tundra of the northwest, the place where she had begun her adventure.

In 1896 the Yukon bonanza began in earnest in the vicinity of the newly established town of Dawson at the junction of the Yukon and Klondike rivers. By 1897 Nellie Cashman was already making plans to join the new rush northwards – Arizona newspapers were carrying the report that she was preparing to 'organise a company for gold mining in Alaska, where she has visited three times. Her many friends in Arizona will wish her success, for during her twenty years residence in the Territory she has made several fortunes, all of which have gone for charity.'[8]

Nellie may have been trying to replicate her Baja expedition of 1883, this time in a geographical area of which she had more knowledge and with a climate which, although grim and hostile, was more conducive to prospectors. If that was indeed the case she failed to interest enough Arizonan miners in abandoning the heat of the southwest for the chill of Alaska. In February, 1898 she made the trip alone. At fifty-four years of age she was about to become one of the few women to join the new Alaskan gold rush. Her journey to Dawson was an Odyssey in itself – she was a lone woman hauling the statutory 900 pounds of provisions (verified by members of the Royal Canadian Mounted Police or else the prospector was to be turned back), through some of the least

7 Chaput, op. cit. p73
8 Ibid. p92

hospitable terrain on the planet. Her journey began at the base of the famous Chilkoot Pass, from which a trail of prospectors would set out each day snaking upwards on a hike that barely half managed to complete. Having negotiated that obstacle Nellie then faced a hazardous journey by barge along the melting waters of the Yukon River. She finally reached Dawson in April, 1898. A few months later her path crossed once again with that of her old friend from Tombstone, John Clum. By then she was clearly doing well (she was already involved in Church charity work). Clum described her as 'robust, active, prosperous and popular'.[9]

For the next six years it was 'business as usual' for Nellie Cashman. She spread herself between mining and the restaurant. In the past such diversification had stood her in good stead in such a highly precarious economy. She was an oddity in a society that was overwhelmingly male and where the preponderance of females were prostitutes. Nellie was approaching sixty, living in a hostile environment but still prepared to buy claims and work them herself. One such claim (according to Clum) produced up to $100,000. Nellie, however, insisted that she had re-invested the entire sum in purchasing other, less rewarding diggings. It is also likely that she gave a large portion of the sum away to Roman Catholic charities.

In 1904 she shifted her attention from Dawson to a new strike in Fairbanks, Alaska. By now she was a tough, resourceful and personally wealthy sexagenarian. She stayed for a winter, made a profit of $6,000 and her departure, in 1905, was a further object lesson in good timing. Within less than a year the business centre of Fairbanks had been burned to the ground!

Most of the final years of Cashman's life were spent on or near the Arctic Circle in the Koyukuk River region. Once again she emerged with a profit from what was, at best, a modest 'boom' with her combination of business skills and physical tenacity. Although her claims in the Nolan Creek area were far from being the most lucrative she had ever worked, she appears to have been

[9] Ibid. p102

content to settle in this remote region. Her newly acquired sedentary ways may have something to do with the slow winding down of the 'gold fever' of the latter half of the 19th century. There were fewer and fewer new 'boom towns' in which a woman could establish a restaurant while working as many claims as she could afford. Perhaps she was simply running out of energy. After all, she was getting on for seventy by the time of the outbreak of World War I.

In 1918, on hearing that the USA had entered the Great War she managed to persuade more than 50 of her beloved sourdoughs to travel (with her of course) 700 miles to enlist in the US Armed Forces. By the time they got to a recruitment centre, however, the Armistice had been declared and their services were not required. At the age of seventy, on one of her frequent returns to civilisation, she managed to mush a dog team 700 miles in 17 days from Koyukuk to Seward, Alaska. It is a record any of today's highly competitive Iditirod drivers would be proud of.

In 1924 she was taken ill with pneumonia and was transferred from Nolan Creek to Fairbanks. She survived the journey and recovered from the illness but died the following year in a hospital in Victoria, British Columbia. Her own money and her fundraising activities had helped to build the hospital.

～ ～

Clare Dowling

Clare Dowling is from Kilkenny and is a playwright, screenwriter and the author of seven novels which have been translated into six languages. Her next novel will be published in 2011 and she currently writes for Ireland's top soap *Fair City*. She lives in Dublin with her family.

Oops *

Clare Dowling

Tara got a positive on a pregnancy test that morning. She held it up to the light and turned it this way and that, wondering if there could possibly be some mistake. Then, because it came in a pack of two, she did the second one, just to be sure. This time the blue line jumped out at her before she'd even hiked her knickers back up.

Aidan would go pure mental.

She said nothing at lunchtime.

'Any luck?' she asked him.

'Naw.'

The baby was crawling all over him. One of the four they already had, that was. Only the first two had been planned. After that, contraception somehow seemed to fail them.

'How? *How?*' they had asked each other grimly on the last one.

Tara's sister June had bought her an apron that said, *'Oops!'* on the front of it for Christmas.

Through the kitchen window Tara watched the three older ones running after each other with hurleys and hula-hoops. It didn't look that friendly.

'They said come back next week,' Aidan said.

'Well, there you go.' She had on her cheery voice, the one that sounded nothing like herself, but that she had been using since Aidan had been let go eight months ago. Everything was, 'Try again tomorrow' and 'They haven't said no yet, have they?' At no point

167

did Tara Delaney, exhausted mother of four, holder of a part-time job in Barney's DIY store, and regular shopper at Lidl, shout, 'This is a load of fucking shite!'

It wasn't as though it was Aidan's fault. The company had herded them into the canteen one afternoon and told them, without having the decency to look all that embarrassed, that they were relocating to Uzbekistan. Nobody even had time to look up an atlas; the plant closed that very evening, at 5 pm.

'They barely let us empty our lockers,' Aidan told everybody in the initial burst of excitement.

There was the usual kerfuffle about redundancy payments, and now the whole mess was winding its way through the courts.

At least Tara had a job. That's what they'd said to each other in those early days, when Aidan would arrive back from town after doing the rounds with his CV. In recent months, this had become, somewhat accusingly, 'At least *you* have a job.'

'Aidan,' she began now.

There was no sense in putting it off. On the plus side, they already had all the baby clothes and equipment. It was the formula and the nappies that were the killer. Maybe she could do the cloth ones. Or breastfeed until the child turned eighteen.

'What?' he said.

The back door burst open and Nicky fell in, his lower lip covered in blood. 'He belted me.'

Following on his heels was Christopher, anxious to make his case. 'He belted me first – he's a scanger!'

'For God's sake!' Aidan thrust the baby at Tara, before grabbing the two lads by the scruffs of their necks and lifting them into the air so that their feet dangled.

Tara sighed. More jumpers ruined.

'Can youse not play happily together for five bloody minutes?' he roared.

The two lads exchanged a little look. Mammy never asked stupid questions like that. And Mammy never had bits of ham sandwich stuck to her bottom lip, either.

The sight of it, together with the fright of the split lip, was too much for Nicky: he burst out in a nervous snigger.

'Oh, so you think it's funny, do you?' Aidan shook him like a rat, scattering blood droplets across the kitchen lino. 'You think it's hilarious, you little pup?'

Chloe waddled in now with the hula-hoop, and was stricken by the sight of Nicky swinging wildly by his neck, amid a red-spattered kitchen.

'Mammy!' she squealed, loud enough for Mrs Brady next door to hear. 'Daddy's killing Nicky!'

Barney's was doing reasonably well, despite the current climate. People who couldn't afford to go away to spa hotels at weekends any more were staying at home instead, laying down their own decking. There was also a tremendous run on paint, the most popular colour being yellow. Either people were trying to bring some sunshine into their dreary lives, or else they were drinking it.

At any rate the car park was full that Saturday afternoon. Tara had to park all the way at the back, and hoof it onto the shop floor as fast as she could, in the hopes that nobody would notice she was late.

'Mrs Delaney?'

Mr O'Neill, the manager, must have been lying in wait for her. His pale blue eyes glittered behind his round little glasses. He was always in a state of nervous excitement at the weekends, their busiest days, although Thursday was seeing a lot of customers too. Dole Day, he maintained. There was never a man happier in other people's misery, and he would fairly fly up and down the aisles in his pointy-toe shoes, his cheeks glowing like apples.

'This can't keep happening,' he told her officiously now, tapping his watch for good measure.

'I know,' she said. She'd had to mop the blood off the floor and placate all the injured parties with fizzy orange and biscuits. By the time she'd rooted out a grubby Barney's overall and applied a lick of lipstick, it was time to go, and she still hadn't told Aidan about the baby.

'Sorry,' she said.

Mr O'Neill looked further irritated by the lack of a grovelling explanation. He had never seemed that keen on Tara, possibly because she was the same age as him, and not as impressionable as the younger ones who worked on the floor. Also, after the baby was born last year – 'Another one!' he'd said – and she had just started back to work at the weekends, her breasts had leaked through onto her top during a stock-take with him, leaving two large milky patches round about his eye level (he wasn't very tall). He had looked at her since as though she were incontinent on all fronts.

'Can you restock the coving? We appear to be running low. Oh, and Sharon?' He grabbed one of the other girls in passing. He always addressed them by their first names, saving the 'missus' tag for Tara. 'Maybe you'd give Mrs Delaney a hand?'

Sharon appeared to have been on her way out for a sneaky cigarette, judging by the bulge of twenty John Player Blue in her pocket. She was fairly cheesed off, anyway.

'Come on, so,' she said ungraciously to Tara, and off they went to the stockroom, but not before Mr O'Neill spotted the gravy stain at the hem of Tara's overall.

The coving was heavy and the stockroom hot. Sharon was no great shakes in the lifting department, either. She looked very surprised when Tara sat down abruptly on a pile of plastic garden chairs (they withstood the fright, thank God).

'Are you all right?' Sharon asked at last, chewing gum furiously, and obviously concerned that she might be called upon to perform CPR.

'Fine.' Tara wished she could take off her heavy jumper. But Mr O'Neill would get the wrong idea entirely if he walked in and found her in a none-too-white bra. 'It's just the heat.'

She hadn't felt sick on any of the other pregnancies. This one looked like it was going to be challenging from the word go.

Sharon decided that she might as well have her fag break, after all. She pulled up another set of garden chairs sat down with a sigh, and fired up. 'Want one?'

'No. Thanks anyway.' Tara waved away the smoke discreetly; there was a plastic plant pot in the shape of a swan nearby should the nausea become too much.

Sharon's belligerence seemed to melt away with each drag, until eventually, when she was near the end of it, she became positively chummy. 'Did you hear that Orla is going?'

Tara was surprised. Orla had been there before any of them. She sat at the cash desk all day long, a voluminous, unsmiling presence. Even Mr O'Neill was afraid of her.

'Where's she going?'

Sharon gave her a pitying look. 'She's not *going*.'

'But you just said –'

'She's being pushed.'

Tara felt herself go hot and cold.

'The recession and all that.' Sharon inspected a fingernail. 'It's just an excuse to get rid of the ones they don't like.'

Tara swallowed her nausea and carefully stood up. She pulled down her dirty overall as far as it would go – never mind about Aidan, what was she going to tell Mr O'Neill? – and said, in her fake happy voice again, 'Come on. We'd better get this finished or we'll be next.'

She didn't get home until nearly eleven that night. Mr O'Neill had asked several of them to stay behind to put up some promotional displays of garden furniture (Tara, naturally, didn't say no). Sharon had dropped a table leg onto Tara's foot, so she hobbled in the front door, to be greeted by darkness and the stale smell of fish fingers and waffles.

Aidan must have gone to bed already. He went off quite early these days. Well, all that rejection was taking its toll. Try again tomorrow, Tara tried to mentally beam at him, as she hopped from foot to foot in the bedroom, taking off her tights. Then she brushed her teeth, and checked that all the children were present and correct, and still breathing.

When she climbed into bed, it felt like years had passed since she'd got out of it that morning. She lay on her back in the darkness, looking at the ceiling, listening to the little whistling noise Aidan made between his teeth. Tomorrow they would drop the kids at her mother's, if she could be persuaded, and they would drive to the Phoenix Park, just the two of them, and she would break the news to him.

She would say nothing about Orla, and Barney's.

Her hand drifted to her belly. With each pregnancy she seemed to explode a little earlier. Even though it was scarcely possible, already her middle felt soft and round. Sorry, she whispered, I haven't made you very welcome so far. Terrible mother altogether. And don't worry about the cloth nappies, I probably won't go through with them.

She wondered if the baby would have red hair, like Nicky. He was always complaining that he was the odd one out. Maybe it would be a girl. Chloe would like that; a little sister to help her gang up against the boys.

Smiling now, she turned over and curled into Aidan's back, her hand still firmly pressed upon her belly.

'What's wrong?' he said, sleepily.

'Nothing,' she said, and kissed his neck. 'Nothing at all.'

In a minute they were both asleep.

∽ ∾

Ana Fischel

Film-maker, illustrator, poet and children's author, Ana Fischel is currently working on a series of twelve books – called *The Twelve Quests*. Six of these are already published and the remaining six will be published in autumn 2010. For further information go to *www.thetwelvequests.com*.

Bluebeard's Key *

Extract from the novel of the same name, Book 1 of the series
The Twelve Quests

Ana Fischel

A Truly Awful Beginning

It was 1849 and in Victorian London times were as hard as nails for most people. It was fine and dandy if you were rich and could afford to dress in posh clothes and eat until your belly was full, but it was pretty dreadful if you were poor and even worse if you had the misfortune to be an orphan living in a dangerous city filled with thieves, murderers and scallywags. Certainly Albert and Florence Leadington knew all about that side of things and then some, because at the grand old age of ten years old, they'd had to endure a lot of hardship.

The Leadington twins wearily followed their new guardian towards Madame Divitan's gloomy creepy-looking mansion, with its spiky turrets and sneering gargoyles, feeling very cold and not at all happy. The January evening seemed more frostily crisped-up than normal, like old icing sugar, and the gas lamps that lined the cobbled street leading up to the house flickered like demented demons in the wind. It had to be said that the visceral feeling which the twins had, as they got closer to the daunting mansion, was not good.

Their minds were clogged up with all sorts of unanswered questions – I mean, after all, what did they really know about their reluctant guardian, Mr Arthur Canarthy? Well, apart from the fact that he was going bald and had recently informed them that their parents weren't dead at all, but had in fact been cursed by a vindictive sorceress, whom he was now insisting they went to meet?

Considering it had been less than two days since the twins had first made his acquaintance, it was rather a lot to take in, especially if you didn't believe in magic (which I hasten to add that neither Albert nor Florence did). It was as if they had slipped in a puddle of time that had turned their lives upside down, changing everything forever, and now the only thing stitched into their future was uncertainty.

'Are you sure this is a good idea?' ventured Albert, through chattering teeth which he tried to grit still as he pulled his thread-bare coat tighter around him.

'Of course I'm sure! I've never had a bad idea in my life. Besides, it is the only way if you ever want to see your parents again,' Mr Canarthy replied brusquely, as he marched forward, his arms swinging like a soldier on parade. 'Believe me when I say I am not overly cheerful about the circumstances either, but I don't see any other alternative.'

'How do we know he's not on her side?' Florence whispered to her brother, as her long tangled hair whipped up against her grubby cheeks. 'He could be, you know, and then we'd really be in trouble, that's if what he's told us is true.'

'Doubt it,' her brother replied, shivering uncontrollably. 'Why go to all the trouble of getting us out of the orphanage then?'

'I don't know, maybe he's just crazy! We don't know if he's really Uncle Charlie's brother or not, we've only got his word! He could be anybody – he could be a mad axe murderer!'

'Don't be ridiculous! He'd have killed us by now if that was the case. Besides, he doesn't look like a mad axe murderer.'

Which was true as Mr Canarthy was a fairly ordinary fellow, and you'd be hard pressed to describe him as dangerous-looking. He had a pasty face and eyes the colour of dirty dishwater, with no real chin to speak of which gave him an insipid air, and enormous ears that stuck out like windbreakers. The few strands of hair that remained on his head were carefully combed over and waxed down from one side to the other, so that even the spiteful gusty night could not ruffle what remained of his balding coiffure.

'Right, here we are then,' announced Mr Canarthy abruptly, as they reached the imposing front door. He lifted the wrought-iron knocker, which was fashioned in the image of a fearsome lion, and let it slam back with a resounding clunk. They waited for a moment or so, but the only sound of life was the barking of a stray dog somewhere in the distance.

Suddenly the door creaked open and they found themselves face to face with the tallest, meanest-looking man that could ever be imagined.

'We have come to see Madame Divitan. These are the Leadington children that I sent word about,' Mr Arthur Canarthy announced, clearly perturbed by the tall man's towering glowering presence.

'You'd better come in then.' He smiled unpleasantly, his lip curling like a sleepy cobra uncoiling. 'Madame Divitan will be most intrigued to meet them, I'm sure.'

Mrs Snagglesnarle's Orphanage

Two days previously . . .

Albert and Florence Leadington awoke to the usual scrum and scurry of the day, with all the inevitable beatings and nastiness that were common at Mrs Snagglesnarle's orphanage. The ten-year-old twins knew it would be yet another dreadful day characterised by horrid chores, such as sweeping sooty choked-up chimneys and scrubbing laundry in steaming vats of water until their hands looked like withered tomatoes. Or, if they were very lucky, they would be sent out onto the grey stenchy streets of London, with its open sewers and disease-spreading rats, to run errands for Mrs Snagglesnarle. Albert and Florence (who actually preferred to be called Florrie) prayed for such days, because even though the streets of London were often chillier than the orphanage, there was a certain freedom to be had running along the roads. However, these sorts of days were few and far between.

There was no denying that Mrs Snagglesnarle's orphanage was a truly dire and dismal place, with its whistley draughts, paint-peeling walls and cracked-up old windows. The house smelt of death and decay, all dank and damp, and cold and mouldy. Truth be known, I've seen graveyards that were more welcoming than this dreadful abode. Indeed, these unfortunate children were even forced to wear dead people's clothes, clothes that had been taken from corpses as they lay cold in their coffins, due to the fact that Mrs Snagglesnarle had an arrangement with the local undertaker.

'Get up, you miserable little ruffians!' Mrs Snagglesnarle screeched, as she poked them with her walking stick. 'Or I will make you sorry that you were ever born!'

She was a spindly woman with a large hooked nose that constantly dripped and she wore an eye-patch over her left eye, which she had lost in an accident with a knitting needle. Her thin mean mouth was always twisted in a permanent sneer, a bit like barbed wire, with the shadow of a moustache perched above it and she had gnarled twitchity fingers that were like snapped twigs. Her grey, wispy hair protruded from an expensive lace bonnet, for whilst she was quite happy to let the children do without, she denied herself nothing.

Outside, it was a bitterly freezing January morning, with frost clawing at the windowpanes spreading a sigh of cold across the floor.

Albert and Florrie dragged themselves up from the flea-ridden mattresses that passed as beds, pulled on their raggedly worn-out clothes, and shuffled down the rickety staircase for breakfast.

The miserable children lined up in silence, as Mrs Snagglesnarle slopped some revolting looking soup into their bowls. Albert forced himself to eat a spoonful of the disgusting mixture, almost gagging as the taste of boiled cabbage and sheep's entrails slid down his throat. As he stirred the congealed greasy gunk, he thought to himself for the umpteenth time how he longed to be back with his Uncle Charlie. It seemed a long, stretched-out time since Albert and Florrie had first arrived and then how different things had been, for if their Uncle Charlie had known the truth about the orphanage, he would never have left them to such a dreadful fate. But Mrs Snagglesnarle had been oh so careful to cover the truth, as she entertained them in her cosy little parlour.

Uncle Charlie, who actually wasn't their real uncle but rather a close friend of their father, had been their guardian since the mysterious death of Albert and Florrie's parents on the eve of the twins' seventh birthday. He had however fallen very ill over a period of time and could no longer cope with bringing up two energetic children. Naturally, he thought he had made a most splendid choice for his charges, and so, on that terrible day, he had handed over his life savings to Mrs Snagglesnarle and with that he was gone.

They were nine and a half years old then, and would never see their Uncle Charlie alive again. It proved to be the worst day of Albert and Florrie's lives.

However, things were about to get a lot worse for the Leadington twins . . .

Mr Felton's Funeral Parlour

Albert and Florrie forced down the rest of their breakfast, hoping against hope that they might be sent out onto the smoggy streets of London and, for once, it would seem that luck was on their side.

'You two vile creatures, come here!' Mrs Snagglesnarle snapped, beckoning with a long bony finger at them. 'Mr Felton has a package of clothes for me which needs collecting from the undertakers. Go directly there now and tell him I will settle my account next week, but no dawdling or Spike will take his belt to you! Do I make myself clear?'

'Yes, Mrs Snagglesnarle,' the twins replied in unison, their hearts bouncing like balls with a barely dared-to-hope-for excitement.

Albert and Florrie quickly pulled on their thin coats, which were more holes than fabric, and ran out onto the streets. Outside, it had just started to drizzle and the skies were all dark and scowling, but the twins didn't care. They just savoured being away from the orphanage, for those moments were always sprinkled with gold dust and a dream that for a short while they could pretend to be normal children, with a normal family doing normal things. But, of course, nothing was further from the truth. I mean, it is hardly normal to expect a child to wear dead people's clothes after all.

They soon found themselves outside Mr Felton's funeral parlour, which, as you might imagine, was an austere and sombre place that smelt of embalming fluid and grief. Albert pushed open the door, triggering a tiny bell as he did so, and they found themselves staring at Mr Felton who was busy trying to console a newly bereaved widow. He was the most dour and humourless-looking man you could think of, all grim and ashen in appearance, his skin waxy and slack with wrinkles.

The adults were standing by an open coffin, and when Florrie stood on her tippy-toes, she could see the death-white corpse of an elderly man laid out inside it, his dead eyes covered with two shiny shilling pieces.

'There, there, and rest assured I shall take care of all the arrangements, Mrs Corby. If there's anything else that I can be of assistance with, then let me know,' he said, ushering her out of the door.

The second that she was out of earshot, he spun round on his steel-toe-capped boots and grabbed Albert and Florrie by the scruff of their necks. 'What do you little whippersnappers want?'

'Please, sir, we're from the orphanage . . . Mrs Snagglesnarle sent us . . . to pick up a package?' stammered Albert, as he tried to wriggle free from the man's vicelike grip.

Mr Felton's expression quietened down momentarily, like a kite that had lost its breeze.

'I see. Have you brought money? She owes me more than eight groats as things stand.'

'Er, no, sir. She said she would pay her account next week, sir,' replied Albert quickly.

'She pays what she owes me – until then she gets nothing!'

snapped Mr Felton, abruptly letting go of the twins. 'Now get out of here or I'll take my switch to you!'

Albert and Florrie didn't need any further telling as they fled the funeral parlour and hastened back towards the orphanage.

'She's going to beat us for sure now,' gasped Albert, as he stopped outside the dilapidated door of the orphanage. He bent over, holding his sides and trying to catch his breath. 'It's not fair, it's not our fault.'

'I know. None of this is fair, but what can we do? Come on, we might as well get this over and done with.'

Brother and sister exchanged a look of resignation as they reluctantly went back inside the diabolical place they had learnt to call home.

Mr Arthur Canarthy

'Ah, you little vermin, there you are!' screeched Mrs Snagglesnarle, stepping out of the shadows, as they entered the grimy entrance. She gave them quite a start and the twins jumped as high as feathers when a duvet is shaken. Florrie ended up stubbing her toe on a rusty nail that was protruding from the rotting floorboards.

'I've been waiting for you! What has taken you so long?' Mrs Snagglesnarle hissed, sucking on a long-stemmed pipe and exhaling a foul-smelling serpent of smoke into their faces. 'Come here this instant.'

'Mrs Snagglesnarle, we came back as fast as we could. I'm very sorry but Mr Felton would not release the goods to us without payment and as we did not have any money . . .' started Albert, as he flinched and braced himself for the inevitable whack of her cane.

'Never mind that, you have a visitor, says he's the brother of your late Uncle Charlie,' she said brusquely, spitting onto a hankie and quickly trying to wipe some of the dirt from their faces. 'He wants to speak to you on a matter of great urgency, looks quite wealthy too, so I want you both to be on your best behaviour.'

'Yes, Mrs Snagglesnarle,' they said.

'Now, listen to me and listen carefully,' she hissed, taking another suck on her pipe. 'You shall tell him how well you have been treated here, and under no circumstances will you say anything that might have an adverse effect on me or my orphanage. Do I make myself clear?'

'Yes, Mrs Snagglesnarle,' replied the twins hastily.

'This way, hurry, hurry,' their odious guardian urged, as she dragged them up the stairs to the parlour, her scrawny fingers biting and pinching into their flesh in a most uncomfortable manner.

A tall wiry man wearing a long frock coat and top hat stood with his back to them, as he warmed his hands by the fire.

'Mr Canarthy,' said Mrs Snagglesnarle in her sweetest, most plummy, and poshest of voices, 'here are your lovely niece and nephew. The delightful little rascals were playing outside. I don't know, if I've told them once, I've told them a hundred times not to play in the rain. You'll catch a chill and we can't have that, can we?' She tried to force an indulgent smile and roughly ruffled their hair with her dirty fingernails. 'Shall I pour hot chocolate for everybody?'

'Actually, Mrs Snagglesnarle, would you mind leaving us? I need to speak to the children in private,' Arthur Canarthy stated authoritatively, turning towards them.

'Of course, sir, as you wish,' she replied, bobbing a little curtsey and flashing the twins a sideways narrow-eyed look that clearly meant 'If you say anything then you'll regret it!'

'Well, sit down then. So you are Albert and Florence Leadington,' the man said curtly, flicking his gloved wrist at them to indicate they should seat themselves on the sofa. 'As I'm sure you have been informed by now, my name is Mr Arthur Canarthy and your Uncle Charles was my brother. Maybe your parents mentioned me before?'

'Er, no, sir, but we were only six, well, almost seven years old when they died,' Albert explained quietly, casting his eyes to the floor and wondering just what this was all about.

182

'I see, well, this is rather awkward. You see, your parents aren't actually dead,' frowned Mr Canarthy, as he began to pace around in little agitated circles.

'What?' cried Florrie. 'But Uncle Charlie told us they were! Why would he tell us such a terrible lie and why would he leave us here if that was true?!'

'It's a long story, but your parents are actually alive – alive but cursed, I'm afraid. I don't want to say any more, prying ears and all,' he continued, as he walked over to the door and opened it to reveal Mrs Snagglesnarle eavesdropping, with the side of her head pressed firmly against the wooden frame.

'Oh, sir, this isn't as it looks. I was just about to see if you needed anything else,' she stammered guiltily, smoothing down her petticoats.

'Of course you were, madam,' Mr Canarthy glared. 'Now, the children are coming with me, so if you could get their things together immediately . . .'

'But we don't have anything!' Florrie exclaimed, looking embarrassed.

'Right, we'll be on our way then.'

'Not so fast! I shall need reimbursing for their lodgings and the like,' retorted Mrs Snagglesnarle, her steely eyes like sharp flints waiting to ignite the spark of an argument.

'Naturally, I shall pay the requisite fee to release them from your care,' he replied, pulling out a bag of coins, which he waved under her nose. 'However, there is one condition, and that is, if anybody asks, you have never set eyes on these children before. Their wellbeing is of no concern of yours any more.'

'It never was to begin with,' Albert muttered to his sister.

'What was that?' screeched Mrs Snagglesnarle, as she raised her hand to clip Albert round the ear.

'You shall not lay a finger on the boy!' Mr Canarthy glowered, as he grabbed her wrist and held it fast.

'As you wish,' Mrs Snagglesnarle hissed as she yanked her hand free again, 'but if you don't beat the bad out of them then they'll run riot, mark my words.'

'That is a chance I am prepared to take. Come along, children, we shall take our leave. Good day to you, Mrs Snagglesnarle.'

A Really Bad Plan

Outside, it had at least cheered up a little and rays of sunshine were dripping down the sky like wet laundry pegged out on a clothesline. Albert and Florrie scurried after Mr Arthur Canarthy, taking just what they were wearing, grateful to be away from Mrs Snagglesnarle's horrid orphanage and, not quite believing their luck, they simultaneously pinched each other's arms to make sure they weren't dreaming.

'Ouch!' each twin cried, glaring at the other, before bursting into a fit of giggles.

'Behave yourselves! I have no time for silliness. You should understand a lot of danger awaits you and there will be little that I can do to protect you from it!' snapped Mr Canarthy from beneath the brim of his hat, as he raised an arm to hail a hansom-cab. 'This is no time for playing games. Just get in and behave yourselves!'

'Where to, Governor?' the driver called out cheerily.

'Bermondsey, Number 6, Cherry Tree Crescent, just round the corner from The Wishing Well Tavern,' replied Mr Canarthy, as they quickly clambered into the creaky black carriage, and found themselves engulfed in the scent of wax polish mixed with a faint hint of horse manure.

When they finally did arrive at Number 6, Cherry Tree Crescent, it was not all nice and delightful as the name might suggest, but instead tumbledown and uninviting. A paint-chipped sign hung above the door – 'The Little Shop of Curious and Odd Things' it stated.

Reluctantly Florrie and Albert followed Mr Canarthy into the shop, which was more akin to a musty museum or someone's attic. Cobwebs snagged down from boxes and chests like torn lace and at the back of the shop there were shelves lined with hundreds of glass bottles.

'Sit down then,' he began, as he took off his gloves and top hat and lit a few candles. 'Are you hungry?'

'Starving,' replied Florrie quietly, wishing that he would light a fire as well, because the cold blanket of winter had well and truly tucked itself into every corner of the room.

'Well, I suppose I should feed you then,' he scowled, clearly irritated by the children's presence. 'Wait here and don't, under any circumstances, touch anything,' he added, as he skulked off through a small darkened archway.

'This is very strange, isn't it? I mean, why would Uncle Charlie tell us our parents were dead if they weren't? And why has it taken Mr Canarthy so long to find us?' muttered Albert.

'How should I know? I'm sure he'll tell us,' shrugged Florrie, blowing into her hands in an attempt to warm up.

'I don't like this, I don't like it one bit.'

'Let's just wait and see what he has to say. So long as we're together we'll be all right,' Florrie said, squeezing her brother's hand.

'Here we are, children. It's not much, I know, but it's all I could find in the pantry,' declared Mr Canarthy, as he returned with a chunk of slightly stale bread and some cheese that had clearly seen better days.

The children divided the bread and cheese between them.

'So you are probably wondering what this is all about?' he began.

'Well, actually, yes, we are,' mumbled Albert, scraping off some mould from the cheese before gnawing at it.

'You said our parents had been cursed,' prompted Florrie.

'Yes, yes, indeed,' Mr Canarthy replied. 'I know it sounds preposterous but there you have it in a nutshell.'

'But how and why and by whom?' asked Florrie, in a tumble of words and breadcrumbs.

'By a witch, of course. Who else goes around placing magic curses on people?'

'I don't know. I didn't think witches even existed,' she retorted.

'Well, clearly they do, otherwise none of us would find ourselves in this predicament now and, speaking personally, this is a dreadful inconvenience to me! I wish I had never come across that wretched letter!'

'What letter?' enquired Albert.

'The one I found in my brother's effects after he passed away a few months ago of course! The one which described how your parents – who so desperately wanted children but were unable to have any – went to a sorceress by the name of Madame Divitan to make it so. The letter describes the deal that they made with her and subsequently reneged on!' spluttered Mr Canarthy, obviously getting more and more annoyed, as he pulled out a crumpled envelope and brandished it at them.

'What deal did they make with her?' asked Florrie worriedly.

'It would appear that Madame Divitan used her considerable powers of dark magic, to ensure your mother was with child, or rather twins, you two, and in return, on the twelfth hour of the twelfth month of your sixth year, your parents were to hand you over to her but when the appointed time came they decided to hide you with my brother Charles,' answered Mr Canarthy.

'So why didn't you come for us sooner?' frowned Albert.

'Well, I didn't want to, did I? I'm a very busy man and besides I was travelling abroad when I heard that my brother had passed away. It's only because Charles's ghost started haunting me, demanding that I help you, that I found it necessary to come and get you. Oh, how he went on and on, until I could take it no more! Finding you children was the only way to get a decent night's sleep again! Always having to do the right thing, even from the grave,' Mr Canarthy grumbled.

'So what's to become of us?'

'We must go and visit Madame Divitan, of course! As she was the one who placed the curse on your parents, then only she can remove it. I sent word to her just before I collected you from the orphanage. She is expecting us tomorrow night.'

Albert and Florrie looked at each other in horror.

And so, having no choice in the matter, that was how the Leadington twins found themselves outside Madame Divitan's front door the following evening . . .

Madame Divitan and The Twelve Quests

'Well, don't just stand there, follow me,' instructed the mean-looking man, his dark sunken eyes boring into them. Florrie and Albert hesitated and glanced at each other, their nerves jittering and leaping around like skittish spring lambs, just before they discover they are destined for somebody's dining-room table.

'I don't want to go in,' whimpered Florrie, grasping her brother's hand and squeezing it a bit too tightly. 'Suppose she puts a curse on us too?'

'Look, we'll just have to take our chances, all right? Besides, you want to see Mother and Father again, don't you?'

'Well, of course I do!' she replied, with a sense of indignation, as the butler led them into a large salon, where Madame Divitan awaited them.

The witch arose slowly and majestically from her chair, her smile thinning like a paintbrush does when you put it in a jar of water, all washed away, until nothing remains but a pale smudge of colour. In fact everything about her was pale, almost ghostly one might say, except for a dab of rouge to her cheeks and her blood-red lips. Several black cats lay lazily around the room, cleaning their fur whilst keeping a watchful eye on the new arrivals.

'These are the Leadington children,' the mean-looking man announced, 'and their guardian, Mr Arthur Canarthy.'

'So I see. Fetch me the contract, Bradshaw.'

'Very good, Madame.'

'Well, let's get down to business, shall we? I have no inclination for small talk and I'm presuming you are here because you want me to lift the curse I placed on your parents?'

'Well, yes, ma'am,' said Albert. 'I mean, Mr Canarthy has explained what happened and we know they made you angry, but we really don't want to have to go back to the orphanage. We just want to see our parents again and Mr Canarthy thought that if we came and spoke to you . . .'

'Mr Canarthy should know better than to think I would be swayed by the pathetic pleadings of children,' she snorted. 'You are mine by rights. A deal is a deal after all! However, I'm not an unreasonable woman. Maybe we can come to an arrangement.'

'That is most gracious of you. You see, children, I told you it was a good idea coming here!' exclaimed Mr Canarthy rather smugly.

'You haven't heard what my proposition is yet,' Madame Divitan purred, a sliver of danger wedged in her voice. 'I propose a small wager, bound on both sides whatever the outcome.'

'What sort of wager?' asked Albert, feeling deeply uneasy.

'You must undertake twelve quests, which have to be completed within twelve months beginning from this very day. If, and only if you can complete these challenges successfully within the allotted time, I shall free your parents. I can't say fairer than that now, can I?' she said, smiling sugar sweetly at the children.

'I suppose not,' replied Albert dubiously.

'What sort of challenges?' enquired Florrie.

'Oh, I just want you to collect a few items for me,' Madame Divitan declared breezily, as she placed a hand on each of their shoulders and squatted down so that her face was level with theirs. 'So, do we have an accord?'

The twins glanced at each other, and then at Mr Canarthy, who gave them a brisk nod.

'I don't think you have any alternative, children,' he said.

'That's the first sensible thing to have come out of your mouth,' said Madame Divitan. 'You children should listen to him. So what's it to be?'

'All right, we'll do it,' said Albert.

'Right then, you just need to sign this,' said Madame Divitan, as Bradshaw returned with a huge sheaf of papers.

'What's that?' frowned Arthur Canarthy.

'Oh, it's just a standard contract to ensure each party honours their part in the agreement,' she replied, as she handed Albert a pen.

'I think I should read through it first,' countered Arthur Canarthy.

'Listen to me, you odious little man, I don't have time for this! They either sign this right now or they will never see their parents again!'

The Leadington twins nodded to one another before each of them quickly scrawled their signature upon the document. Madame Divitan rolled the contract up and handed it to her butler.

'But what happens if we fail?' asked Florrie nervously.

'Then your innocent little souls will be mine for all eternity,' she hissed, as the disguise of her compassion dropped away like a snipped shadow, 'and make no mistake, I will collect if you fail.'

The witch raised herself to her full height, stalked over to a nearby cupboard and pulled out a small box which she gave to them.

'Inside there are twelve matches. You must strike them one at a time and they shall reveal the quests that you must embark upon.'

Albert cautiously took the matches, a sinking feeling glugging down to the pit of his stomach.

'Remember, you have just twelve months to complete these challenges, not a day more. Oh, and I do hope you like fairy stories, my dears, because it's the only way you'll find the happy ending you're looking for,' she hinted cryptically, tagging an evil laugh on the end for good measure. 'Now, run along! You don't have a moment to waste!'

The twins and Mr Canarthy were duly shown back out onto the street by Bradshaw, where they stood momentarily under a night that was bleeding with stars.

'Well, there we go then, quests and fairy stories, eh? Doesn't sound too bad. I mean most of them end well, don't they?' commented Mr Canarthy, digging his hands firmly in his pockets, 'So I'll be off then – you know, places to be, people to meet! Do look me up when you're back in London next. Farewell and good luck.'

And with that, he turned on his booted heels and disappeared into the darkness . . .

Striking the First Match

Albert and Florrie stood shivering in the inky shadows, each as shocked as the other that Mr Canarthy had just left them there with no money or food. Indeed, he hadn't even left them with a playing card of advice that they might use at some stage in this game – because it was clearly just that, a nasty and uncertain game that Madame Divitan had concocted and now they were her pawns.

'Oh well,' shrugged Albert at last, 'best we get on with it then!'

'But how?' asked Florrie, her eyes beginning to well up with big ploppy tears and her mouth going all trembly with worry. 'We've got nowhere to stay, it's freezing cold and I'm hungry. Maybe we should try to find our way back to the orphanage. We might be able to persuade Mrs Snagglesnarle to take us in again.'

'Are you mad? We're not going back, not ever. Look, it'll be all right, Florrie,' Albert said, wrapping an arm round her. 'We've got each other and that's the main thing. Besides, things could be worse.'

And, with those words, the skies sliced open and a big storm broke loose, unleashing a torrent of rain and, oh dear, things did indeed get worse. Albert and Florrie ran to take shelter under a nearby tree and were just wondering what to do next, when a hackney carriage pulled up beside them, splashing them as it drove through a nearby puddle. The door opened and a familiar, albeit rather terse voice called out, 'Well, what are you waiting for? Get in out of the rain, children!' Mr Arthur Canarthy poked his head out of the window, 'Come on then! Before I change my mind!'

Florrie and Albert didn't need to be told twice, as they scrambled in feeling all damp and musty, like old stinky socks.

'You came back for us!' cried Florrie, awash with surprise and hope.

'That would be stating the obvious, now wouldn't it?'

'But why? What made you change your mind?' asked Albert, looking at him suspiciously.

'Well, upon reflection I thought that it might have been a tad remiss on my part to leave two ten-year-old children to fend for themselves on a night such as this, so out of the goodness of my heart and though I never wanted anything to do with this whole sorry situation in the first place, I thought that I'd better make sure you were all right.'

'Uncle Charlie's ghost came back to haunt you, didn't it?' interrupted Albert, pulling a face that clearly meant 'you don't fool me!'

'Well, there was that too,' muttered Mr Canarthy, somewhat sulkily. 'Anyway, it looks as if the only way he's ever going to leave me alone is if I help you. So here I am and it would appear that we are all tangled together in this mess until those quests are completed.'

'So you're going to help us then?' asked Florrie.

Arthur Canarthy scowled a little and slicked an agitated hand over his balding head. 'It doesn't look as if I have much choice. So, do you know what the first challenge is yet?'

'No, we haven't struck any of the matches,' replied Albert, pulling the box out of his coat pocket. 'Shall I do it now?'

'You heard what Madame Divitan said – time is of the essence, young man,' nodded Mr Canarthy curtly, as he took out his bronze fob watch and snapped it open.

Albert gingerly slid open the box and picked out one of the matches, striking it quickly. Immediately the carriage was filled with a strange and eerie light that contained a picture within the flame.

'What is it?' asked Florrie, peering closer to see, as she widened her eyes. 'It looks like a door and there's somebody walking towards it.'

'Yes, it's a man and he seems to be holding a key or something,' interjected Mr Canarthy frowning. 'Goodness me! He's got the longest beard I've ever seen!'

'He looks pretty evil to me,' Florrie shuddered.

Suddenly a voice began to speak to them, all thin and quiet, like somebody skating on ice.

'*Your first challenge is to travel to Paris. Just outside the city you will find a château that belongs to the Duke de Mauvais. There is a secret room inside which can only be unlocked with one key. You must acquire this key, and once you have completed the remaining quests, return with it to Madame Divitan. If you fail you shall never see your parents again and your souls will be doomed to eternal damnation.*'

And with that, the match burnt itself out, leaving just a suggestion of sulphur hanging in the air and Albert's fingers almost singed.

'Where's Paris?' asked Florrie, who had never travelled abroad before, nor even so much as looked at a map.

'It's in France, which is miles and miles and miles away. This really is a bother! We shall have to find passage on a boat,' grumbled Mr Canarthy, as he stopped to ponder for a moment. 'We must head to the docks. I have associates there, and maybe one of them can help us.'

'Driver, make haste and take us to the North Thames Estuary!' shouted Mr Canarthy, leaning out of the window again.

With a snap of the reins they were away, galloping fiercely through the rainy chill of the night and the twins began to nod off. Though they were exhausted by the bizarre events of the past few days they did at least have a thimbleful of hope now that they might see their parents once again.

Derek Foley

In real life Derek Foley is a reporter and columnist with the high-circulation *Irish Daily Star* (420,000 readers daily); in fiction he owns Lillie's Bordello nightclub, appearing as one of Ross O'Carroll Kelly's mates in the popular series of novels. A novel *There is Only One F in Fatal* is due out in the summer of 2011.

Bright Lights, Big City **

Derek Foley

There has always been a melancholia to supporting Manchester City, an infinite sadness about a club without a major trophy since 1970.

It was a European Cup Winners Cup, following on from a 1969 FA cup win, a year on from winning the Championship in 1968. And that was a league win completely overshadowed by Matt Busby and Man Utd's first European Cup win.

As the most famous book about being a Man City fan espouses in its title, *Manchester United Ruined My Life* . . . Yet at the same time, despite 40 years in the wilderness, Man City have always been cool . . . rock'n'roll enough for Oasis to wear on their sleeves.

Man Utd will always have Simply Red, Spurs Chas'n'Dave, Leicester City Kasabian and so on, but they can't hold a candle to the Gallagher brothers.

And then this season, a sheikh-up.

Before a 2009/10 Premiership ball had been kicked, the bookies more or less agreed on Man Utd (2/1) as favourites to win out, Chelsea (9/4), Liverpool (3/1), Arsenal (8/1) with next up and under new owners Man City (12/1).

It was a seismic leap from City at 12/1 to the next-rated side Spurs at 100/1 and that's despite them owning four top-rated international strikers – Defoe, Keane, Crouch and Pavlyuchenko. Last season at City the only player to get into double figures in the

Premiership was Robinho and 10 of his 14 came in the 2008 half of the season. There was also a highlight, a 5–0 pasting of Sunderland, straight out of Copacabana on a day Stephen Ireland looked as Brazilian as Robinho or Elano.

I've seen other amazing Man City things but they have been from different eras: Giorgi Kinkladze; Paul Power's 1981 Holt End FA Cup semi-final winning free kick; 5–1, 3–1 and 4–1 Manchester Derby wins; 5 entry for all against Aalburg last March. I've seen bad days: last days of the season against Luton Town; a 1999 Deva Stadium FA Cup first round game where the top team in Division Two (us) played the bottom team in the entire Football League (Chester); the 1994 Derby at Old Trafford, 0–5. But here City are, having won their very own lottery, being taken over by oil-rich gazillionaires who have so much money they have even sheikh-en UEFA awake.

'There is certainly disquiet in the corridors of power here, that clubs such as Real Madrid and Man City are destabilising the market,' said UEFA's General Secretary David Taylor at one point. It's flattering the mandarins who run European football have even heard of Man City who, in their history, have had only one European Cup outing, two Cup Winners' Cup and six UEFA Cup seasons.

Getting mentioned in the same breath as Real Madrid, a club who have just splashed out £217m on players this season, has its novelty effect; we're more used to getting mentioned in the same breath as teams with odd tag-on names such as Wednesday, Wanderers and Orient.

I've reservations about City's 109m shopping spree all the same. For instance, the cumulative 2008/09 Premiership goals total from Tevez, Adebayor and Santa Cruz was 19. Carlos Tevez is admired for his work-rate but for 33m, I want 22 goals from him. It is not a new complaint: I have supported a club that has celebrated the signing of a man called Jim Tolmey, a small Man Utd striker called Terry Cooke, paid 5m in 2002 for John Macken, lived with the Incredible Sulk of Nicolas Anelka.

I fumed as fans pretended Shaun Goater was anything other

than battering-average and then there was the 21m paid in 2008 to CSKA Moscow for Jo! In search of that 21-goal-a-season player and to be backed up by Robinho's 14 and Stephen Ireland's 9, the pressure is on Emmanuel Adebayor to reproduce a goal-scoring touch that was parked last season at Arsenal.

And/or on Tevez and Roque Santa Cruz, none of whose goal-scoring prowess last season was overly impressive. There is not just me out there either, loading a six-gun with hope in a tough's town – City fans may be an idiosyncratic bunch but they are dotted about.

David Cassidy, ex-Dublin 5 but now of Greystones, is one of City's longest-serving and hardest-travelling fans; between Premiership, Division One, Division Two and FA Cups it is probable he has visited more league grounds supporting his club than any Irish-based fan of any club.

There is Foxrock's Dr Joe Curry, Bartley 'Mr Finn Harps' Ramsay, Joe Trainor, long-time suffering Hon Sec of MCFC Supporters Club Dublin and his wife Róisín, Brian Douglas of Fairview CY and latterly Dollymount FC fame, amateur football referee 'Gilly' Smart.

Some years back there was even an Irish Man City fan who lived in Meath who was voted BBCs Radio 5's Supporter of the Year. Did I mention Ireland's greatest ever amateur soccer international Tony O'Connell of Bohemians and Tolka Rovers managerial fame, the AUL's Dick Redmond, Julian Davis who organised the Special Olympics here, Leinster rugby, IRFU, St Pats and RDS announcer Declan King, *Daily Mail* soccer journalist Philip Quinn . . . Now this menagerie may appear to have little in common but what they don't do is wear anything coloured red, shout so loud as to invade your personal space and appear to lack any empathy with the weak, the down-at-heel or dissolute.

There is also the sheer unavoidable pratfalls, in my case stemming from a request to watch the Manchester derby while a guest of the Sheikhs at the Dubai World Cup at Nad-al-Sheeba. Now, the Astra satellite is blocked in Dubai so a dedicated limousine ferried me across an emirate's border. City top on, I travelled in silence for five hours through the desert sun, arriving at Sharjah's Hilton Hotel and a big sign, '*United v City Live, Shepherd's Pie, Beer, Ale, Crisps, Air-conditioning*'.

My stay, I'd been warned beforehand, was set at a minimum of four hours as it was the Moslem feast of Ramadan and my driver had to obey certain religious rules. Walking in five minutes before kick-off my heart sinks: there are 250 people in the bar, every one a 'UK ex-pat' and every one wearing red and my arrival is greeted with the kind of roar reserved for the pork at a pagan feast. I later counted 55 televisions, some high, some low, essentially one for every side of every pillar, every corner, nook and cranny.

This proved particularly awkward as no matter which one I looked at Man City lost the game 0–5 (Kanchelskis ran amok) to the background noise of 250 United fans enjoying rubbing it in. As for City singing, there is the wistful 'Blue Moon' but I also know Man City's older and better nickname is The Citizens. Have you ever heard '*La Marseillaise*', the most rousing anthem in the world, and its best line, '*Aux armes, citoyens . . . Marchons, marchons!* '? After 40 years in the wilderness, the revolution can't come soon enough.

∞ ∾

Teena Gates

Teena Gates has more than twenty years' experience as a journalist, presenter and media trainer. She heads up the PPI award-winning newsroom at Dublin's 98FM, where she presented breakfast news for two decades. Teena is a board member of Learning Waves, a training network established for the Independent Radio Industry. She has also lectured in communications with FÁS, and in journalism and media studies with BCFE.

Tapping into Hope **

Teena Gates

The tap, tap of the stick comes with me as I gauge the distance between the cab and the door to Fallon & Byrne. I estimate the walk between the door and the lift and wonder if the girls are sitting at the table near the bar. Avoiding the eyes of a woman in the lift and leaning slightly forwards, I push the small of my back into the cold panel . . . small relief. The doors open and I breathe in heavily, trying to ease past the unmoving woman, avoiding her thoughts. Shuffling down the corridor, I feel my back begin to seize. When it happens in the supermarket I lean on a trolley or bend on a knee pretending to look at the tins on the bottom shelf, stretching out my back to ease the pain and hoping no one will notice. I don't bring my stick to work, preferring to make it to my seat and sit there all day, accepting coffees from the world, and never making my own run to the kitchen. Somehow it felt easier to be seen as lazy, than disabled. Can't figure why, even now. Looking around the corner as I hold my side, my heart sinks; the girls are at a great table on the other side of the room. Moving from table to table, leaning on people's chairs, and trying to pick a route that doesn't require too many happy diners to move their seats, I make it to safety, pin on a smile, and drag my 23 stone onto the stool, on the third attempt. I've arrived. Pass the menu, life is great, let the show begin.

I've never believed in crystals, or faith-healers. Not that I don't have beliefs, I believe in the Universe, in Karma, perhaps in God,

201

and certainly in the human spirit. But my friends have laughed as I rained on the 'fakey Reiki' parade and snorted at moonstones and moonbeams. My search to find a cure for the pain in my back took me on an eight-year trek from hospitals to doctors, to physiotherapists, chiropractors and acupuncturists; and had very nearly brought me around to crystals and pendants when I ended up in hospital, extremely sick for a different reason. Diagnosed with gall-bladder problems, the choices were bleak – lose weight for keyhole surgery or face an eight-inch incision and major surgical event. I don't blame the consultant for looking sharply at me when I promised to lose 4 stone, but I didn't hesitate. I headed off to the South of France for two weeks, to eat olives, drink a little good red wine . . . and swim for hours every day! I cut the weight, and five months later headed for surgery, suddenly relieved of my new goal, and suddenly terrified of what lay ahead.

Waking up in surgery I thought I'd reach for my stomach, for my scars, to assess the damage and check I was still there. But my first waking thought was the lack of pain in my back – loving the anaesthetist, and wondering where I could get a permanent supply of drugs like that! I didn't have long to wait. The drug was life and freedom and energy; the ability to move and put the mask away. The pain never returned. For eight years I'd lived with what we all believed was scar-tissue from a riding accident. Gone; as quickly as it came, with as few answers now as then; and the rush of life, of hope, the glowing, beaming, joy of being me. Glittering, gleaming, glorious Gates. I loved me, and the world loved me too. Turbo-charged Teena threw herself into living, and clawing back every second of wasted opportunity. Gym guru David – who'd helped me climb that initial four-stone mountain, got dragged into further demand as I determined to repay my body for coming back to me, by working it, and minding it. I'd also joined Weight Watchers, and never missed a meeting, thriving on my colleagues' support and advice. Intensely private despite being in the public eye, I threw open my life, told my story on Facebook and Twitter, and accepted every bit of help along the way. The tap, tap of my stick was replaced by the tap, tap on my keyboard as I posted Wednesday weigh-ins on the Web . . . knowing, whatever the result, encouragement was just a keystroke away.

Suddenly – with six stone lost, and six more to go to reach goal – I stumbled, and a random post called on my new FB friends for motivation. 'I need a new mountain to climb,' said the thread.

Reading it, Rosaleen Thomas from The HOPE Foundation frowned, as her fingers went tap, tap. 'I've got a mountain for you,' her email read.

It's June 2010. A year ago I couldn't walk but today I'm catching a train to Kerry, to meet Pat Falvey and the rest of the Expedition of Hope. We'll be climbing mountains for the next few days, a tough training camp to judge our progress in preparation for later this year. What better way to test a new body than go for a stroll to Base Camp Mount Everest – the highest point on the planet? As the tap, tap of my climbing polls replaces the tap, tap of my stick, I'll think of the incredible challenges and privileges that my whirlwind journey has brought me, as it crashed through so many peaks and valleys to the foothills of the Himalayas.

Trying on dresses for The HOPE Foundation Ball last March – my 82-year-old mum laughed and giggled as we ran between bedrooms. I'd dropped so many dress sizes I was giddy with excitement and Mum was grinning too, from ear to ear. Finally deciding, we hugged and parted before going back to our rooms.

But moments later she was back: 'Is that it? You're sure we've tried them all?'

'Yes, Mum, that's the lot.'

'So the fashion show is over?' she said.

'Yep, Mum, the fashion show is over.'

'Well, it's got to be the red,' she said.

Laughing, I agreed.

We hugged and kissed again, said 'Goodnight, God bless' and went to sleep.

Hope won't drag or drive me up Everest. But it stops me from giving up and giving in. It opened the door and whispered in my ear, telling me I could walk through it; and walk I will.

I'll never wear the red dress. Mam never woke up.

But when the time is right, I'll wear red again and remember her with love and laughter. And her strength and her spirit and her endless supply of hope come with me to Everest. It's not just my challenge any more, it's Mum's too. And everyone's who needs a bit of Hope.

Noëlle Harrison

Noëlle Harrison was born in England and moved to Ireland in 1991. While based in Dublin in the early 1990s she wrote and produced plays, setting up her own theatre company, Aurora. She has written extensively on visual art in Ireland. Her first novel, *Beatrice,* was published in 2004, followed by *A Small Part of Me* in 2005, and *I Remember* in 2008. Her last novel, *The Adulteress,* was published in 2009. Its film rights have recently been sold.

At the Coalface *

Noëlle Harrison

It is dark down there. Tommy pokes the bed with his oar and clouds of mud billow into the pond. Underwater is not so different from underground.

'Daddy, look!' Anita points to a tiny flicker, a small fish gliding beneath them. 'What kind of fish is it?' she asks, clasping her hands in excitement.

'I don't know, love. What do you think, David?'

He glances over at his son but the boy isn't interested. Nothing he says seems to rouse him. The child looks like he has shrunk over the past weeks. He sits at the end of the boat, hunched, his knobbly knees pressing into his chest, his eyes blank and expressionless. He hasn't cried once, not like Anita who sobbed every day for two weeks.

Tommy thought this trip would do them all good. He hoped the Butlins slogan – *Holidays are Jollydays* – would live up to its promise. He worked hard, sold stuff, saved up for weeks. He believed if he took the children to Ireland, her country, it would help them feel close to their mother again. Help him. But it had made it worse. He had booked them into a holiday camp full of young couples and other families. No fathers, not even mothers, on their own with children. How could he have been so stupid? Every day his son and daughter were reminded their family was incomplete. And every night he sat in the bright chalet, listening to

207

the incessant rain. Bronagh was right. Ireland was wetter than Wales.

He would sit in silence. The distant sounds of the evening's entertainment washing over him and he would think of all the other chalets filled with sleeping children, unprotected while their parents danced the night away. He listened attentively to his own two. He was afraid one of them would stop breathing. Any disaster was possible now he had lost Bronagh. He sat in the tiny living room of the chalet, his loneliness reflected in the shiny countertop, stainless-steel sink and flawless pine table. He longed to be back at the colliery, down the inky pit, picking away, where he could sweat out his grief.

She was like that fish, his darling wife. Darting through his life like a flash of silver. She had lifted him up from the riverbed, made him light. Now his feet feel so heavy he wants to sink down to the bottom, never to rise again. If it weren't for the children he believes he would kill himself, throw himself off a bridge and have done.

'Daddy. Look at David.'

Anita sits in the bow of the boat, pointing at David. Tommy twists round, the oar still in his hand. David is standing up in the boat, his back to them, his tangled hair blowing in the breeze and his arms reaching out in front of him.

'David. Sit down, there's a good boy. You're making the boat wobble.'

People in other rowing boats begin to look at them.

'David!'

But his son ignores him. It is as if he and Anita are not there, nor the boat, nor the water. All David can see is one thing, one person.

'Mummy!'

David points. A woman sits with her back to them in the bow of a small rowing boat. For a second Tommy's heart does a tiny flip of hope because she does look like Bronagh. She has the same narrow shoulders, the same long silvery blond hair dipping to the small of her back, the shape of a duck's tail, and hadn't Bronagh worn exactly the same pink shirt once?

'Mummy!'

David leans dangerously out of the boat.

Tommy shakes himself. 'No, David, that's not your mummy. Sit down now.'

Tommy glances back at Anita. The little girl's face is pale and she is close to tears. Oh God, what a disaster. He can't cope with his own children. He can't cope with anything.

'Sit down David. *Now!*'

He shouts, no longer caring people are turning around in their boats, including the Bronagh look-alike, whose face is uncannily like his late wife's. David doesn't hear his father's call, or notice him reach out to try to grab him, making the boat lurch to the side and nearly causing Anita to tip out of it. No, all the five-year-old sees is his mother as he steps out of the boat, arms outstretched as if he is about to walk on something solid, as if the miracle of his mother returned is enough to make him walk on water.

'Mummy!' the child bleats before going under the surface of the sludgy pond.

Tommy watches his son drop like a stone. He cannot speak, or move. He is frozen in horror, paralysed just like he had been six months ago when he found Bronagh dead.

'Help!' he manages to croak.

There is a lot of commotion. Other boats come towards them, people shout but all Tommy sees is his wife's angel stand up in the boat in front of him, and dive expertly into the pool of dark water thick with pond weed and churned-up mud. For only an instant she is under the water but everything around Tommy is falling apart. His little girl is shaking, hands over her eyes and the murky water laps menacingly against the boat. He is invaded by tiny flies which buzz around his head and a sick oily smell from the churned-up water. The sun goes in behind a cloud, the rain beginning yet again. It feels like the end of the world.

'Here, take him,' a woman's voice breaks through the nightmare.

Tommy suddenly jolts into action, leaning forward and dragging his son over the side of the boat. The little boy is alive, coughing and spluttering but alive, and red in the face and angry. He screams at Tommy, who tries to hold him in his arms as he thrashes about the boat.

The girl who looks like Bronagh holds on to the side of the bobbing boat. There is mud streaked on her face, and weeds in her blond hair, the same rare shade as Bronagh's. But her eyes are different. Blue as well, but different. She watches Tommy trying to calm David down. Then, without saying anything, she leans on the boat, tipping it to one side and drags herself in over the edge. Her pink shirt and white shorts are clinging to her. She is thinner, slighter than Bronagh, younger.

'It's okay, darling.'

She wobbles over to Anita who is whimpering in the bow of the boat. She puts her arm around the little girl's shoulders, drenching her with pond water.

Tommy looks over at the woman's boat and sees a couple in it. They stare at them curiously.

'Are you all right?' the man asks.

Tommy nods.

'It's okay, Jim,' the girl in his boat says. 'I'll meet you both back at the chalet.'

Her friends wave in reply, and begin rowing back to shore.

'Thank you,' Tommy whispers. 'I don't know what happened . . . I just . . .'

'Don't worry about it.' She smiles kindly. 'It was a great opportunity for a swim. I was dying to go for a dip.'

She winks at Anita who has stopped crying and holds on to her hand. David has calmed down, but he won't let go of his father's shirt. Tommy can feel the strength in his son's fingers as he holds on tightly as if for dear life.

The girl in his boat looks at them.

'Will we be feminists?' She turns to Anita. 'Let's row the men home.'

She picks up the oars and starts to row. Droplets of water trickle down her front, and her hair is dark now and stuck to her forehead.

'No redcoats to be seen of course! Never one when you want

one. Then they're all over you when they want you to join in their silly games.'

'I'm sorry,' Tommy stutters. 'I can't swim. You see, I can't swim.'

'That's okay. Don't worry about it. I grew up on the river, spent my life diving into muddy pools.'

'Here, let me row at least.'

'Not at all. The little boy is freezing. You'd best keep him warm.'

'What's your name?' Anita pipes up.

'It's Concepta.'

'Con . . . what?' Anita says. 'I never heard of that name.'

'It's a very Irish name. My mammy is a great believer. Con–cep–ta,' she repeats. 'And what's your name?'

'Anita.'

'Ah, now that's a lovely pretty name.'

She looks over at Tommy, smiles again, and he thinks how nice it is to talk with a woman. He hasn't talked to anyone, except his mother and the children, since Bronagh died. People back home think he is the strong silent type. He never did talk much, but it is because he is shy. Painfully. Bronagh had spoken for him. Now it seems he has no voice.

'I'm Tommy,' he stutters. 'And this is David.'

His son is still in his arms. For the first time since he was pulled out of the water he looks directly at Concepta.

'Daddy,' he whispers. 'She's not Mummy.'

'No, David, she's not.'

Concepta stops rowing. She catches Tommy's eye but he looks away. Raindrops speckle the pond. She says nothing and the boat begins to move again. He listens to the steady rhythm of the oars and feels the motion of the boat in water. In, out and pull back, in, out and pull back, in, out and pull back. It is as if the water doesn't want to let them go, the same way he can't let Bronagh go.

Later he sits in near-darkness. The children are both sleeping, exhausted by the day's drama. He listens to their steady breath, innocent and trusting. What can he ever do to make life for them whole again? They have lost its most important part – their mother. Anita is seven, David five. His children are damaged and there is nothing he can do about it. It makes him furious. He bangs his cup into the sink and it shatters. The dregs of his tea spread onto the steel basin, the same shit-brown as the pond today. He scoops up the broken china and throws it into the bin. He wants to smash something else but the chalet is too small, neat and tidy. He could go outside, but he can't leave them. A sudden gust of wind knocks against the chalet and rattles the window frames. He doesn't feel safe here. Not like in the pit. So black the only light is the gleam of your mate's eyeballs. So dark you can show your feelings and no one will see.

After Bronagh's funeral Tommy had gone back to work as soon as he could.

'Keep busy,' his widowed mother had told him. 'It's the only way, son.'

He couldn't bear the glare of pity from all those around him, even management. He hated them to feel sorry for him because he felt guilty. So he had got back into his overalls, left the children with his mum and worked as many shifts as he could. He dug himself a hole deep underground, where he could sink and beat and pick, pick away, each chunk of black coal like a piece of his black heart. Each seam he came across was like a raw nerve-ending which tore at his grief. Often he would be sobbing as he picked away, all on his own. But that was better than being above ground because up there, in daylight, he couldn't feel a thing.

He turns off the garish lamp and lights a candle. The soft glow makes him feel better. He closes his eyes. He can hear Bronagh chiding him and laughing with him. They had known each other nearly all their lives; since her father had come over to Wales to work in the mines when she was eight years old. Their dads had been pals and Tommy and Bronagh had been sweethearts. Everyone could see it. How they belonged together. When they were first married, Bronagh swung out of Tommy all the time. She hated him going down the pit, said she worried all day especially after his dad died. He sees Bronagh from those days. Her long hair flying loose and blowing across his face when they went on his bike. He would find strands of silver everywhere – in his lunch, on his jacket, stuck onto his stubble. They were still in the house even now, precious threads, priceless. He was afraid to let his mother sweep.

Tommy remembers the early years of their love-making before the children. Her hair would tumble over her forehead, so that he could hardly see her face, only her full pink lips, with the tiny scar on the left corner of the top one. Her hair would cascade onto his bare chest, and he would stroke it with his sore hands. It was silk binding his rough flesh, soothing him.

The day she gave birth to Anita he had held Bronagh's hair for her, one hand pulling it into a tight ponytail, back from her face so as to keep her cool. He was bending down now, listening to her breath, short, fast, breaking through the pain.

A branch taps against the windowpane. And now, in his little holiday chalet in Ireland, the country in which his beloved wife had started her life, Tommy re-visits her death. It had been a Saturday and all day she complained she had a headache. He hadn't believed her because she said it so often and he thought it was an excuse so that she didn't have to go out with him to the pub. So that she could be asleep when he came home. If she had a headache she didn't have to touch him and he couldn't touch her. She had said she didn't want another baby. Tommy grips his hands and shivers. They hadn't made love in months. He can't even remember the last time he kissed her and now she is gone. He never would again.

He left her alone, dropped Anita and David to his mum's, and went out that night. There was a singer and a band and they were doing Sinatra numbers. He loved Ol' Blue Eyes, thought he was cool. He had danced with other women. He had even kissed one of them.

Tommy slams his hand down on the kitchen table so that the new pine cracks. For Christ's sake, he has to face it. He made love

213

to another woman. Someone he did not care about at all. She was another miner's wife, whose husband didn't want her. In their drunkenness they had found each other outside the pub, and with no words they had come together, their sexual frustration uniting them. He still remembers the freezing cold air on his bare buttocks as he pushed into her, on and on, and her little gasps of breath as if she could cry at any moment. That girl had come to his wife's funeral.

On a Saturday night like no other Tommy had gone home filled with remorse, suddenly sober and disgusted at his betrayal of the wife he loved. He vowed he would try to talk to her. He began to hum her favourite song. He would woo his wife yet again. But when he went up to their room the bed was empty, crumbled where she had lain and her fluffy pink slippers were still on the floor, her nylon dressing gown draped on the end of the bed. The music stopped in his head, and he could hear nothing just the swish, swish of lost time. He went downstairs into the kitchen and the back door was open. He went into the garden and it was a full moon and then he could see her. She was lying face down in her white nightie like a dead swan he had once seen on the riverbank killed by foxes. The doctor later told him Bronagh had had a massive brain haemorrhage. It would have been swift. There was nothing he could have done. But that didn't help because he hadn't been there. She had been alone when she died.

The tapping on the window continues and then turns into a knock. Hesitant but nevertheless someone is at the door. He gets up, opens it. The light is not completely gone from the long summer's day and it is still dusky. She stands in front of him in a shimmering silvery grey dress, a shining halo of hair piled on top of her head.

'Hello there, it's me, Concepta. Jesus, are you all right? You look like you've seen a ghost.'

He steps back inside the chalet, angry at the irony of her words and afraid she will see his tears.

'I'm all right. What do you want?'

She colours, pulls her cardigan around her slight frame.

'I wanted to see if your little boy was okay. I've obviously disturbed you . . .'

She turns around and walks away.

'Wait!'

She stops, twists around to look at him.

'I'm sorry. Come in, please come in and have a cuppa.'

She smiles shyly, walking briskly back down to the chalet.

'That would be grand.'

They stand awkwardly inside the dimly lit chalet. Tommy wonders whether he should turn on the light but the flickering candle gives the sterile surroundings a welcoming ambience and he is reluctant to break the spell.

'Are the children asleep?'

She sits down at the kitchen table, smooths over the crack he just made in it with the palms of her hands.

'Yes. They were exhausted, especially David.'

She nods, and he looks at her and knows he doesn't have to tell her anything at all. It is obvious.

'There's a dance on,' she says as he hands her a cup of tea.

'Right.'

'And a singer. Apparently he's a dead ringer for Frank Sinatra. Very good. I might go.'

'Where are your friends?'

'Oh that was my sister Deirdre, and her fiancé Jim. They've gone into Bettystown. I don't know why Dee asked me to come with them. They've just got engaged. All lovey dovey. And the chalet is so small.'

He smiles and his jaw aches. He realises it is the first time he has smiled in a long while.

'So you're playing gooseberry?'

'You've got it.' She sips her tea.

And then something strange happens. It is as if his customary shyness has abandoned him.

'And what about you? Surely a beautiful girl like yourself has a fiancé or at least a young man on the scene.'

She blushes, shakes her head, unable to speak.

'I cannot believe that now.'

Concepta stands up suddenly.

'I'd better go,' she says, moving hastily towards the door.

'I'm sorry, Concepta, I didn't mean to upset you. I'm an old fool. Please stay and finish your tea – that is, unless you want to go to the dance.'

'Oh, I'm not going now. Not on my own . . .'

'But your dress?'

She stands in front him, her cheeks deep crimson.

'I'm such an eejit,' she whispers.

Before he can stop himself Tommy picks up her hands. They lie limply in his palms, like two little white doves.

'What happened to you?'

He looks into her eyes, blue and sad.

'I had a fiancé, but he died. In a motorbike accident last year.'

She sniffs, and removes her hands from his, taking a small white handkerchief from out of the sleeve of her cardigan and blowing her nose.

'And your wife?' she asks.

Tommy says nothing, just stares at her.

'I thought so, when your little boy called me Mummy I thought it was something like that. The poor wee things.'

Tommy looks at Concepta. The more he talks to her the less like Bronagh she looks.

'How do you get over it?' he says hoarsely, his voice barely audible.

'You don't.' She pauses, sighs, passes her hand over her face. 'When someone you love dies, you have to learn to live again. Step by step. Day by day.'

She walks out the door of his chalet. It is darker now, and she becomes an insubstantial pale shape in her silver dance dress, with her silver hair. She glides across the grass, quickly, fast, away from him.

'Concepta!' he calls.

She stops walking.

'Yes.'

He runs up the hill so that he is a few inches from her. Her face is hidden by the approaching shadows of night but he can feel her benevolence, her growing care for him.

'Will you teach me to swim?'

'You want to learn to swim?'

'Yes. Tomorrow. In the swimming pool. Will you teach me?'

She rustles in her dress, and laughs softly.

'Sure I will, Tommy.'

She speaks like Bronagh, a soft Irish lilt. She is slightly above him, iridescent. Her hair is a shining orb on top of her head.

'You'll get the hang of it, no problem. It's all about trust.'

He watches her walk away until she is a tiny light flickering in the opaque night, eventually vanishing. He stands for a while listening to the music as it floats over to him, mixed with the sound of the sea brushing the shore nearby. He can hear the Frank Sinatra look-alike singing one of Bronagh's favourites – 'Stella by Starlight'.

My heart and I agree,

She's everything on earth to me.

Bronagh had been his whole world. Concepta could never replace her. Yet she is lonely too. Tommy decides right there and then, as he listens to Frank Sinatra on the doorstep of his flimsy holiday chalet, he will marry this girl. He needs someone to hold at night and his children need a mother. He can't bear this terrible grief any more. He fiddles with his fingers and looks down. He is twisting a strand of blond hair around his hand. He pulls it off, and presses the coil of silvered gold into his palm. It could equally belong to Bronagh or Concepta.

Nothing will ever be the same again. Yet he can choose to keep picking away at the coalface until his black grief buries him and his children. Or he can let Bronagh pass through them like quicksilver, and find a vein of hope. Concepta. She could be a lamp at the pit face and moonbeams on water. He will go towards her light for he hopes she can teach him to stay afloat.

Julia Kelly

Julia Kelly was born in 1969, studied English, sociology and journalism in Dublin, and escaped to London for the mad, bad years of life. Her first novel, *With My Lazy Eye,* won the 'Newcomer of the Year' award in 2008. She lives in Bray, Co. Wicklow, where she is currently finishing her second novel.

Hope Springs Eternal *

Julia Kelly

They arrive early, as the elderly do, in a minibus fusty with talcum powder and TCP, stiff with their sticks, dickey hips, plastic bags of medicines and swimming togs in Delta Airlines bags or sausage-rolled under arms. Once they've paid the off-season rate of $3 for the day, they organise themselves poolside, positioning Zimmer frames and oxygen tanks within safe reach of the water, wedging towels between the plastic slats of rickety loungers, which immediately flap themselves free.

They undress with the insouciance of old age – flat posteriors in the air, egg-bellied paunches hanging loose over elastic, armbands on, hair tucked into caps, togs pulled into place around soft-skinned thighs – and lower themselves into the water with trepidation, groaning, exhaling, faces as textured as elephant hide, disconcertingly uniform teeth. Their gashed knees and bandaged ankles a testament to limbs they can no longer trust.

At the foot of the snow-capped San Bernardino Mountains, above the San Andreas fault line, the mineral water destined for Desert Hot Springs percolates beneath the surface at 140 degrees but is tempered to bath-water warm. A hunkered-down motel that was fashionable in the 1950s, it is twenty miles on the wrong, dusty side of Palm Springs. Monkey-brown Buicks and Lincolns are parked in carports of a cement block that's home to vast palms, mocking birds, sandstone, spirals and swirls, pea-green carpets, panel-effect beauty-board. There's a forest of wind farms on the horizon; tumbleweed blows through the high street.

If the Salton Sea is where people go to get lost, Desert Hot Springs is where the elderly idle their final days. The water in the mineral pools is not just the perfect temperature; it's soft, unchlorinated and textured with ripples from the wind. Once immersed, faded beauties, bit-part players, former good-time girls are eased from their arthritis, lumbago and all those other ailments of the aged. In the water, they are free and graceful; their limbs fluid in movement again.

'Hallo, cutie,' says a man with a baseball cap and a moustache that's flour-white against a freckled Californian tan. He squeezes lemon into a hipflask of tequila, takes a slug and sidles up to an octogenarian, on her back, arms outstretched on the tiles behind her, kicking her legs vigorously, like a child. He asks her if she is in showbiz. They chat, words lost in bubbles under water, others not heard or misunderstood. Another man joins them – he claims he can yodel, a chuckle becomes a choke and conversation comes back, as it always does, to where it began – the temperature of the water.

A damaged man-child in a hooded wetsuit and a spittle-flecked goatee screeches and flaps as he lopes from pool to pool, loose-hinged feet like paddles, his father or nurse behind him, in polo shirt and slacks, holding a towel in the air like a matador trying to tame. As the palm trees bend in the breeze, a Japanese man searches for his wife. He has the sort of face that looks as if he's permanently searching for something. His wife sits in the sauna watching him, without gesturing, through the one-way window.

'Are you sure you're not a film star?' says the baseball-capped man to the cutie. She smiles with flattery but doesn't reply. 'I was Alfalfa in *The Little Rascals*.'

The handyman is in the Sunshine Café, swinging on a naugahyde stool. He fingers the swizzlestick in his Jack Daniels as he chats up the waitress who's sexy in a tired way. He tells her about the darndest thing he saw in LA: a hobo who'd worked his way into the window display of a home-furnishing store on Third Street and sat there unchallenged for an afternoon, counting his change on a chaise-longue.

She lifts the hatch, a J-cloth in her fist, and wipes tables, half-listening. Through the window, the handyman watches an ancient woman, supine and floating towards the deep end of the Olympic-sized pool. Water wings keep her buoyant, her bathing cap of white roses sits high on her head; her waxen feet are flexed and afloat. She hums loudly and tunelessly as she goes, eyes shut against the sun.

No one needs to be anywhere else. The day meanders into dusk: filters at pool edges gurgle and suck, the rhythmic clink of a flag stay against a pole, clouds charge silently across a vast sky, a chamber-maid billows a sheet over a balcony, a radio plays somewhere.

'This is about as close as we're going to get to Heaven on Earth, right here,' says the handyman aloud to himself.

⌒〜 〜⌒

Brian Keenan

Brian Keenan was born in Belfast. He has degrees in English and Anglo-Irish literature. He became a lecturer at the American University of Beirut and was taken hostage in 1986. Four and a half years later, following his release, he wrote *An Evil Cradling*, which won *The Irish Times* Irish Literature Award for Non-fiction, the *Time/Life* PEN Award, the Ewart-Biggs Memorial Prize and the Christopher Award in New York. He is also the author of the novel *Turlough* and two travel books, *Between Extremes* (with John McCarthy) and *Four Quarters of Light*, an Alaskan journey. His most recent book is *I'll Tell Me Ma*, a childhood memoir. His next project will be a book of short stories set in contemporary Lebanon. He lives in Dublin with his family.

I'll Tell Me Ma **

Extract from his memoir of the same name (RANDOM HOUSE)

Brian Keenan

Every Monday morning my mother gave me five shillings to purchase five dinner tickets, which I had to exchange every day for a hot meal at the dinner hall. It took me about six months to realise that I could do better things with five shillings. If I added to that a week's worth of bus fares, I would have something to make my visits to Smithfield more interesting. Dad rarely took me there now, and maybe that was one of the reasons for my own secret escapes on Saturdays. I don't know why or how it came about, nor do I even recall the first time it happened or where I went, but it became a major part of my weekend for a long time after.

I suppose it was a chance thing. A momentary impulse which, once acted upon, could not be stopped. I think it was one of those Saturdays when everybody else was doing something. There was a second-hand shop on the Newtonards Road where you could exchange comics for a few coppers. Dad had gone to watch football and Mum was busy with our new baby. I didn't want to be about the house with her and Brenda. Neither did I have much interest in the Saturday matinee at the cinema any more. I had my five shillings, plus several days' bus fare, which I kept in the box under my bed where I stored my comics. I had quite a varied collection and knew the bookshop would be happy to exchange some of them for me. There was a big pawnshop on the way to the bookshop that seemed to do more business than anywhere else. I had been to it several times with my mother, usually at the start of the school year to buy cheap shoes and 'mutton dummies', a very basic canvas and rubber gym slipper. That was when she had cash. On other occasions she obtained a Provident cheque from Billy the 'Provident' man. With this cheque she could buy my complete school uniform and clothes for the new baby. Every week Billy from the Provident would arrive at our house at 6.30 pm and Mother would pay him seven and sixpence towards the cheque. It was a form of moneylending and our house, along with everyone else's, was furnished on the Provident. The pawnshop fascinated me the way Smithfield did. There were things in the window that no other shop had. Some weeks before, I had noticed a fabulous harmonica there. The silver plates on the top and bottom were elaborately carved and beside it was a fancy leather case with a handsome silver clasp. There was a blue and white cardboard box embossed with a design that looked the same as that on the instrument. On it I read the inscription 'Alabama Blues Harmonium Company'.

I was unable to forget the mouth organ. I remembered the name of the harmonica player that I heard in the market at Smithfield, Sonny Boy Williamson. I was too young to know anything about music but Sonny Boy's mouth organ music was frenzied, magically inventive and always caught me up in its rhapsody. I had learned from the back of an album cover that as a boy the musician used to walk about with half a dozen harmonicas stuck in his belt. That impressed me. I fancied myself wandering around with this gleaming instrument hanging out of my back pocket – it would be better than any dagger-edged steel comb! And when I blew my harp people would really take note. I was so carried away by the idea of me and this mouth organ that I even began to make up names for myself. I don't know what made me think of it but one of them was 'Licorice Lips'. It had something to do with the fact that Sonny Boy's real surname was Rice and that his music wasn't blues, it was black and he was black.

I stood outside Geddis's pawnshop that Saturday admiring the gleaming harmonica. I knew the money in my pocket wouldn't be enough to buy it, but I had to know how much it was. Inside the shop I stood at the long wooden counter. 'Yes, sir?' asked the pawnbroker. However intimidated I may have been, the way he addressed me made me cocky. 'How much is that old mouth organ in the window?' I asked. The pawnbroker looked down at me, then answered, 'Seventeen shillings and sixpence.' My heart sank. My head reeled. I would have to starve myself for the next six weeks at least! The man reached into the window, lifted out the instrument and proffered it to me. 'Try before you buy!' he urged me. 'No, no,' I said, stumbling over the words in panic. 'I just wanted to know how much.' The man smiled, then said knowingly, 'The man that owns it will be back for it before you have time to buy it.' He paused for a moment, then added, 'He always plays a few bars of "Goodnight, Irene" when he brings it in. Just so as I know it's working.' He leaned forward and said in a half-whisper, 'Doesn't like to leave it without saying goodbye, I suppose.' Then he winked at me and returned the instrument to its spot in the window.

I left the pawnshop dejected. I could always buy another one, I told myself half-heartedly. But I knew it would never be as special as this one which had come all the way from the Alabama Blues Harmonium Company. Then I wondered who owned it and always said goodbye to it by playing 'Goodnight, Irene'. I remembered a photo I had seen of Sonny Boy. He had a tiny wispy growth of hair extending from the point of his chin and he wore a black beret. His hands were huge with long bony fingers. I wondered what my mysterious harmonica owner looked like. I half knew the tune of 'Goodnight, Irene', and knew that Sonny Boy would never play it the way I had heard it sung. The mystery man who owned the Alabama harmonica, how did he play? Where had he learned? Behind all these questions I was starting to believe that because the song 'Goodnight, Irene' was, in a way, my song then maybe the harmonica could be mine also! I looked at my small hands. I was thirteen. I think I knew from reading a record sleeve that Sonny Boy had been playing since he was five. Even then, I thought, his hands would still have been bigger than mine.

I was standing at the roadside waiting to cross with my comics in one hand and my dinner money in the other. I didn't know it, but I was standing at a bus stop and just at that moment a green double-decker pulled up beside me. Green buses were country buses and the sign on this one read Holywood, which everyone pronounced as Hollywood. Without thinking about what I was doing, I stepped on and climbed the stairs and sat on the front seat. Hollywood was in America, but I knew where I was going wasn't America. I knew it was somewhere miles from the city. What I didn't know was how far, or why I had stepped on the bus. 'Fares, please,' said the conductor. 'Where are you going, son?' 'Holywood,' I said as that was all I knew. 'Single or return?' 'Return,' I answered. 'Half return, ninepence,' he said as he handed me a pink ticket, which he had punched with a pliers-like instrument. I handed him a shilling from my dinner money. He returned an octagonal three-penny piece and walked off with the coins in his purse making a muffled rattle. I looked at the ticket. At least I could come back from wherever it was I was going.

It was some weeks before I ventured off on another expedition. I am not even sure where I went. It seemed to be another unplanned thing: a spur-of-the-moment compulsion. I had gone back to the pawnshop to see if the harmonica was still there. I was unable to get it out of my head. I had already decided that it was mine and that eventually I would somehow acquire it. Another part of me hoped that if I kept going to see it I might meet the man who owned it. I fantasised that if I could tell him how important it was he might give it to me. If not, maybe he would teach me how to play it. I was sure my dinner money would cover the cost of these lessons. The lure of the mouth organ was incredible. With that mouth organ I just knew that my life would change. I stood at the pawnshop window staring at the harmonica. It was in a different place but it was still there. I would have done anything to get it. The impossibility of possessing it was crushing me. I turned to walk home and, as I was waiting at the roadside to cross over, a bus came towards me. I recognised the place-name on the bus from Dad's map and hopped on, knowing my dinner money would get me there and back. I liked the idea that only I knew where I was going, even if I didn't really. I repeated this bus-hopping intermittently for several months. I didn't have any reason for it except that the word 'hobo' had lodged itself in my head. I liked the sound of it and I loved the idea of it. Occasionally, if I spotted somewhere interesting en route to the bus's destination, I would get off as near to the places as I could on the return journey. I rarely stayed long at the places the bus took me to; I simply wandered round looking for something to attract my attention. I liked railway stations, old cemeteries and bridges and rivers. I think I really enjoyed the journey. I liked to be moving. Usually I was the only kid on the bus and this made me feel special in a way. Sometimes I had weird notions that I was the only person on the bus who was really moving, and everybody else had somehow stopped!

These sorties into the countryside came and went, but they always began and ended with me standing at the pawnshop looking at 'my' harmonica. If I could never have it, it seemed to have become a talisman or good luck charm. If it was in the window waiting for me then all was well with the world. Of course, there were times when the weather did not permit bus trips. Then I would go alone to Smithfield just to look at things and sometimes at people. All the time I was absorbing classic blues and jazz without understanding any of it. It made me feel like I was keeping faith with Sonny Boy and my mouth organ. It was a world of its own and I had become one of its residents. One day, a stallholder who recognised me from my frequent appearances in the place called me over. 'Here, son, mind this place for a few minutes. I'll be back in ten minutes or so,' he said, and off he went. I felt pretty important being left in charge. The man never knew who I was except that I was one of the habitués of the place. He was only selling old furniture and odd pieces of bric-à-brac that no one would think of stealing but by choosing me to look after his things he had accepted me into the colourful confraternity of the disciples of Smithfield. The thing about Smithfield was that you didn't have to buy anything. You could own everything.

Kate Kerrigan

London reared of Irish parents, Kate Kerrigan worked as a leading magazine editor in London before moving to Dublin, in 1990. She is currently a full-time writer and lives in the historic village of Killala in Co. Mayo on the west coast of Ireland with her husband and two sons. Kate writes a weekly column each Thursday in the *Irish Daily Mail* and writes screenplays in partnership with fellow novelist Helen Falconer. Her novel *Recipes for a Perfect Marriage* was nominated for Romantic Novel of the Year in 2006, and her current novel *Ellis Island* has been selected for the Channel 4 TV Bookclub.

Tom **

Kate Kerrigan

I was ten weeks pregnant when my brother died suddenly in London. It was a beautiful day in Killala. The tide was in and the sea was as still as glass. The phone call came in at 2 pm on 6th February 2009 from the Metropolitan Police in Central London. Tom lived alone, and had been found by a neighbour that morning and taken to the coroner's office. I threw the phone down and started to howl like a trapped dog. My husband picked up the receiver and hurried out of the room. When he came back he carefully gathered me back into myself and we did what had to be done before making the journey into Ballina to tell my mother that her only boy – her magical, musical son – had died of a haemorrhage.

Over the coming days the family gathered and were swallowed by the vast wave of sympathy and support that happens when you lose somebody in Ireland. People brought us hot dinners, filled our kitchen with cakes and apple tarts. Old school friends of my mother's distracted us with anecdotes; new friends of mine fed and entertained my son. Our husbands stood sentry over all of us women. The usually noisy, overpowering feminine gaggle of our female-heavy family now muted by grief, they quietly took care of our business and prayed they'd get us back soon and in one piece.

Like many second-generation Irish families, ours is divided. I have always felt more Irish than British, and have worked and lived in Ireland for almost twenty years. My mother moved back to her

Mayo birthplace after she retired, and my younger sister and her family followed her while my other sister and one brother stayed in London. Tom never understood the appeal of rural Ireland. He spent every spare moment exploring the galleries and concerts and museums of London. He sucked up the culture of his city and sent us postcards from the Tate Modern telling us about some wonderful exhibition we must see. Up to our elbows in work and nappies, we never took much notice of his pleas to expand our cultural horizons. But when the time came we knew that London was the only place Tom would rest in peace.

My two sisters and I went into overdrive organising the funeral. The English don't really 'do' funerals – and there were two weeks between Tom's death and his burial. So we used that time to give our only brother the 'wedding he never had'. We tracked down school and university friends. We catered and flower-arranged and designed orders of service: we organised and bossed and bickered, three capable control freaks trying to distract and demote our shock and grief to a more manageable size.

My younger sister, who was early for her own wedding, managed to get us to the church almost a full hour before the funeral service began. We sat on the wall outside Our Lady of Dolours, Hendon, our childhood church (where Tom had been an altar boy and tortured us into giggling while taking Communion) and marvelled at the mild, sunny day that was in it. We were able to greet everyone as they arrived, and all agreed that the early arrival had been a blessing. There was a huge turnout. 'More like an Irish funeral than an English one,' an author friend of my mine commented. People travelled from Ireland but from all over London too. Our oldest and closest English friends were there for us, and brought back memories and feelings I thought I had left behind. An old friend (the great love of his life) organised the music, a cellist played his favourite piece, and members of a Westminster choir he sang with came, bursting quite unexpectedly, and gloriously, into the Gospel acclamation. Although burials in England are generally private, family-only affairs, we invited the entire congregation up to the grave where we made them stand and say a decade of the rosary. I met friends of Tom's that I had never met before and was reassured that he was loved and cherished by a wide circle of good people, living the life of a single man in central London – a world away from his henpecking bossy Irish older sister.

All in all it was a wonderful funeral. Full of old and new friends – and every moment drenched in love. In that one day that we buried him, we also brought him back to life with stories and laughter and music.

Then came the hard bit. Back to normal life – away from the distraction of sandwiches and seeing friends and the suspension of life that death brings – it hit me. *He's gone. Oh my God – my baby brother Tom is dead.* I had become temporarily lost in the drama of his death, the constant reassurances from kind religious, the comfort of being with my mum, aunt and sisters every day – but back in my own life I struggled to accommodate my overwhelming grief. Some stupid tune we once danced to at a Catholic Youth Club disco came on the radio and I slid down my kitchen wall, sobbing.

Nothing anyone said seemed to help.

'*He's at peace now.*' 'I don't want him to be at peace,' I felt like screaming, 'I want him back, my unreasonable, annoying brother so that I can finish the last row we had – and even let him win it!'

'*He's with you all the time, ask him for a sign,*' spiritual friends said, but try as I did, I couldn't feel him. I couldn't grasp Tom as an ethereal floating ghost. He was a solid, chunky, visceral presence – except when he played music. Then he existed on another plane. And so I set the car radio to Lyric FM and let my brother send me messages through music. But the only message he ever sent me was 'I'm dead – and I'm never coming back.' Every five minutes I was looking for a lay-by to pull into and weep.

My husband, my rock, who had been so supportive, so strong and silent throughout, began to waver. I could sense his exhaustion with my unprompted crying jags and relentless sadness. Grief is a frightening thing to live with, especially when your sleepless red-eyed wreck of a wife is carrying your baby.

He was worried by the way his usually sturdy wife was

unravelling. I was worried myself. So I did what I generally do when I am really worried about something, which was take a deep breath and get busy. I knew I wasn't ready to start writing again, so I threw myself into organising a couple of charity events. I put on my lipstick, got myself blow-dried to within an inch of my life and faced out into the world. Let's rein in the horses and turn this chariot around, I said to myself. I spoke at a book launch in aid of Ballina Arts Centre and everyone marvelled at how great I was doing. In the moment I was being bombarded by admiration and approval, I felt good. But as soon as I was alone, out of sight, the empty grief washed over me again.

Niall announced our pregnancy on Facebook.

'I'm going to be a dad,' he said.

'Does Kate know?' my sister replied from London.

Everyone laughed. Everyone was delighted for us. People made the connection between Tom's tragic death and this new, growing life. I grabbed onto the idea that my pregnancy might become the antidote to Tom's death. *'My brother died but hey! Guess what? I'm pregnant.'* The joy of new life cancelling out the messy awkwardness of unwelcome grief. I had waited for this second pregnancy for seven long years and, in my mid-forties, it had been as unexpected as the tragic events that followed it. Although I tried to be cheerful and push myself forward, I was frightened by my lack of control – and not just over the event of my brother's death. The feeling of helplessness was spilling over into the pregnancy. In its early stages I had been shown how terrible, unexpected things could happen to people we love. Just a year older than Tom, my life, as far back as I can remember, had been defined by my 'taking care' of my younger brother. Right or wrong, as the eldest child I had always felt a sense of responsibility towards my younger siblings – especially Tom. He was artistic, vulnerable, the only boy – a special, talented person. I had always believed myself to be his keeper – where in reality I was just a controlling bossy older sister. Now that he was dead I could not help but feel I had failed him. I didn't want to be in charge of anybody any more and yet here I was taking the ultimate responsibility for another human being. This growing being was inhabiting me, dictating what I could and couldn't eat, giving me chubby arms and legs and a swollen stomach, taking over my body with the same insistence that Tom's death had taken over my emotions.

Last week we went for a private scan – one of these state-of-the-art 3D jobs, where the baby actually looks like a real human being instead of a black and white blur. I wanted the three of us to bond with the baby. Mostly, though, I wanted to find out the sex so I could feel in control again. Pick a name, decorate the nursery. I wanted to stop pretending to be happy when I was, in fact, just terrified and angry and sad. In a selfish recess at the back of my mind I was hoping for a girl: someone who would grow into a strong woman who would hold me up when bad things happened. A daughter to do what we girls had done for our mother: take me to the hospital when my hips need replacing, break bad news to me. Boys were too painful, I had decided. They abandon you by marrying bad women – or die before their time.

Leo, our seven-year-old, sat up on my husband's knee and gazed at the screen as the baby came into focus. I watched its limbs and features writhe around slowly as if it was on a TV screen.

The radiographer cooed and chatted and eventually said, 'It's a boy.'

My husband looked at me nervously as I let out a muted cry.

'Have you got a name for him yet?' the lady asked Leo.

'Tom,' he said without hesitation, 'after my uncle who died.'

'I lost my brother recently,' I explained.

'I'm sorry,' she replied – but I could hear the silent append: *'Still never mind, you're having a baby eh?'*

And then it happened. I saw the unborn boy push his legs against the walls of his watery sac. As I felt the familiar kick I realised, for the first time, that this small life we had made was as inevitable and uncompromising as my brother's death had been. This child would be born, in September, and I would love him with the same passion that I love our other son. And that love would expose me to the same pain I had felt at losing my beloved brother – but it would also enrich my life in so many ways – even if I was in too much pain to imagine them right now.

With the certainty of our new son's coming I felt – not the untrammelled joy I'd been hoping for – but a small measure of acceptance and yes, a little hope.

We took Leo to McDonald's to celebrate and I rang my mother to tell her the news. She was thrilled.

'You know Tom adored his sisters,' she said, 'but he always longed for a brother.'

For a fleeting moment, I felt he was there.

Hazel Katherine Larkin

Hazel Katherine Larkin trained and worked as an actress back in the 1990s before running away to Asia when she was twenty. She now holds an honours degree in psychology, has written extensively for stage, screen and publication both here and in Asia and makes regular contributions to programmes on *Newstalk* radio. Hazel is currently working on her memoir, entitled *Gullible Travels* – which details the ten years she spent in Asia, married to the wrong men.

Asha *

Hazel Katherine Larkin

You are the song of my soul. You are every dream I have ever dreamt. You are every prayer I have ever prayed. You are my past. You are my future. You are every hope I have ever hoped. You are the manifestation of all the love in the Universe. And now you are here, asleep in my arms, and you are every love I have ever loved across time and space and lifetimes.

I am humbled with gratitude for the woman who birthed you. The woman who felt that her circumstances precluded her from keeping you with her. I have no idea what those circumstances were, and I will probably never know. The documents merely tell me that you were born of 'an illicit relationship'. I understand the antiquated language – as well as the meaning behind the words and between the lines. Still, I cannot help but wonder how any relationship that produced a child as wonderful as you could possibly be deemed 'illicit'. I am angry that such a dirty word is used in connection with you – my precious, precious baby. I marvel at the courage of the woman who held you one last time before handing you over to a stranger. A stranger who, I imagine, promised her that you would have a better life away from, rather than with, her. I feel a flash of anger at a society that presumed to tell her that it was 'unacceptable' for her to keep you. At the same time, I am profoundly indebted to her for carrying you so that I could have you – when she could easily have chosen to destroy you when you were in her womb.

You grew in her womb – but you took root in my heart the

243

moment I laid eyes on you; and today is the day that you become legally mine. Our destinies became inextricably linked from the moment Radhika, the social worker, called me from the orphanage to say that they had found a little girl for me. I left work early and dashed through the busy Mumbai streets to get to you. Tenderly, Radhika placed you in my arms.

'This is your daughter,' she told me.

'Really?' I asked, tears forming in my eyes.

'Yes,' Radhika smiled at me. 'God has given her to you.'

You were completely still in my arms and I laid my cheek on your downy head.

'Thank you, God,' I whispered.

'Please sit.' Radhika indicated the chair under the window of her office. I sat.

'Congratulations,' Radhika continued in her educated Indian accent. 'You're a mother now.'

With your head resting in the crook of my elbow, I looked at you. You lifted your sloe-black eyes to mine and I felt as though you were looking into my soul – and that you *knew* me.

'When can I take her home?' I asked Radhika.

As I was resident in India, it was possible for me to take you home that very evening. A quick trip to the courthouse allowed me to take guardianship of you immediately. The finalisation of the adoption procedure would give you to me eternally.

Very few people knew I was involved in the process at all. I didn't want people to know. I didn't want to be judged. I didn't want people to make assumptions about my motivation. I didn't want people asking me constantly for updates when the process would be slow and updates would be infrequent. Part of me hardly dared to hope that I would manage to adopt at all. Sometimes, I would lie awake, imagining all the things that could go wrong – all the shortcomings that might be found in me and my situation.

I was widowed on September 11th, 2001. When Jagdish died, so many of my hopes died with him. He shouldn't have been in New

York that day. He should have flown home to Mumbai – to me – the day before. But the final meeting of his trip had been postponed, so he'd ended up in the First Tower when the plane hit. We had planned on having children, and hoped to have two – one of each.

'I hope we have a girl who looks like you,' Juggi said, running his index finger down my nose.

'I hope we have a boy who looks like you,' I smiled at him.

'But with your eyes,' he said. 'I'm hoping for blue-eyed babies. No point marrying a *gori* otherwise!'

We weren't putting it off, either; we had hoped I'd be pregnant by the end of 2001 – but, of course, those hopes were dashed.

When Juggi died, my family expected me to return home to Philly, but I stayed in India. I felt closer to Juggi there. India – where he'd been born and grown up – was where we'd planned to live and raise our family. Our hopes and dreams were to be realised on Indian soil. Sentimentality aside, I'd lived there for six years. I had an apartment there, a job, friends, a community, a routine. I stayed because I was happy to stay. Now I'm so glad I did.

'Sorry we're late!' Radhika is breathless, having hurried up the three flights of stairs at the courthouse. With her is Swathi, the advocate.

'You're not late – I was early.' I smile at the women.

There are three other families adopting from MSSK that morning, but we are first on the list. This is the final hurdle; and even though Swathi has told me exactly what will happen, and exactly what to say, and even though I know it is really just a formality, I am still nervous in case something goes horribly wrong at this late stage.

We are summoned. The judge, a kindly older man, entreats me to sit and I do. The proceedings are conducted in English. The judge has already read the documents pertaining to the adoption. He has read my home-study report. He knows I have been approved by CARA (the Central Adoption Registration Agency) as a parent. He knows that I have been caring for you for the past six months. He can see with his own eyes that you are thriving. He asks me to swear that I will treat you like a child born to me. I swear. He asks me to set up an education fund for you and asks me how much I will put into it every month. I name a figure. He nods and writes it down.

Before pronouncing you mine in the eyes of the law, the judge asks one final question.

'And what will be her good name, madam?' he asks.

I smile before replying. I have given you a Sanskrit name. It is short and sweet.

'Asha,' I answer.

Hope.

∾ ∾

Monica McInerney

Monica McInerney grew up in a family of seven children in the Clare Valley of South Australia, where her father was a railway stationmaster. She is the author of the bestselling novels *A Taste for It, Upside Down Inside Out, Spin the Bottle, The Alphabet Sisters, Family Baggage, Those Faraday Girls* and a collection of short fiction, *All Together Now*, published internationally and in translation. In 2006 she was the ambassador for the Australian government initiative Books Alive, with her novella *Odd One Out*. *Those Faraday Girls* won the General Fiction Book of the Year at the 2008 Australian Book Industry Awards. *All Together Now* was shortlisted in the same category in the 2009 Australian Book Industry Awards. She currently lives in Dublin with her Irish husband. Her new novel, *At Home with the Templetons*, will be published in 2010.

The Long Way Home *

Monica McInerney

Shelley made the age limit for the ten-city *Rave* tour of Europe by two months and three weeks. The woman in the travel agency pointed out that fact as she ran her eyes down the application form.

'You're thirty-four? Nearly thirty-five? Our clients do tend to be the younger end of the age group. You're sure you're happy to go ahead? We've other tours with more of a focus on culture, less on –'

'No, I'm very happy with this one, thanks.' Shelley had her hand on the brochure on the desk between them as if she was staking a claim.

The woman lowered her voice. 'They're usually all single, not really into the history side of things. More out for a good time.'

Shelley dug out a bright smile from somewhere. 'I am, too, I promise.' A pause. Then her confidence faltered. 'Don't I look like I am?'

The other woman seemed relieved when her phone rang.

At home, on the new sofa in the centre of the living room which still felt nothing like home even after three months, Shelley leafed through her ticket folder and read the brochure. All the people in the *Rave* photos looked like models. Happy models. Happy and high-on-life models. She'd have to do her best to look like them. She had obviously not dressed casually enough that morning. She pulled her hair out of its current plait. Made a mental note to buy some T-shirts. Decided to wash her jeans a few unnecessary times to fade them. She automatically went to the towel cupboard to get the washing powder when she realised that was where she'd kept it in her old house. In their old house. In her new house, she kept it under the sink.

She'd seen the *Rave* ad on TV the previous week, rung the toll-free number for the brochure and picked out the tour that lasted two weeks and took in ten European cities, finishing with a visit to Edinburgh and the highlands of Scotland. She read the description, fighting her way through the exclamation marks that surrounded the brief eligibility questionnaire. Yes, she was between eighteen and thirty-five. Yes, she was single. As of three months previously. Yes, she was out for a good time. 'Are you looking for carefree days of fun, adventure and romance? We supply three out of three!' the *Rave* copywriter promised.

Travel was the key, Shelley had heard. Lose yourself and find yourself at the same time. She had a different motto in mind. Run, run, run as fast as you can. She couldn't get away from her own life fast enough.

Her taxi was delayed the morning the tour group left. She heard the driver make his excuses about heavy traffic and oil spills but she was too nervous to console him the way she normally would. She needed him to concentrate on his driving and get her there before she changed her mind. She was the last to arrive at the meeting point in the departure area. She knew immediately it was a mistake. She should have got there first. She could have welcomed the others, been someone they came to and wanted to talk to, instead of having to edge in and join the group, feeling left out on the sidelines. She hated being late. She was always the first to arrive anywhere. Harry said it was from being the daughter of a schoolteacher.

They'd been late for the first appointment at the maternity hospital. She'd been fidgeting in her seat, willing the tram to go faster. He'd taken her hand and squeezed it.

'*Shell, relax. We're about a minute late, that's all.*'

'*What if they give our appointment to someone else?*'

'*I'll tie myself to the receptionist's computer until they give us another one. Go on a hunger strike. Hire a brass band and march up and down outside until they see you.*'

They'd had to wait another hour in the reception area for an appointment that lasted less than five minutes. It only took that long to confirm a pregnancy these days. Outside they'd sat on a stone step, in the sunshine, not speaking, just gripping each other's hands and smiling at each other and at everyone who walked past.

On the plane, a hitch with the seating arrangements meant she was in a different section from the rest of the tour group. She didn't mind. She took every distraction on offer. She watched five movies, one after the other. She ate everything put in front of her. She drank red wine. She left in the earphones when the movies finished, hoping they could block the thoughts.

'*Shelley, at least send me emails. Let me know where you'll be.*'

She could barely look at him. It hurt too much. '*Harry, there's no point. Please, can't you accept –*'

'*An email. Just now and again.*'

'*It has to be over. We have to make a clean start. Away from each other.*'

How else could they recover from something like this? It wasn't a normal fight.

London was the first stop. The sky was grey, the weather cool, even though it was spring. They visited Big Ben, took a cruise down the

Thames, stood outside Buckingham Palace discussing whether the Queen really was inside.

The guide called her. 'Shelley? Come on, the bus is waiting.'

'Sorry.'

She'd been looking at a couple further down the footpath, peering through the gates into the palace like everyone else. The woman was her age. The man was about Harry's age. About their height, too. There was a pram between them. The father's hand kept absently reaching into the pram and stroking his son or daughter's head.

Two nights in Paris. A joke party with everyone wearing berets and an impromptu quiz. The tour guide was good at impromptu activities. Name three famous French people. Shelley couldn't. She could name three French restaurants in Melbourne. She could remember three meals she'd had with Harry in those restaurants, one for their first date, the second when they got engaged. The third for no reason at all.

She could remember telling him in detail about something funny that had happened at work and him interrupting her.

'I love you very much, you know.'

'You're dropping it into the conversation? Just like that?'

'Just like that. Sorry, go on.'

In Amsterdam she followed the group down the canal paths, through the red-light district, into the clog factory and the cheese shops. The guide was talking but Shelley was remembering different conversations and attempted explanations.

'I don't understand. I get home from work and you tell me it's over. You're moving out. Without even talking about it with me?'

She didn't understand herself.

252

'I need the space, Harry.'

'It's not about that, is it?'

It was about the pain she felt every time she looked at him. She was trying to get as far as she could from that, not from him.

Venice. City of love. City of food. The forty members of the tour group took up three long tables in the cheery restaurant. The waiters were friendly. There was no European snobbishness.

'We're worth too much to them,' the guide had whispered to Shelley as they walked in.

'*And here for poor tired Shelley who has had a long week and needs to spend the weekend with her feet up being spoiled is a glass of shockingly expensive Italian wine and the speciality of the house,* crostata di pastore, *colloquially known as shepherd's pie –*'

She needed to remember the bad times, not the good times.

'*You're running away, that's what you're doing.*'

He was right. She was running away as fast as she could. But she wasn't getting anywhere. Everything that made her feel bad had come with her.

Rome. She wanted to be pinched. She stood hopefully in Piazza Navona. She watched confident, curvy Italian women walk past, watched the promenade – the *passeggiata,* the guide told them. The women glanced over their shoulders, knowing they were being watched.

She remembered him walking in and finding her standing side-on in front of the full-length mirror in their bedroom.

'*Is it showing yet, do you think?*'

Harry coming up behind her, with a pillow, putting it in front of her, the two of them laughing. '*Now it is.*' He grabbed another pillow.

'It might be twins.' A third pillow.
'Triplets, even.'

●

The guide organised football and basketball matches in Madrid. Shelley didn't play. She sat on a wooden bench back from the park.

'You need to relax. Promise me you won't do anything while I'm away.'

'Sit still for three days? Harry, I'll go mad. And I want to get the room painted while I can still move.'

'It'll wait. I'll do it when I get back.'

'It'll take me less than a day.'

'But should you be doing all that sort of climbing around?'

'I'll be fine.'

She'd been up and down the ladder, moving the chest of drawers, wriggling the cupboard side to side across the floor, wincing at the screeches it made on the floorboards, out to the car, carrying in heavy pots of paint, singing to the radio. She'd felt a twinge, so attuned to every movement in her body. Then another. Then something worse.

It was all over by the time Harry got home, even though he'd left the conference centre the second he heard her voice on the phone.

Hands held in front of a doctor the next day, but this time no smiles.

She'd asked the question. *'Doctor, did I make it happen?'*

He was an old doctor. He hadn't looked at her, making notes as he spoke, pulling open a drawer beside him, taking out a fresh prescription pad.

'I can't say. It mightn't have helped.'

Outside, at home, the next day, the day after, the week after, they discussed it, over and over.

'He said it mightn't *have* helped. *He didn't say you killed your own child.*'

'But I did. It's what you think, isn't it? You think I killed him.'

'Shell, I don't.'

'That's what you think every time you look at me.'

It was what she felt every time she looked at herself in the mirror.

'Shell, I –'

She couldn't listen to the rest. She could see it in his eyes. He didn't want it to be that way, but she knew that's what he thought.

In Munich she came across a carpet shop that wouldn't have looked out of place in Morocco. The rest of the group were in a beer hall. She'd run out of things to say to them, and they had run out of things to say to her. She wanted to tell them that a year ago she would have been different, a year ago she would have loved this. Two years ago she and Harry might have been on a trip like this together. But she couldn't find the words. She hadn't been able to find the right words for anything for three months.

There was a deep red carpet in the front window. It had a purple and green border of flowers and leaves. The longer she looked at it, the more she found hidden in the pattern. It wasn't as beautiful as their rug at home. It was the only thing she had taken with her. The carpet that had been in the hallway of their house. She'd found it in a second-hand shop a week before their wedding. It had come with a spiel from the shop owner, a second-generation Afghani. The patterns signified the future, happiness, growth. She and Harry had made love on it that night. At first on the rug itself but then it had tickled and started to burn and then she'd got the giggles. So he had put a quilt on it. She wasn't fanciful enough to think that's when their baby had been conceived. The timing was wrong. It had been a practice run.

The rug didn't look as good in her new flat. It looked out of place. It didn't quite fit. The edges pushed up against the sides of the hallway.

In Prague the bus driver tried to make a pass at her. He'd had too much wine at dinner.

'Isn't this against the company rules?' she said.

'To hell with the rules. There's something special about you.'

She'd heard him say the same thing to one of the other girls the previous night. For a moment she gave in. This was what she needed. A new experience, the feel of a different body, to cancel out and cover over memories of Harry's body. The bus driver was a good kisser. That made it easy at the start and easy for a little while. It would have been simple to sink into it, to let feeling take over from thinking even for just an hour. To cover the traces. To try and forget about everything. But when his hands strayed beneath her shirt, against her skin, it was like she was burnt. She pushed him away.

'I'm sorry, I can't. I'm married.'

'Come on. No one comes on these tours if they're married.'

'I'm separated, I mean.'

'Then you're not married, are you?'

She still felt married.

Back in London she heard music in shops, from car radios, that reminded her of him. She saw places she'd heard sung about. She imagined Harry seeing them with her. She bought a CD for him. She would send it to him. No, he had the key to her flat, he was keeping an eye on it. He'd insisted. She'd give it to him when they met after she'd got back. A thank you. A farewell present.

'Let me be sad with you. It was my baby too.'

'But you didn't hurt it like I did.'

'You didn't hurt it. It wasn't the right time for it. We'll try again.'

'*We can't. We can't go backwards.*'
'*Then we'll go forwards. Don't give up on me.*'

In Edinburgh there was a free afternoon of shopping time. On the second floor of a large shopping centre she found herself at the entrance to a Mothercare store. She had avoided any babywear shops since it happened. She would leave a shopping centre if she saw on the directory that there was one inside. This one surprised her.

In a basket in front was a collection of pale yellow, pale blue, pale pink and creamy white knitwear. Little booties. Little hats. It came up from deep inside her, the hurt and the anguish and the sorrow and the guilt. There, in a strange city, she cried for the first time. The same woman who was embarrassed if she discovered she'd walked around town with a ladder in her stocking, now standing in public, in the middle of a shopping centre, crying hard. Sobbing. The younger girl inside the store looked shocked. An older woman didn't.

'Come in here with me, pet.'

There was a small room at the back of the store. The woman didn't need to ask. She seemed to know. She handed Shelley a cup of hot tea.

'When did it happen, lovie?'

'Three months ago.'

'How old?'

'He wasn't born yet. I was five months pregnant.'

The woman nodded.

'We thought we were over the danger time. We thought we had nothing to worry about.'

'He was your first child?'

Shelley nodded.

'Is your husband all right?'

A pause.

'We separated.'

'Not for good.'

'It was my fault.'

'It wasn't your fault. It was nobody's fault, not yours, not his. Nobody's. I know.'

Shelley looked at her.

'Five times,' the woman said.

'Five miscarriages?' At the woman's nod, 'Did you ever . . .'

'One daughter, just when I'd given up hope. And she's had five children. I'm Supergran. Keep talking to him, pet. Keep loving him. He needs you as much as you need him. The two of you made this baby together, so the two of you have to grieve together. Where is he?'

'At home.'

'Here in Edinburgh?'

'Australia.'

'Go home to him.'

'I'm on a tour.'

'Go home to him.'

'Promise me you'll email. I need to know you're all right. Let me collect you at least.'

She sent it from a crammed Internet café. She didn't know if he was checking his emails regularly. She wasn't due home for another five days. He'd be expecting her to go on to other parts of Scotland. He had the itinerary. He'd said he needed to have it, to know where she was. She could remember everything he had said to her and she could remember everything she had said to him.

Her plane arrived at Melbourne Airport before dawn. The queue was long through passport control, through baggage reclaim, through the double doors out into the airport. Dozens of people were waiting. There was no sign of him. He wasn't in the line of people pressed against the barrier. He wasn't there with a cardboard sign with her name written on it. He wasn't in the group of people near the door having cigarettes, or outside, double-parked in their old Holden station wagon, ready to whisk her away.

He was under the meeting-point sign. He was standing on a rug. Her rug. Their rug. She was crying as she moved towards him. His arms were open. She moved into them and pressed her face against his chest.

'I'm so sorry, Harry.'

'Welcome home, Shelley.'

He didn't say anything else. Not yet. He just held her tighter.

∽ ∾

From the short story collection *All Together Now*
PAN MACMILLAN

Ferdia MacAnna

Ferdia MacAnna was born in Dublin. He has worked as a television producer/director, journalist, magazine editor and scriptwriter. For some years he toured Ireland as lead singer and songwriter with Rocky De Valera and the Grave-diggers and The Rhythm Kings. He has written numerous plays and screenplays and published three novels: *The Last of the High Kings* (made into a Hollywood movie starring Gabriel Byrne), *The Ship Inspector* and *Cartoon City*. His memoir, *The Rocky Years,* was published in 2006. Ferdia has taught at various colleges and institutions, including DCU, NUIM and IADT.

Elvis Costello Saved My Brain **

Extract from his memoir *The Rocky Years* (HODDER HEADLINE)

Ferdia MacAnna

Dublin 1985

The first thing I heard was a yelp.

I woke up in a white bed in a white room with the worst hang-over ever. The sun blazed in through high windows turning everything in the room ghostly, stabbing fingers of light into my eyes.

I had a metallic taste in my mouth, as though I had been sucking an empty spoon. My teeth felt as though someone had removed them and stuck them back in upside down. I sat up. I felt stiff all over, and now I tasted blood in my mouth.

Opposite me there were two beds. In one, an old guy sat reading a paper. A teenage lad lay in the other bed, looking bored. Next to me was a white screen. Soft snores came from behind the screen. I tried to figure out what I was doing in a hospital bed, but nothing came. No memory at all.

Another high-pitched yelp. The yelps were coming from outside the room. Somebody must have brought their dog in, except that it didn't sound like a dog.

The yelps made me angry. Finding myself in hospital made me angry. Having no idea how I got there made me angry. Now I just wanted to get away. I wanted to go home. A new thought struck me – I don't know where my home is. I can't remember where I live. I can't even remember my name.

263

A milky nurse came over, looked at me and asked me if I was OK.

'Yes, I'm grand.'

'You sure?'

'I'm sure. Now go away, please.'

I didn't want her looking at me. I didn't want her asking me stupid questions. I wanted to ask her if she knew what had happened to me, but I didn't want to look thick.

I was convinced that I had done something bad. Along with my anger, I felt guilty and confused. Nothing felt right. I didn't want to see anyone until I had figured this out. I didn't want anyone to see me.

Milky Nurse said something else but I didn't get it. Either I didn't hear it properly or I just couldn't understand.

'Please go away.'

She shrugged and then walked off, consulting a chart.

Now I could get some peace.

A blonde woman walked in. She came over to look at me, face tight and concerned.

Immediately I felt mad at her. I didn't want anyone coming here to see me like this. I didn't want her looking at me either. I didn't want her asking me if I was OK. But I recognised her. Her name was Maria.

'Are you –?'

'Yes, I'm OK,' I told her abruptly.

She said something but I ignored it.

'You don't have to be here,' I snapped at her.

'Do you know who I am?'

'Of course I do.'

'Who am I?'

'You're Maria.'

Maria looked shocked. 'That's what you were calling me last night. Who's Maria?'

I didn't need to be bothered with this now. Her name was Maria. She obviously had some kind of problem with her name.

Another yelp from the corridor.

I felt the urge to move. I had things to do, stuff to find out. I wanted to make sure somehow that nobody found out that I was in hospital. That seemed important to me.

Maria wouldn't let me alone. 'I've been outside all night. I'm really worried about you.'

'Well, you can go now, I'm fine. Don't tell anyone I'm in here.'

The word 'outside' scared me. Outside where? Outside this ward? Outside the hospital? Something bad had happened to me 'outside', but now suddenly I didn't want to know what it was. Everyone else seemed to know something I didn't, and that pissed me off. I wanted to ask Maria what had happened but I was afraid of what she might tell me.

'How are you feeling, Ferdia?'

'Ferdia?'

My own name came back to me, as though it was trailing a banner at the head of a parade of small memories. Ferdia. A sudden flood of recollections rushed through me because of that one word: I often got letters from people who thought I was a woman (for the attention of Ms Ferdia Mac Anna – the name sounded feminine); people had trouble pronouncing it (in London they called me Fred!); I had grown up in Howth (in a little white bungalow near the top of the hill, just below the Summit Inn); I didn't think that I still lived there; I couldn't remember my parents or brothers or sisters, if I had any.

Then there was a sudden yelp from the corridor.

'Somebody give me my clothes and let me out of here. I want to go home.'

I knew that there was a reason why I couldn't go home to the little white bungalow in Howth. I could feel answers stirring deep within me as though trapped somewhere in my stomach. I could feel knowledge slowly working its way up my body until it evaporated somewhere just before it could pop into my mind and illuminate me. I couldn't understand it or rationalise anything. I was like a sheet of paper with some doodles and scribblings on it.

It felt strange not being able to remember, as though all of my memories had been wiped. Except for basic functions – like knowing what a fork was or recognising a window or realising that I was in a hospital bed – I was basically blank. I knew my name and I recognised Maria, but that was about it. The loss left me feeling empty and angry.

I wanted to blame someone for all of this.

The nurses pissed me off. The two blokes on the other beds pissed me off. The person snoring behind the screen pissed me off. The mystery yelper down the hall pissed me off. I wished that they would all go away and let me have a big think so I could work out what was going on. Except that I couldn't think. I couldn't figure anything out.

'Are you OK?' Maria asked.

'Yes.'

Maria's questions pissed me off.

I wanted Maria to go away and quit annoying me.

I closed my eyes and Maria disappeared along with the white room.

I woke up a few seconds later. Maria was gone.

In her place stood Milky Nurse, looking at me. 'Your wife will be back later – she's gone for something to eat. She was outside all night, you know.'

'My wife?'

'Yes – Kate,' Milky Nurse looked at me.

She asked the OK question.

'Of course I'm OK.'

'How many fingers am I holding up?'

'Two.'

'Now?'

'Four.'

'Good.'

The blonde woman was my wife? Kate. Not Maria. Who's

Maria? Kate was American. We had met . . . I couldn't remember when I had met my wife. I couldn't remember getting married either.

My wife's name is Kate.

I was shocked to find myself married. I wanted to ask Milky Nurse if we had any kids but when I looked up she had vanished.

I shut my eyes. Tried to think. Nothing came. Better idea. Don't think. Shut down. Save the energy. Veg out on the hospital hum.

A yelp from the yelping man.

A nurse came in with a plate of dinner on a tray that she placed in front of me. I sat up and tried some. The food tasted like paste and I spat it into my napkin. I couldn't eat it. I rang a bell and when the nurse came I asked her to take it away. I asked her why the food was so crap.

'Is it always this inedible?'

'Well, everybody else likes it.'

She looked annoyed, but she took the tray away.

Hospital food was crap.

Outside the windows, it was dark. I had a tight feeling in my head, as though I was wearing a crash helmet that was too small. I was awake but incredibly sleepy – except I couldn't sleep. I kept thinking but there wasn't much to think about because no more memories had returned. My mind was firing blanks.

I just lay there, listening to the hospital drone while counting the seconds between yelps.

The next morning Kate was back. She had the same tight look on her face. I asked her about the yelps. She told me the story of Yelping Man. It seemed the guy had been out jogging when he had suffered a sudden massive stroke. The last sound he heard was that of a dog yelping. Soon after he came to, he yelped. That's what he'd been doing ever since. Maybe he thought he was a dog. Kate said that he was in the next ward, sitting up in bed normal as anyone with his eyes open, giving a yelp out of him every thirty seconds.

Apparently, Yelping Man's ward was doing a big turnover in patients. Most lasted a day before asking to be moved.

'You're very lucky to be in here,' Kate said.

I didn't know what to say to that.

I refused to eat hospital meals. Everything tasted awful, even the toast.

I couldn't read or concentrate on anything for very long. I didn't notice days changing into night. I remembered mornings only because the white light was so bright through the windows that it poked my eyes awake.

The following morning, the old man in the bed opposite had gone. In his place was a man with a white beard. I recognised him – my dad knew him. More memories. My dad was a big man with a massive face. He could throw a deafening scowl if he was mad at you. Whenever Dad came back from America he brought me an album. Once I got *The Doors*, then it was *The Flying Burrito Bros.* The best one and my favourite was *The Allman Brothers Live at the Fillmore East*. I remembered that I had a big record collection at home. I just couldn't think where my home was. I didn't want Dad to know that I was in hospital. I wanted to hear 'In Memory of Elizabeth Reed' by the Allman Brothers – it was my favourite piece of music. Listening to it always made me feel as if I was flying.

The man with the white beard had something to do with the Dublin Theatre Festival. I had met him several times. It triggered a new memory. Dad worked in the Abbey Theatre in Abbey Street, Dublin – a big, rectangular, ugly building. Outside on the side-walls and in front of the main entrance posters of plays were displayed. I had spent a lot of time there as a child. I could feel Dad. Big man. Big presence. Schooldays when I would sometimes call into the Abbey for lunch money or a lift home. Dad sitting in the auditorium, directing actors on a stage. Dad's big, broad, dark back in the seat. The cigarette in his mouth, trailing wispy smoke up into the lights. Dad directing *The Plough and the Stars*. The standing ovation at the end. Dad directing *Borstal Boy*. The Tony Award on our mantelpiece at home. All those plates on the wall – those weird colourful plates.

I remembered being in the audience one night when all the lights suddenly dimmed and we heard a car approaching from the alleyway outside. Slowly, this ancient thirties jalopy drove onto the stage, its headlights gradually illuminating a group of actors dressed as Chicago gangsters. The remainder of the scene was played out in the headlights over the soft murmur of the car engine. Somebody got bumped off on stage. The lead gangster looked like Hitler. The title of the play jumped out at me: *The Resistible Rise of Arturo Ui* by Berthold Brecht. Then the headlights switched off and my memories went into darkness. I chased the images for a while but got nothing more. It was as though titbits of memory were being filtered through, enough to tease me but not enough to lead me anywhere. I remembered that I had loved the play. That memory made me feel good for a while. I liked plays about Chicago gangsters. I liked old jalopies.

Mr White Beard got up, quietly put on his dressing gown and slippers and walked out of the ward. A few minutes later a nurse gently brought him back, helped him out of his dressing gown and put him back to bed.

As soon as the nurse left, Mr White Beard got up again, put on his dressing gown and slippers and walked out purposefully, like he was going to a meeting. Moments later, the nurse led him back again. This went on most of the night and the next morning. Mr White Beard didn't once make it past the end of the corridor.

Kate told me that I was supposed to remain in hospital for a few months until they had a chance to figure out what was wrong with me. They wanted to observe me and do more tests.

A few months?

No chance.

I wanted to go home.

I had a row with Milky Nurse over the taste of the tea, so she took it away. I refused to eat dinner and made a big fuss about it. I made a fuss about everything. I was obnoxious. Hospital food was crap and somebody should do something about it. Everyone else in the ward thought the food was fine.

In the end, it was decided that I could leave. The nurses thought I was an arrogant shite and couldn't wait to get rid of me. They preferred the yelping man. The next morning Kate came to collect me. I had everything packed.

Mr White Beard was standing by the side of his bed in his dressing gown, just standing with a blank expression. He seemed to have lost interest in going anywhere.

Before we left the hospital, I wanted to see Yelping Man – I needed to put a face to the yelps.

We paused outside the next ward and looked in. Kate pointed out a normal-looking fellow in his late twenties or early thirties. There he sat in his bed. He looked perfectly normal, but he wasn't reading or looking at anyone. He just stared ahead as though contented.

We waited. He gave a sudden yelp. He made no big deal about it – it seemed like a normal thing for him to do.

We left the ward and walked down the corridor to meet my doctor. His office was small and murky with medical books stacked on the table, along with a bag of medical implements. The walls were covered with charts of the human brain and body. Neatly folded papers and forms lay piled on the desk. The doctor was an elderly skinny man with a quiet manner. He asked me several questions. He made notes. He held a small bottle with the cap off under my nostrils. 'Do you smell that?'

'Yes,' I replied.

Then I realised that I hadn't smelled anything. I was surprised. 'No,' I said quickly. 'I don't smell it.'

Alarmed, he removed the cap from another small bottle and put it to my nose. 'That one?'

'No.'

He made some more jottings. At one point he gave my knee a

whack with a small hammer. He seemed relieved by my reaction. He told us that he could not say for sure what had happened to me. The word 'aneurysm' was used. I didn't know what it meant. He explained, but I still didn't get it. The phrase 'spontaneous bleed in the brain' came up. I understood enough to know that I was very lucky to be alive and even luckier not to be a vegetable. Then I heard him tell Kate that there was some permanent brain damage. He said there was a good chance of epilepsy.

Permanent brain damage?

Epilepsy?

I didn't believe him. I knew I was fine. I didn't want to hear any more. I wanted to get out of that murky room and get clear of the white rooms and the yelps and Milky Nurse and Mr White Beard and the quiet doctor as well. I shut out the doctor's voice. I didn't want to listen to the stuff he was telling Kate.

Kate drove us home to our small basement apartment on Crofton Road in Dún Laoghaire. As far as I was concerned, I had been in hospital for a few days and nights. In reality I had been in the public ward in St Vincent's for two weeks.

I recuperated at home for what I thought was a week, only it was really two months.

I had no dreams. Memories came back slowly, though some didn't come back at all. Nothing tasted good. It took me a while to realise that I had no sense of smell. I couldn't smell the dinner cooking or the toilet or perfume. I don't remember any visitors. Now and then something would trigger the memory of a particular smell, but it never lasted more than a second.

I was lucky. Things could have been a lot worse. If I had to lose one of my senses and I'd been given the choice, smell would probably have been the one I'd have picked.

Kate looked after me on her own while she continued working as a journalist for *The Irish Times*. I saw her walk past our bedroom door to the kitchen. I heard the kettle boiling and then tea being poured. Moments later, Kate walked past on the way to the front room and her typewriter. We were assigned no aftercare.

I knew I was also a journalist. I worked as arts editor for the *Evening Herald* but I had no memory of the job or of my colleagues. I still couldn't remember my parents or brothers or sisters. I couldn't recall my wedding to Kate. I didn't even know who Kate was. She was just there with me, my mysterious wife. I felt resentful of her. I wanted to blame someone for what had happened to me and Kate was the only one around – even though I knew that she was entirely blameless. My wife had saved my life and was now looking after me.

I was incapable of rational thought, and I immediately blocked out any emotion that frightened me or made me aware of my own fragility. I had no idea why I had called Kate 'Maria'. Sometimes memories just arrived unannounced.

I had grown up in Howth. I remembered long walks home from town whenever I missed the last bus – the number thirty-one. I had a friend called Nessan. We were two boys with weird names hanging around Howth together. My favourite soccer team was Crystal Palace. They used to have a centre-forward named Gerry Queen. One time he got sent off for fighting and the headline in the sports pages read 'Queen in Row at Palace'. I went to see the movie *Woodstock* when I was fifteen. Ten Years After were brilliant and I really wanted Alvin Lee's big red Gibson guitar with the peace sticker on it. Richie Havens kept strumming and strumming forever and wouldn't finish his song. I really wanted him to get off the stage so that the next band could come on, but he just kept strumming. Even when he stood up to leave he kept playing. Irritated the shit out of me.

I couldn't read because I couldn't follow a train of thought. I watched television but had trouble concentrating or absorbing information. Often a programme would leave me behind after five minutes and I would be totally lost, unable to recall how it started or even what it was about.

I was grumpy all the time. I couldn't even enjoy music.

I was a nightmare.

Over the weeks, I pieced the day of my accident back together. I remembered being in the *Herald* offices and my work, typing up a film review. I remembered enough to make a story out of what happened.

It had started as a normal day. A columnist, Dominic Behan, wanted to meet me and Colm (the design editor and a good friend) for a lunchtime jar. We met him at noon in The Oval, next door to the *Independent* building. Dominic sat at the bar, under a portrait of his late, world-famous brother, Brendan, though I don't know if he had noticed the portrait.

We drank pints. We talked. We laughed at Dominic's stories. He was living in Scotland. He said he felt accepted there and that he had never really felt accepted in Dublin. He was good company, but he got drunk quickly and turned bitter.

We went somewhere for lunch, or perhaps we walked around intending to go somewhere for lunch and then decided to go back to the pub instead.

I remember bumping into Nick O'Neill, the filmmaker, outside Bruxelles. Nice guy. Big smile. We chatted to him a while before moving on. I remember bright sunshine in Grafton Street, like it was the start of summer.

We went to Larry Tobin's pub for another pint. Then, somehow, Dominic disappeared, Colm was gone and I was in a taxi.

Now it was night-time. I arrived at my friends John and Sally's apartment for dinner. I remember that Kate was annoyed with me for turning up a bit drunk. I denied being drunk. 'Just a few pints,' I said.

John and Sally had an old black pay telephone with an *A* button and a *B* button on the money-box part. I showed them how to tap the phone so that you didn't have to put money in and then tapped out a call to my brother Niall, and had a chat with him.

We sat at a table. I talked too much. A plate of spaghetti carbonara appeared in front of me. I kept talking away about something.

John put *West Side Story* on the stereo as I stood up to go to the toilet. A male voice sang about a girl named Maria.

That was the last thing I remember.

Apparently, I walked off towards the toilet only to collapse like an empty coat in the doorway. At first they thought I had passed out because of the drink. They tried to wake me up but couldn't. I was completely gone. That was when Kate noticed that there was blood coming from my ear. She phoned an ambulance. She saved my life.

The ambulance arrived and they carried me out on a stretcher. I came to for a few moments on the stretcher. One of the ambulance men had recognised me from my time as a rock-and-roll singer. 'Don't worry, Rocky, we won't tell anyone,' he said.

He thought I was drunk too. Everyone thought I was just drunk – everyone except Kate.

We went for walks. I couldn't remember much but I grew familiar with the small area between our apartment and the Dún Laoghaire Shopping Centre. Sometimes we bumped into people we knew, though I never recognised them.

It was hard to tell if I was getting better. It took me ages to do the simplest task, like opening a can or boiling the kettle. Then one day we saw a small man wearing glasses in a big overcoat walking in our direction. I thought I recognised him, but he passed without a sign or a nod that he knew me.

A few seconds later I knew who he was. 'That was Elvis Costello,' I said to Kate.

Kate was used to me rambling. I told her that I had seen him at the Stella in Rathmines around 1976. 'He was brilliant. He said that it was great to be playing in Dublin. That it was great to be playing in front of real people.'

I was very happy. I had recognised Elvis. He lived in our area. That was something I remembered from before. Everything was going to be fine now.

Elvis Costello had saved my brain.

Liz McManus TD

Liz McManus TD, who was born in Montreal in Canada, is a Labour TD for Wicklow. First elected to the Dáil in 1992, Liz was the Deputy Leader of the Labour Party from 2002 to 2007. Currently, Liz is Labour's Spokesperson on Communications, Energy and Natural Resources. Liz established the Women's Refuge in Bray in 1978, was Chairperson of the National Taskforce on the Needs of Travellers and was Minister of State for Housing and Urban Renewal 1994–97. Liz is a previous winner of the Hennessy, Listowel and Irish PEN awards in fiction. Liz's first novel, *Acts of Subversion,* was nominated for the Aer Lingus/*Irish Times* Literature Prize.

Foundation of Hope **

Liz McManus TD

Going abroad on a charity walk didn't appeal to me. I envisaged too many early starts in the morning and too much *bonhomie* at night, but the temptation was irresistible; to be offered a chance to go to the top of the world, and to salve my conscience at the same time. So I ended up travelling with a group to a remote place, high in the Indian Himalayas. Ladakh is a land of fertile valleys and austere, arid mountains. Known as Little Tibet, it is the closest I will get to Shangri-La, or what I imagine Shangri-La to be. For centuries people have been shopping in Leh, its capital, where trade routes between China and India crisscross, and where Tibetan refugees have flowed over the border to set up their markets. In summer when the snows clear, the streets are filled with Indian Hindus, Kashmiri Moslems, Ladakhi Buddhists, Western hippies and visitors like me, lost in wonder.

In the middle of a market I was surrounded by stacks of carved wooden animals, turquoise jewellery, cloths of gold, mysterious board games, Buddhist prayer wheels; a hoard raked up from the history of India. I was bewildered by choice. I didn't know what to buy. In my mind I was already going home. The plane was dropping out of the dry air between the great mountain ranges in order to take me back to familiar territory. I had a sudden idea and turned to the woman behind the stall.

'I'm looking for a musical instrument, something small enough to carry.'

The woman smiled. Her hand moved over the brass bells and wooden recorders and then it came to a stop.

'This one,' she said.

The pipe was delicate, thin and grey with a pitted texture. At one end it had a bulbous, open-ended bowl made of silver. When she blew through the pipe it responded with a plaintive cry. I took it and rolled the pipe in my hands. It looked vaguely familiar.

'What is it?'

'It's used in the monastery in Tibet.'

'Yes, but what is it?'

'It is the thigh bone of a girl.'

I was conscious that my companion, Rakesh, a guide from Sikkim, flinched just like I did. Both of us were unnerved by the woman's explanation even though the Tibetan tradition of sky burials is well known. I had read about them. When a Tibetan dies their corpse is not buried. Instead it is cut up and left out on a mountain top to be picked clean by the vultures and sometimes the bones are used for ceremonial purposes. This is the practice of *jhator*, 'of giving alms to the birds'. According to Buddhist thought, the body, once it is dead, is empty and the spirit gone. Although I'm not a Buddhist I believe that too. I am here to learn, I told myself, and not to judge. Even so, the pipe felt eerily potent in my hand. I put it back on the stall and settled instead for a wooden whistle.

To learn and not to judge . . . It is not easy. The touch of dry brittle bone stays with me. There are so many sensations I cannot absorb them all; the smells of spices and sewage; the sound of a wind yowling up a mountain pass; the thick taste on my tongue of tea mixed with yak butter. India's assault on Westerner sensibilities is celebrated but when you travel there with The HOPE Foundation there is a further dimension to the experience. You leave any certainty behind. Preconceptions need not apply. This is not the slum tourism sparked off by *Slumdog Millionaire*. It is more complicated, more challenging and a more hopeful experience. It is not even tourism. It is immersion. Plunge in.

My story begins in Calcutta.

In this age of Global Positioning Systems and Google Maps, when we can spy into the backyards of strangers in New York or Tunbridge Wells, it is an astonishing fact that nobody has succeeded in counting the population of Calcutta. Nobody knows how many people live in the sprawling city that reaches out to capture us, a little cluster of wide-eyed, pink-skinned Irish, into its unnumbered millions.

Day and night, the streets of Calcutta heave with people. They are thronged with women, their saris fluttering, and men on bicycles piled high with goods. The mass of Indian generations is swollen by immigrants slipping over the border from Bangladesh to set up in slums that spring up on the outskirts. Calcutta is a vast, decrepit metropolis that roars with life. It is also the place where a handful of Irish women and local people work to make life better for children of the city. They run classrooms in the slums, a hospital for the homeless, a house for former prostitutes, a hospice for AIDS victims . . . Compared to the enormity of needs of Calcutta their projects may seem like a plaintive cry at reality but they have a potency beyond their reach.

'It is remarkable,' says a Bengali teacher standing in a shaded classroom in the middle of a slum, 'that people from a country so far away from us have done this for our children.'

It is remarkable, yes, but it didn't happen by accident. It required a suspension of disbelief to accept the premise that a small Irish charity could make any difference in this Third World mega-city. It also required nerves of steel and an unsinkable optimism.

'There are just too many people for us to manage,' says an

official of a large Indian trade union. 'And the industries we had are closing down or leaving . . .' He sits in a shabby room with the door and window open for any breath of wind that comes. On the ceiling an electric fan thuds hypnotically. A tall man, he is dressed in cotton dhoti and loose tunic. His elegant hands rest on the table. The tone of his voice is polite and laden with fatigue.

'Child labour is against the law in India,' he says.

Our group was travelling through the city of Calcutta. We were somewhere near the docks where giant trucks plough up the streets, spraying up sheets of mud onto passersby. Dark wheels, dark earth, dark faces. Traffic lodged around us, car-horns howling. Then suddenly, like a flake of sunlight on water, a tree appeared. And then another. Leaf upon leaf played around our heads as we stepped down from our jeep onto a puddled track. Angry flies clouded around us.

So this is what a slum is like . . . Hundreds of low shacks made from bamboo, cotton, metal sheeting huddled together with rutted tracks between. Children crowded around us as we approached. Liquid eyes and the gentlest of hands grasped ours.

'Auntie! Auntie!' they cried. 'How are you, Uncle?'

I see a girl. On a mat in the clearing she is hunkered down. She is ten or eleven maybe. In her hand she holds a broad sharp knife. She is one of a group of children who are splicing wood into splints for reinforcing kites. Her hands move frenetically as she works. She barely looks at us. A man will come in the evening and collect the bundles and pay her. If she cuts 1,000 splints she will earn 5 rupees. It is a pittance, we know, and I think *'alms for the birds'* . . .

An old woman complains to us in a sing-song voice.

'She's her grandmother and wants the girl to get more money for the work she's doing,' our guide explains.

At the sound of his voice the girl stops and she looks around at the other children. Then her head goes down and her knife flashes.

'Do the children go to school?' I ask.

'Yes,' the guide says proudly. 'They go for two hours a day and *this* one –' the girl looks up momentarily – 'she is the first from our slum who is going on to secondary school.'

For the first time since we have arrived in the slum, the girl smiles a child's smile. Our group responds with a burr of spontaneous comments. Like children we clap our hands and around us, the children laugh and join in the clapping. We are out of our depth but, in this unfamiliar world, we are learning fast. The terrible poverty that pervades our senses and fills us with helplessness hasn't lessened in any way but we have made a discovery. Poverty has its limits. On a rare occasion such as this, we can see with the eyes of a young girl that, beyond the edges of a Calcutta slum, there is a foundation of hope. Not only can we see it but we also see that, in our small way, we are part of it.

∽ ∽

Mary Malone

Mary Malone lives in Templemartin, Bandon, Co. Cork with her husband Pat and sons David and Mark. As well as being a novelist and freelance journalist, she works in the Central Statistics Office in Cork. She has three published novels, *Love Match* (2006), *All You Need Is Love* (2007) and *Never Tear Us Apart* (2009). Her fourth novel, *Love Is the Reason,* will be published by Poolbeg Fiction in November 2010. For more information, visit her website, *www.marymalone.ie.*

A Crazy Little Thing Called Love *

Mary Malone

Sarah pulled her convertible into Jack's driveway, her apprehension increasing when she saw him standing in the doorway. He looked divine in dark denims, a fitted white T-shirt (either it was new or he'd become very adept at doing his own laundry!) and brown loafers. His shock of dark hair had a messed-up look, a look Sarah guessed he'd spent ages perfecting.

'Punctual as ever, Sarah.' He strolled towards the car.

'Aircrafts don't wait,' she said, fixing her long blonde hair into a tight ponytail.

'A few more bits of luggage and I'm ready.' His blue eyes held hers for a split second. Then he tossed his khaki rucksack into the boot and returned to the house.

Sarah's jaw dropped when he reappeared with his golf bag slung over one shoulder. 'You cannot be serious?' she gasped, her resolve to remain calm instantly evaporating.

'Shame not to take advantage of the courses in Praia do Vau.' And yet again he disappeared into the house. Their house. The house she'd walked out of six weeks before.

Speechless, she watched while her husband stuffed the laptop carry-case onto the back seat. What was he trying to tell her? That if she wanted to rekindle their relationship, it involved playing second if not third choice to his computer followed by his time on the golf course! She pursed her lips, knowing that if she opened her mouth there would be no trip to Alvor. Instead, there would be a heated argument about his obsession with work. Like the millions they'd had before she'd barged out of the house, screaming at him that things had to change, refusing to accept he had no choice.

Pressing her foot hard on the accelerator, she revved the engine and pulled the car onto the road, barely giving him the chance to fasten his seatbelt before whizzing off in a cloud of exhaust fumes. Casting a swift glance in Jack's direction, she focused on her main reason for taking this trip. To get her man back.

In the weeks they'd been apart, Sarah had taken up residence in her sister's spare room, twisting and turning late into the night, visualising a life alone and hating the prospect. After marathon wine-fuelled chats with her sister, they had finally decided to coax him away from distraction. Sending the email invitation at three in the morning after copious glasses of chardonnay had seemed like a really great idea! But now, in the sober light of day – not to mention his luggage content – she knew the odds were stacked against her. All she had were five days – and nights – to achieve results.

'Let me take the bags and you go and park,' Jack offered, when Sarah brought the sports car to a screeching halt outside Airport Departures.

'Just take yours, I'm used to managing alone now,' she replied curtly.

His 'just out of bed' look had taken a sharp turn for the worse. She couldn't help feeling a childish satisfaction.

'But your case looks a ton weight!'

She passed him an envelope. 'Here's your boarding pass. You have remembered your passport?'

'Yes!' He stepped out of the car. 'Sarah,' he began, his luggage beside him, his laptop clutched firmly in his hand. 'I don't think this is . . .'

She gripped the steering wheel. Surely he wasn't going to change his mind about travelling. Not at the airport doors!

286

As luck had it, Airport Security chose that exact moment to intervene. 'Can you move along, please? This is a set-down area only.'

She let out the breath she'd been holding and headed for the long-term car park, slipping into the first parking space available. It took huge effort on the rough and uneven surface, but she managed to drag her suitcase to the bus stop, climbing onto the shuttle already waiting. Unable to get Jack's unfinished sentence out of her head, she willed the bus driver to hurry and was first to get off when they arrived at the airport doors.

Running towards the appropriate area for the Faro flight, she crashed her suitcase against a man's legs.

'Ouch! Sarah, will you watch where you're going!'

She stopped and turned around, relief coursing through her. He hadn't abandoned her.

Thank you, God, she mouthed silently.

'Sorry, Jack,' she said aloud.

'Let me,' he offered, reaching out to take her case.

She accepted his offer of help, anxious not to irritate him again. At least not until they were safely in Portugal.

'Drink?' Sarah asked, when they'd cleared security.

'No, thanks. I've tenders to recalculate and business calls to make before boarding,' he explained, taking a seat in the nearest coffee dock and unzipping his laptop case.

Sarah walked away, her enthusiasm wavering. Work, work, work. Everywhere he went, it followed. Had she brought them both on a fool's errand?

Browsing through Duty Free, she was overcome by a sense of finality. Unexpected tears sprang to her eyes, forcing her towards the sunglasses section where she hid behind darkened lenses until she was confident she had her emotions in check.

What happened to us, she wondered, stealing a glance at Jack, noticing his head bent in concentration. But she knew the answer:

Jack's obsession with his financial enterprise had left no time for her, no time for them to spend together. She'd tried everything to distract him: pleaded with him to turn off his phone, issued ultimatums and wagged her finger that his health would suffer. But her efforts were fruitless, his drive and ambition impossible to curb.

'12A and 13B,' the stewardess advised as they boarded the aircraft.

'Seats apart?' Jack raised an eyebrow.

'Late booking,' Sarah lied. She hadn't wanted to put herself through the agonising intimacy of having his thigh touch hers for two hours and twenty minutes. Not until she was convinced he still wanted her.

She slowly descended the steps of the plane, savouring the heat from the strong sun. She was glad she'd dressed lightly, excited – yet apprehensive – at the thoughts of donning her swimwear and lounging around the pool, glass of wine in hand, husband at her side – at least that's how she imagined it.

'You haven't told me which hotel we're staying in?' Jack steered their luggage trolley towards the taxi stand.

Wanting to keep their location under wraps for a short while longer, she pretended she hadn't heard and turned her attention to hailing a taxi. She couldn't but wonder about the days ahead. Would they be reunited? Or would they be further apart than ever?

The taxi journey through Faro's suburbs and along the picturesque Algarve coastline was a silent one. As she stared at the expanse of ocean and foaming waves behind their four-star accommodation, the Jardim Do Vau apartments, Sarah was instantly transported back to their honeymoon – two heavenly weeks of treasured memories. She felt a lump in her throat at Jack's intake of breath beside her. Could it be that he was remembering too? Could this be the first glimmer of hope?

'Of all the hotels in Portugal, you had to bring us back here!'

The blood drained from her face, the hope in her belly wilting like a snowdrop in late spring.

'Dragging me back here isn't going to work miracles, Sarah,' he continued, as she led the way to their apartment, room key in her hand. 'I'm still the same guy. Under even more pressure! But, Sarah, if we're patient . . .'

'Patient!' God damn him, she thought, closing the apartment door.

She took her suitcase through to the larger bedroom, her eyes filling with tears when she heard Jack banging wardrobe doors and settling himself into the room next door.

'I'm going for a swim,' he announced shortly afterwards, knee-length khaki shorts and well-worn flip-flops being the full extent of his dress.

She stared after him as he walked to the door, more than surprised when he stopped and invited her to join him.

'You didn't travel all the way here to stare at the view from the window, did you? Now that we're here, we might as well take advantage.'

We, she thought! He said 'we'! Her heart soared, her anger abated and in that moment Sarah truly believed that he wanted to swim in the bright blue sea and relax in the warm summer sun.

'I'll be right down,' she told him, dashing to the bedroom and slipping into a bronze-colour bikini, dancing in celebration on the gleaming marble floor.

Skipping out of the apartment a few moments later, Sarah fixed her Gucci sunglasses on her nose. She stopped in surprise to see Jack running towards her. And past her.

'You go ahead without me,' he called over his shoulder. 'I've a business call coming through from Canada.' He waved his phone at her and disappeared from view.

Sarah stomped blindly towards the pool. Still furious with Jack, she wasn't watching where she was walking and stubbed her toe on the footpath. Yelping in pain, she glanced down, her stomach heaving at the sight of blood streaming over the straps of her sandals. She flopped onto a concrete step to investigate, jumping up again when the intense heat burnt her skin. Suddenly, she felt exhausted. Yet again, regardless of the fact they were in beautiful sunny Portugal where everybody around them was lazing in the sun, she was on her own. Nothing at all had changed and, as far as she could see, she was the only one fighting to give their marriage a chance. Having plenty of experience of Jack's business calls, she didn't expect to see him before sunset.

'This is all?' the cashier enquired when Sarah brought a packet of Band-Aids, a large bar of chocolate and a magazine to the supermarket checkout.

Sarah nodded and smiled. 'Can you charge it to Apartment B125 please?'

The girl shook her head. 'You must pay cash.'

Damn, she thought, looking from her bleeding toe to the Band-Aids on the counter. She had no intention of giving Jack the satisfaction of returning to the apartment within the space of ten minutes. It would make her look like she was waiting for him. Sighing, she left her purchases on the counter, limping her way towards Reception. Surely they'd have a first-aid box there.

Sarah gave Carlos – she read his name on his jacket nameplate – her most charming smile. 'I've cut my toe and . . .'

Carlos immediately came around to her side of the desk, seeing the congealed blood on her foot and assuming the worst. 'You stay and I will call emergency.'

'No, please!' she insisted. 'I just need a Band-Aid. It's not serious.'

'But you're in pain? No?' He put an arm around her waist and led her towards the soft leather furniture adorning the foyer.

'Only a little,' Sarah admitted.

'You travel alone?' Carlos enquired, his arm still supporting her.

'No, she bloody didn't! Now would you mind taking your hands off my wife?'

Both Sarah and Carlos swivelled around at the sound of Jack's voice, Carlos's hands dropping to his side.

'You will be okay?' Carlos enquired.

'Yes. Yes, Carlos, I will,' she said, furious with Jack for making such an ass of himself, embarrassed that Carlos had witnessed it and confused as hell by the treacherous leap in her heart when Jack had referred to her as his wife. 'Perhaps you could get me that Band-Aid now?'

'Certainly, madam.' He gave her a curt nod, cast a disapproving glare in Jack's direction and disappeared into the office behind the Reception desk.

'What was that about?' Jack glowered.

'A bloody toe!'

'Arrogant oaf,' he muttered, glancing down at her foot. 'Here, lean on me and we'll go back to the apartment and get you cleaned up.'

'But what about Carlos?'

'What about him?'

Not wanting a scene, Sarah acquiesced, annoyed by his masterfulness, yet secretly clinging to the small shred of evidence that he still cared.

Three days later, Sarah sat on the balcony of their second-floor apartment watching the sun going down. Jack's voice filtered through the open patio doors. He was discussing unit prices with a potential client. She listened without hearing, visualising him running a hand over his evening stubble. He'd been on the phone intermittently for the past three days, negotiating deals and placating clients. Sarah had lazed by the pool with magazines or walked barefoot on the sandy beach stretching from Vao to Praia da Rocha, ending her days with a light snack from the restaurant on the ground floor.

Laughter from other balconies travelled in the still night, making Sarah restless, drowning out the chirping crickets. The strain of remaining polite was taking its toll, her efforts to hold Jack's attention fruitless – apart from the few moments he'd spent attending to her bloody toe on the day they'd arrived. And that reaction had only been fuelled by his annoyance with Carlos the receptionist. She sat up a little straighter on the patio chair, a germ of an idea formulating in her mind.

'I'm off out for the night, Jack,' she called, making sure she had her room key, planning a late return. Slipping a cool cotton cardigan over her tanned shoulders (the only positive outcome of her holiday so far), she waited for the lift to take her to the ground floor. Too impatient to call a taxi, she walked the brief distance to the main road and hailed the first one available, instructing the driver to take her to the local town of Alvor.

She stopped to watch a chef cooking fish on a huge grill outside his restaurant, heat emanating as he added olive oil to the iron plates.

'Table for one, madam?'

'Please.' Sarah's mouth watered, the scintillating aromas arousing her taste buds.

'Some homemade bread, madam?' A smiling waiter placed a basket of mixed breads on her table, opening a menu and handing it to her. 'And wine?'

She was about to refuse but at the last minute changed her mind.

'A half bottle of house white, please,' she responded, 'and some of your grilled fish.'

'Excellent choice, madam.' And whisking away the menu once more, he was gone.

The waiter hadn't lied. The fish was indeed an excellent choice. As was the wine. And indeed the company of three Scottish girls at a nearby table who invited her to join in their conversation.

'You cannot be serious! You have never tasted *caipirinha*, Alvor's finest cocktail!'

Sarah giggled, shaking her head. 'Aren't they lethal concoctions?'

'Exactly!' they replied in unison, exploding into laughter.

'You're coming to Bolan Bar with us. We're not taking no for an answer.'

Ten minutes later, Sarah linked arms with them and they walked four-abreast down the steep hill in Alvor, laughing hilariously at nothing at all.

It was 4.00am. Sarah still hadn't returned.

Jack wasn't quite pacing the floors but he was agitated. And worried. Who is she with? He clenched his fists as that guy Carlos flashed in his mind. That bastard, he thought, making a bee-line for Reception.

'Carlos? Is he on duty tonight?'

'No, sir. Can I help?'

'Did my wife order a taxi earlier?'

'Room number, sir?'

'B125.'

'Nothing charged to your room tonight, sir.'

Jack stormed outside, looking left and right, not knowing where to begin searching. The local strip of bars and cafés closed at midnight. How could I have been such an idiot? he screamed inside. Why did I think she'd accept being ignored while I tried to recoup our losses?

Leaning against the hotel window, he rested his hands on his knees. For the first time in weeks his fear of bankruptcy faded, his concern for Sarah utmost in his mind. Breaking into a frantic run, he followed the cobbled pathway in the direction of Praia da Rocha until finally he came to the landmark fountain at the edge of the town. Stopping to catch his breath, he muttered aloud, 'Where is she? Where is she?'

He noticed a police car pulling up outside a nightclub, ordering a lively group to keep the noise down. Jack's heart skipped a beat. In Praia da Rocha, he realised, the night was still young. Terrified his wife would spill out of the club on the arm of a stranger, he turned and ran as fast as he could, beads of perspiration sticking his polo shirt to his back, his feet moving faster and faster as he faced up to the truth. Yet again, he'd lost.

Sarah's shoulders shook with laughter as she waved to her friends in the waiting taxi. She managed to unlock the apartment door, despite the copious number of cocktails she'd consumed. Twirling into the apartment, blushing as she remembered climbing onto the table to dance, she called for Jack.

No answer.

'Jack! Can't we please be friends? For one night only . . .' She collapsed into giggles again, revelling in the numbing oblivion of alcohol, willing to forgive and forget anything.

A very despondent Jack returned to the apartment.

'Sarah! What's happened?'

He hurried to the coffee table, gently putting his arms on her shoulders. She remained in a slumped position, her long blonde hair tipping the floor, her mascara-stained face turned to one side, her lips the colour of raspberry.

Jack's hands shook as he turned her around. The buttons on her blouse were undone, her breasts partially exposed, the ghost of a smile on her face.

She wriggled in his arms, opening her eyes and focusing on his face for a split second. 'Jack, can we go dancing? And drink *caipirinhas*?'

He was too choked to respond.

She was too drunk to repeat her request.

As though she were a small child, he bundled her into his arms and carried her to the bedroom. His bedroom.

Tonight he would watch over her.

Tomorrow he would explain.

❧ ❧

Róisín Meaney

Róisín Meaney was born in Listowel, some time after the Famine. In 2001 she travelled to San Francisco to write her first novel, *The Daisy Picker*, which won the Tivoli 'Write a Bestseller' competition. Róisín has written six adult novels and two children's books. Three of her novels have made the top five in the Irish bestseller list (with one going all the way to the top!). Her latest adult novel, *Love in the Making*, will be published in the US in early 2011.

William's Birthday Party *

Roísín Meaney

As his eighty-seventh birthday approached, William Brosnahan considered the idea of a party, and eventually decided in favour of it.

Of course he had a birthday party every year, but the memory of the last one had long since faded by the time the next one came up for consideration. If you had trouble each evening recalling whether your breakfast egg had been poached or scrambled, what hope had you of remembering anything that happened three hundred and sixty-five eggs ago?

'I'm thinking of having a party for my birthday,' William said to his sixty-three-year-old daughter Eleanor at dinnertime. 'Make a bit of a fuss, get a cake, do a few nibbly things on sticks. What do you think?'

'Why not?' asked Eleanor, tucking his bib into the collar of his white shirt and handing him a soupspoon. 'It's not every day you're eighty-seven.'

'Eighty-seven?' William repeated indignantly. 'I'll have you know I'm going to be ninety-five.'

'Of course you are, how silly of me,' Eleanor said quickly. 'Blow on that soup, it's hot.'

'Daddy's birthday party is coming up,' Eleanor reported to her husband, but Dick hadn't spoken to her in fourteen years, ever since his car had skidded on black ice one February morning and landed him in a coma, so the only response she got was the wheeze of his ventilator, which as far as she could see was his stock reply to everything she said. You'd think he'd have shown a bit of interest in his father-in-law's birthday party.

'Daddy will be eighty-seven,' she reminded her husband a little sternly, and Dick wheezed gently in reply.

'My grandpa is having a birthday party,' their thirty-nine-year-old son Gerard told Patrick, who had come to French-polish Gerard's dining room table three months previously and never left. 'He has a party every year, and I always bake the cake. I'm thinking Zucchini and Hazelnut Sponge.'

'Wouldn't the nuts get stuck in his teeth though?' asked Patrick, who wasn't partial to zucchini, and who had gained seven pounds since moving in with Gerard. 'What about a nice Sour Cream Coffee Ring, or maybe the Lemon and Ginger Roulade again?'

Gerard's Lemon and Ginger Roulade had been the highlight of their recent Eurovision party.

'And of course lots of canapés,' Patrick added. Gerard had a wicked way with filo pastry, cranberries and goats' cheese – not to mention smoked ham, semi-sundried tomatoes and sweet cucumber pickle.

'The tulips are up early this year,' Gerard's forty-one-year-old widowed sister Veronica wrote to her only child Sophie. *'The pink ones are particularly splendid. Your great-grandpa's birthday party is coming up, not that you'll be able to come, of course, but he'd love it if you could – and so would I. Mrs Greybeard's cat was in the garden again this morning. I'd swear she's looking for a place to have her kittens.'*

'My great-grandfather is having a birthday party in two weeks,' nineteen-year-old Sophie said to Mother Superior. 'I was wondering if I might . . .' She trailed off, seeing the expression on Mother Superior's face. 'Of course I could just send him a card.'

'Sister Magdalene, as you know, we don't normally allow novices to leave the convent during their first six months,' Mother Superior whispered, having succumbed on the previous Tuesday to a nasty dose of laryngitis, which she was offering up for a special intention. 'However, as I assume your great-grandfather is quite advanced in years –'

'He'll be eighty-seven,' Sophie said – forgetting, once again, the golden rule about never interrupting Mother Superior. 'Sorry,' she added hastily, lowering her eyes to the wooden crucifix dangling from Mother Superior's giant rosary beads (which were a little unwieldy when it came to counting off the Hail Marys, but which served them admirably as belts).

'However,' Mother Superior repeated, her whisper containing a new note of irritated yet resigned martyrdom, 'in the light of your relative's advancing years, perhaps we might make a small exception, just this once.'

'Thank you, Mother Superior,' said Sophie humbly, wondering if she'd have to wear her white habit to the party, or if she could get back into the red halter-neck dress she couldn't bear to add to the charity-shop bag when she'd been getting ready to enter the convent. As she left Mother Superior's office she began murmuring the first of the ten Acts of Contrition that a vain thought demanded.

Eleanor bought her father a white shirt (collar size fourteen and a half) and a six-pack of Mint Aero. She wrapped them in paper printed with racing cars, and signed the card *Eleanor and Dick*, even though Dick hadn't contributed a cent towards his father-in-law's present for the past fourteen years. Still, you couldn't be petty at a time like this.

'So who's going to be there?' Patrick asked as he and Gerard tried to decide between a Harris Tweed tie and a pair of Galway Crystal martini glasses.

'Well,' Gerard replied, holding a glass up to the shop's fluorescent light and twirling it, 'my parents of course, since it'll take place in their house –'

'But you told me your father is in a coma,' Patrick said.

'Yes, but mother doesn't like him to feel left out,' Gerard answered. 'We'll cut the cake in his room and offer him a slice. It's all we can do really.' He sighed. 'Although he probably won't eat it.'

'No,' Patrick said faintly. 'And . . . the other guests?'

'My sister Veronica, who'll bring the champagne – well, the Jacob's Creek Sparkling – and possibly my niece Sophie, if she can escape from her convent.'

'Your niece is a nun?'

'Training to be. I wonder,' Gerard added, giving the glass another twirl, 'if we should get these for ourselves. They're really quite beautiful, and I think after all Grandpa would be happier with the tie. He's not what you'd call a martini kind of person.'

Veronica knit her grandfather a scarf in rusty orange, her favourite colour. Her needles clacked rapidly as she watched *Inspector Morse*, Hannibal's long wet nose buried, as usual, in her brown corduroy lap.

'You want your dinner, I suppose,' she said to him, and Hannibal woofed hopefully. 'Just wait till the ads, will you?'

Grandpa William didn't need another scarf – Veronica had knit him one for the past three birthdays; and anyway, he hardly ever went out – but it gave her something to do with her hands as Morse solved another grisly murder in sleepy Oxford. She always felt terribly self-indulgent just watching television.

Sophie waited until Sister Gabriel left the convent kitchen garden unattended, and then she quickly dug up a clump of mint and stuck it into a little terracotta pot she'd found in the ancient wooden shed at the bottom of the rose garden. You couldn't call it stealing, with Gabriel moaning constantly about the mint being so hard to control. Sophie was helping to tidy it up a bit, that was all. And Great-Grandpa

William had always loved a drop of mint sauce with his lamb, so she was keeping everyone happy.

'I've been given permission to go the party,' she wrote to her mother. *'Will you take my red dress from the wardrobe and give it a wash? 40 degrees, and a gentle spin and no iron. Did Mrs Greybeard's cat have her kittens yet?'*

It was all right about the dress. Mother Superior hadn't said anything about Sophie having to wear her habit. And she was so tired of white.

The day of the party dawned sunny and bright. The sky was a perfect blue, the clouds white and fluffy – right up to eight minutes past ten, when the sun disappeared and the heavens opened.

'Never mind,' Eleanor said to the birthday boy, mopping egg yolk from his chin. 'It wasn't as if we were planning to have a barbecue.'

'Barbecue?' snorted William. 'I should think not. Nasty new-fangled idea. Perish the thought. Barbecue indeed!'

But Eleanor had left the room by this, so William huffed into silence and gazed out at the wind-whipped, rain-soaked garden, and wondered if perhaps this year he'd get the present he'd always hoped for.

'Daddy is disappointed about the weather,' Eleanor told Dick, 'but he's bearing up. We got him a shirt, did I mention? Or rather,' she added pointedly, 'I got it, seeing as how I seem to do everything around here these days.'

Wheeze, wheeze, went Dick.

'That's right, pretend you don't hear me,' Eleanor said. 'I'm used to it. I got him Mint Aeros too, just in case you're interested.' She looked disapprovingly at her comatose husband. 'I suppose you'll be expecting some of the cake later on.'

'It's raining,' Gerard said, pressing angelica violets carefully into the coffee icing. 'I daren't wear my Versace.'

'What about your Paul Smith?' Patrick suggested, tying the belt of his paisley dressing gown. 'Much more weather-friendly – and single-breasted is so flattering. Not,' he added hastily, seeing Gerard's face, 'that you need to be flattered, of course. Want me to wrap the gift?'

'No, thank you,' Gerard answered icily, stabbing a prosciutto roll with a cocktail stick. 'I obviously need the exercise.'

Veronica folded the orange scarf and hunted in the kitchen drawers for a ribbon. Hannibal sat nearby, panting asthmatically. 'It's Grandpa's party today,' Veronica told him, pulling out another drawer and rummaging among the tape measures and candle stubs and clothes pegs. 'Do you think he'll like my scarf?'

But Hannibal, not hearing 'walk' or 'dinner', made no reply.

'It's not much,' Sophie said, zipping up the red dress, 'but it was all I could think of. There aren't too many opportunities to get a birthday present in a convent.'

'Darling, it's lovely,' Veronica replied. 'Great-Grandpa will be delighted with a little plant for his window.'

'Actually it's mint,' Sophie said, 'for his roast lamb.'

'Oh yes, of course it is.' Veronica didn't like to point out that William's doctor had advised him to give up red meat at his last check-up. 'How very practical of you. Now come out to the shed and see the kittens. Hannibal,' she added, looking sternly at the dog as they left the kitchen, 'try not to get up to any mischief.'

Hannibal wagged his tail, which could have meant anything.

The birthday cake was a big success with everyone except Dick, who showed no interest whatsoever in the slice they cut for him.

'He's probably just not hungry,' Eleanor told Gerard, to spare his feelings.

'That'll be it,' Gerard answered, thinking that his mother was definitely losing it, and hoping he and Patrick wouldn't have to take Dick and William in when she went completely gaga. 'Should we do the presents now, do you think?'

'Presents?' William asked in surprise. 'You didn't bring presents, did you? What do I want with presents, at my age?'

He'd been wondering when they'd get around to the presents.

'You shouldn't have,' he said to Eleanor, thinking of the five white shirts already hanging in his wardrobe. 'And Mint Aero, my favourite,' he added, recalling the heartburn he'd been getting lately whenever he ate chocolate. 'Thank you, my dear.'

'How nice,' he said to Gerard, trying to remember the last time he'd worn a tie, and resolving to overcome his aversion to lilac. 'Many thanks.'

'Splendid,' he said to Sophie, wondering what you did with mint when you no longer had any use for mint sauce. 'Just what I wanted.'

'Which just leaves me, Grandpa,' Veronica said, handing him a mobile phone.

'How thoughtful,' William said, never having had the slightest desire for a mobile phone. 'Very useful.'

'No, Grandpa, it's not the phone – look at the photo,' Veronica said. 'It's a photo of your present.'

And William peered at the screen, and fumbled for his glasses, and peered again. And slowly, his face began to crease into a million lines.

'It's a kitten,' he said softly. 'It's a black and white kitten.'

'It's yours,' Veronica said, 'or rather, it will be, when it's old enough to leave its mother. I had a scarf all ready for you, but Hannibal chewed it, and this was all I could think of to replace it. If you don't want it, I can get something else tomorrow.'

Everyone looked at William, but William was too busy gazing at the phone to notice. 'I always wanted a kitten,' he said. 'Every single birthday I hoped someone would give me one, and nobody ever did.'

'Until now,' said Eleanor, who couldn't help thinking about litter trays and cat hairs and puddles on her terracotta tiles. 'Isn't that lovely.'

'It's got a black moustache,' William said. 'I'll call it Groucho.'

'Maybe we should get a kitten,' Patrick said to Gerard, hoping he'd been forgiven for his earlier faux pas, because if Gerard threw him out he'd be heartbroken.

'It would have to be Siamese,' Gerard answered, hoping that their earlier squabble was forgotten, because if Patrick left he'd be heartbroken.

'By the way,' Sophie said to her mother, 'I've decided to leave the convent. I hope you don't mind.'

And Veronica, who'd missed her daughter desperately for the past six months, did her best not to burst into happy tears, and failed miserably.

'Hello?' a voice came faintly from the far side of the room.

They all rushed over to Dick, who was blinking in bewilderment. 'Where am I?' he asked, looking from one face to another.

'You're back,' smiled Eleanor, who'd only been cranky to hide her loneliness. 'Would you like some coffee cake?'

'It's my birthday,' beamed William. 'I'm one hundred and eight.'

Dick's pale face became slightly paler.

'Don't worry, he means eighty-seven,' Eleanor whispered. 'You've only been unconscious for fourteen years.'

'I see,' Dick said faintly. 'Maybe I'll have some of that cake now.'

'I got a kitten for my birthday,' William said. 'I got exactly what I hoped for.'

'Me too,' Gerard said, looking affectionately at Patrick.

'Me too,' Veronica said, looking fondly at her daughter.

'Me too,' Eleanor said, looking lovingly at her husband.

They all had seconds of cake to keep Dick company, and then they sang 'For He's a Jolly Good Fellow' twice, once for William and once for Dick.

'This has been my best birthday ever,' William said happily.

And so say all of us.

Anita Notaro

Anita Notaro is a television producer/director who left RTÉ in 2003 to write. Her fourth book, *Take a Look at Me Now,* won the Irish Book Awards Popular Fiction Book of the Year in 2008 and she has a new book, *No Ordinary Love,* out at the moment. She works occasionally as a director on RTÉ's *Fair City* and directs a few other projects just to keep her hand in. Her books have been translated into several languages and she is also published in the US.

With a Little Help from My Mammy **

Anita Notaro

I always thought I was afraid of hospitals and that's because my mother was terrified of anything medical – and that extended even as far as watching *ER* on telly. She was so scared of doctors that her four daughters were born at home and even then rumour has it that she only barely tolerated the midwife. When she was pregnant with me – her first-born – there were complications and she was told she'd have to go into hospital for observation. She flatly refused and simply carried on as normal. Because everything turned out okay, she felt justified. In fact, even way back then she decided that she knew medicine better than anyone, especially doctors. She adjusted her medication frequently as she got older, read the 'contraindications' that came with her pills the way some women read *Hello* magazine and diagnosed herself most weeks, usually with a rare tropical disease that none of us had ever heard of.

'If I ever get sick, don't tell me,' she told us over and over again, 'because the fright of having to go near a hospital for treatment would kill me anyway.' She meant every single word.

We laughed at her and told her that everyone has to go to the hospital at some point. 'Stop worrying about it, hopefully it will never happen and if it does you'll be fine,' we jollied her along.

When the time came, she wasn't and this was just as an outpatient! A year before she died she fell off a ladder (she was painting the ceiling) and fractured her wrist. I just about managed to get her to the doctor and even then she tried to insist that 'the nice girl in the chemist will give me tablets – that's all I need.'

'Your arm is swollen and deformed, tablets won't do it this time.' I tried to remain cheerful but stood well back, afraid she'd kick me in the shins.

The lovely Dr Mary Murnaghan said she'd need an X-ray. My mother refused point blank. My eyes were out on sticks as I silently pleaded for help from her doctor and we eventually reached a compromise and Mam agreed to come with me to a private clinic. Once there, they confirmed the diagnosis and whispered to me that she'd have to go to A&E for a cast. She clung to every car in the car park on the way out until a security man – who initially thought I was trying to kidnap her or something – intervened and helped me get her into mine. I locked the doors and headed for the nearest hospital, calling the entire family en route for back-up. Several times she tried to grab the steering wheel and turn the car around – on the M50 motorway! On arrival, we practically had to call the police to get her inside and by the time she was seen she was shaking so badly that they thought there was something else wrong.

It took a while before she forgave me but we were friends again long before the last time I saw her.

She waved me off from her front door one sunny Sunday evening, and the last thing she told me was that she loved me very much. Two days later my sister Jean and I called to visit her at lunchtime and found her dead, and somewhere in the midst of all that grief we found a minute to give thanks for the fact that the only time she ever found herself in an ambulance she knew nothing about it.

So I always assumed that I'd inherited her fear, but thankfully had never had to put it to the test until, less than a year later, I clutched my new husband's hand very tightly as I prepared to face my worst fear. I was to spend two days in hospital. And the visit came totally out of the blue.

You see, from the time I was in my twenties, I've found it very hard to examine my own breasts because to me they were, well, lumpy, I suppose. And they changed, depending on the time of the month. Also, two people I knew were diagnosed with breast cancer, one in her twenties and one in her thirties. So off I went to my GP who examined me and thought I was fine. For some reason I persisted and asked for a referral to a specialist. My mother thought I'd lost my marbles – going near a hospital when I didn't have to – and after a doctor told me I was healthy! She kept saying she didn't know where she'd got me.

A very kind consultant told me that my breasts were perfectly normal, but advised me that many women – just like me – found it very hard to self-examine because there were lumps and bumps which appeared and disappeared at various times of the month, so he suggested I have a proper check-up every two years if I had any concerns whatsoever. 'Start now,' he told me. 'Hopefully, you won't have any problems but if you do, early detection is vital.'

So I did as he advised, but as the years went by I felt a bit silly, to be honest. I thought I was wasting their time. And my mother nearly had me admitted to a hospital of a different kind – fearing for my sanity. No matter how hard she tried she could never fully understand anyone not 'leaving well enough alone' and only the fact that she loved me to bits kept her encouraging me – sort of.

Initially it was examinations and then ultrasounds and on my last visit I was due to have my first mammogram – four years ago – but I almost didn't go. I'd been to my GP for a routine health check and everything was perfect. Blood tests all came back normal, blood pressure was fine and on paper I ticked all the boxes. A breast examination revealed nothing. Still, I'd been keeping a check on my breasts for so many years now I felt I might as well continue. However, I forgot to ring the clinic and went off on holiday, came back relaxed and glowing and forgot all about it until one day as I sat at my desk the appointment card fell out of my diary. I decided it was a sign from my mother and rang immediately.

A week later, I was called back for an ultrasound. I wasn't really worried, assuring myself that I'd know if anything was wrong. Everything felt the same and I was in great shape. As soon as I was told I needed a biopsy, fear set in and I couldn't stop shaking. Everyone was so kind to me and so positive but the following thirty-six hours were truly awful as I waited for the results.

That was Wednesday and my appointment was for three o'clock on the Friday afternoon and an hour later as Gerry and I walked out into the warm September afternoon I was more scared than I'd ever been in my life. No lump, no pain, no symptoms whatsoever. I felt fit and healthy but I had cancerous cells. I needed surgery. I was about to experience hospital life and it wasn't a routine visit. I was diagnosed on Pink Ribbon Day.

'I'm here to check in,' I told the receptionist in a very high voice a week later. Maybe I was just wishing I was in a hotel.

'Em . . . my wife is being admitted,' Gerry explained, smiling at me, arm tightly around my waist to stop me shaking.

I waited for them to bring the wheelchair. They simply directed me to my room. When I needed an ultrasound, I expected to be whisked off on a trolley. The nurse cheerfully told me I could walk. Two hours later, in theatre, I was scared to go to sleep in case I didn't wake up and was definitely *not* going to count backwards from ten, under any circumstances. I'd seen that trick on *Grey's Anatomy*.

A smiling man asked me what I did for a living.

'I'm a writer,' I said proudly, 'and I'm just . . .'

Two hours later I woke up. Gerry told me I talked gibberish for a while and promptly fell asleep again. Next thing I remember was watching Pat Kenny on *The Late Late Show*, a programme I'd worked on for two years. This particular Friday night was a far cry from the ones where I'd whizzed around Studio Four, buzzing and happy.

A lovely nurse plumped my pillows and brought me tea and toast. Gerry held my hand and scoffed all the grapes. My consultant, Mr Enda McDermott, called to see me and told me he was very pleased. I felt safe and warm and slept like a baby all night. Forty-eight hours later I walked home, marvelling at how well I'd survived the experience. I couldn't believe it when they told me a couple of days later that I wouldn't need chemotherapy. All the prayers and candles had paid off and there were major donations due to various saints. It was the greatest lesson in faith and hope I'd ever had.

Not long after I'd fully recovered, I went hill-walking in Wicklow with Gerry and the dogs on a glorious summer Saturday afternoon. I felt in top form. I'd changed my car that morning and drove to Wicklow exploring all my delicious new gadgets, pressing buttons here and twiddling knobs there. I sweltered for the entire journey because I was determined to have my heated seat on – despite the temperature on the plush dashboard telling me it was 25 degrees outside. I stacked my CDs before I set off and sang my heart out all the way there, delighted with myself. An hour later, as I danced along the cliffs on the coast road near Brittas Bay, my leg went from under me on wet grass and shortly afterwards I was introduced to Ian and Sean.

Along with six hunky firemen they stretchered me off the cliffs and I had my first ride in a 'nee-naw'. I'd broken my leg in three places.

Another visit to the same hospital, another look at the theatre ceiling, another quick question and another few hours of my life lost forever, while the rest of the world mowed lawns and had barbecues. This time I didn't stroll home. Life as I knew it came to a full stop. I couldn't walk – obviously. My leg was, well what I was told was that I had a 'nasty fracture' and that meant a plate, pins, you name it. I couldn't settle at night, either. 'Sleep on your back with your leg raised,' they'd told me cheerfully in hospital. Impossible, I now realise. I couldn't shower. And I had to drink my tea at the counter top in the kitchen – ever tried carrying a cup of boiling liquid anywhere while hopping? And every time the phone rang it was at the opposite end of the room. In the first week, I invented new swear words. I could go on, but you'd die of boredom listening to my moans.

My friends kept me sane – and I'm not exaggerating. They shopped for me, brought me to the hairdresser's when I cried in frustration and toured the coffee-bars of Dublin with me in search of the perfect latte. Caroline, who doesn't drive, took a taxi to the shops and had it wait while she bought me organic vegetables so that I could keep juicing and 'stay healthy' – that gave me a laugh, anyway. I was a crock, in spite of all their efforts. On days when I managed to hobble anywhere, I discovered the world was divided into two types of people. The man coming out the bank just as I was trying to get in and who let the door close in my face was one type and the very old lady who carried my bag as I tried to get up an escalator to buy my husband a birthday present was the other. I learned another lesson, which was how much I took my life for granted. St Anthony's box groaned under the weight of my coins and St Rita would have been sick to death seeing me except that she was too far away in John's Lane church.

Six weeks later the plaster came off. There was talk of a crutch, or a special boot or something, as white coats floated about and made odd noises. I did a mammy on it and flatly refused. I even sounded like her as I told them they were not putting anything else near me.

'I'm worried you won't use the leg.' The consultant sounded weary.

I quickly decided he'd never spent even an hour of his life in plaster.

'Give me thirty seconds, then look out the window and watch me try to jump that wall over there,' I told him cheerfully and, just like my mother, I meant every word of it.

'Walking will be your physio,' he warned me, staring at my face for a few seconds as if trying to come to a decision. What he didn't know was that he was battling me *and* my mother all rolled into one, so he hadn't a hope.

'Well, let's see then, try and take a step towards me.' He held out his hand.

My leg felt like wobbly jelly and I was sure I couldn't put any weight on it, but the thought of not having anything to do with a hospital in the foreseeable future was the greatest incentive ever.

Okay, Mam, you've made your point, I told her silently. It's official. I hate hospitals too. Now get off your fluffy white cloud and help me get the hell out of here, I begged her, and gritted my teeth as I took a baby step forward, a jumble of arms and legs.

I don't know which of us was more surprised to find my leg worked, but I suspect it was me.

'Well done,' he beamed and signed the discharge. 'You've done very well, very well indeed. Someone up there must be looking out for you.'

If ever I'd doubted the power of a mammy, or that we all have a guardian angel, I was converted in that moment and now I ask for their help all the time. In fact, most of the time I'm such an optimistic, hopeful person that I drive everyone who knows me mad. I keep giving them reasons to be cheerful, no matter what happens. And I don't intend to be back with a doctor any time soon. And, Mam, you've made your point, so you can quit laughing at me!

Denis O'Brien

Denis O'Brien is one of Ireland's leading entrepreneurs, with extensive investments across several sectors. Denis founded Esat Telecom Group plc, and is also Chairman of the privately owned Digicel Group, which has operations in 32 markets. Outside of his extensive business interests, Denis is the Chairman and co-founder of Frontline, the International Foundation for the Protection of Human Rights Defenders. Based in Dublin, Frontline works to ensure that the standards set out in the UN Declaration on Human Rights Defenders are known, respected and adhered to worldwide. In 2000, Denis established The Iris O'Brien Foundation to identify and assist projects in Ireland and internationally which help disadvantaged communities.

Dust Yourself off and Get Going Again **

Denis O'Brien

Every country encounters difficulties at some stage or other in its history. Ireland's past is pock-marked with extremely turbulent periods. I often think of the Famine in the mid-19th century as the most traumatic time for the Irish nation in recent centuries. Millions died, bodies were left to lie and rot all over the country. Can anyone imagine the impact such sights had on fathers, mothers, sons and daughters as they watched helplessly as their loved ones breathed their last?

Such images are far from Ireland today. Yet as we endeavour to cope with the sharpest economic downturn in living memory . . . we are still a country that is rich. How, you may ask?

Let me digress for a few moments. Since January of this year the people of Haiti have had to cope with the truly shocking fallout from the earthquake. Here was one of the poorest countries before the earthquake. Imagine what it has been like since then . . . But in my frequent travels all over the world, the most striking feature of all is that where the people are poorest the children smile the most. The faces of young boys and girls light up the darkest situations with their curious smiles.

A country is rich when it has an educational system which is available and accessible. It is rich when parents make sacrifices to ensure their children get the academic access to match their ability and their ambition. Ireland is such a country.

Our own parents grew up in an impoverished Ireland where holidays were sacrificed and car ownership was forgone in favour of sons and daughters obtaining a proper education. Together with the religious, that generation are truly the parents of Ireland's emergence as a successful nation – renowned and respected throughout the world. And indeed it is an indictment of us all that many of our elderly are denied those services that are essential for them to enter the autumn of their lives with dignity and respect . . . rather than as some burden on our society.

Ireland's future will be vested in those young Irishmen and women who are currently recipients of the guidance and interest of this country's educational staff at national, secondary and third levels. The winning combination – and it is a winning combination – of committed parents and enthusiastic educational staff will see this country return to its rightful place – as a leading international player in the key sectors of business, entertainment and culture. We have a tendency to 'over egg' the good times and wallow in pity with our current predicament.

The economic problems are bad but it is the social and community impact of the situation that would concern me most. We will delay our recovery if we succumb to a belief the future holds scant promise. Remember how our parents buoyed us up when things were not working our way: pick yourself up, dust yourself off and get going again.

Young people are more ambitious, more positive and more idealistic than their elders and such traits should not be dented or displaced by their more cynical and more senior peers. More than ever, Ireland needs to invest in the next generation. And the best way for this to be achieved is to ensure that our educational system is geared to avail of the global opportunities that will present themselves in so many sectors and in so many places.

The Digicel experience has been an enormous education for me because I have found myself in countries in the Caribbean, Central America and the South Pacific where young local men and women have tremendous skills to take on any task. Invariably, I ask them about their schooling and more often than not they mention the name of an Irish nun or priest or brother who taught them.

Equally, the Irish who have journeyed with me as Digicel rolled out its services have a wonderful ability to take on any challenge and adapt to any situation. Yes, they work hard – and they can play that way too.

The countries that tend to achieve the most dramatic economic growth are those that have withstood natural disasters and wars. For example, look how Japan, South Korea and Vietnam achieved phenomenal growth in post-war periods. Remember when the only car an Irish person would buy was made in Britain or in Germany?

I believe that Haiti – with the appropriate supports from the government and the developed world – will emerge in the next few decades as a strong economic force. It has an abundance of natural resources and it has a young intelligent population.

One of the insights one gets when travelling abroad is that Ireland is still highly regarded as a country that has achieved so much in recent decades. Yes, we have made mistakes and we are suffering from a dramatic economic downturn, but we are too critical of ourselves.

We need to move on. We are not alone in the banking crisis and if we learn from the recent past we can emerge fitter, stronger – and better.

Lia Mills

Lia Mills is a novelist who also writes short stories and literary non-fiction. She is the author of two critically acclaimed novels: *Another Alice* and *Nothing Simple* (shortlisted for the Irish Book of the Year Award, 2006) and a non-fiction account of her experience of cancer, *In Your Face* (2007). Her short stories and essays have appeared in many publications, including *The Dublin Review*, *The Irish Times* and *The Stinging Fly*.

Under Weather *

Lia Mills

'You're not going out this morning, Mother. Are you?' There's
more exasperation than concern in Breda's voice as it clatters down
the phone.

May reminds herself that Breda has a lot on her plate. That
boring man of hers finally decided to do something interesting, and
upped and left her after twenty-five years, just last summer. Her
two daughters left home soon after, as if they were afraid to be
caught on the wrong side of the door when it slammed behind him.
As if that wasn't enough, she's been let go from her job in the
Trustees' Department at the bank, a job that has given her a pessimistic
outlook on life. 'People's affairs get into such a state, you've no
idea,' she says. 'And all of a sudden they're not able to take care of
themselves. The trouble it causes. You should be prepared, Mother.
No one ever thinks it'll happen to them.'

The same could be said of anything, May thinks. Redundancy,
for example. Or a marriage ending.

Poor Breda is nervy, of course she is. She has spent her entire
adult life looking after other people, and look where it's got her.
Rattling around on her own in a three-bedroom house on an estate
full of families with young children. While she was busy raising her
own, the neighbours she'd known had moved away.

'You need a hobby,' May says. 'Some kind of project. To keep
your mind off things.'

323

Until the hobby comes along, Breda is often cranky, as she is now. May has to be patient.

'Actually, I was just on my way –' May smiles into the receiver – it's an old trick, to soften the voice, defuse a row.

Breda never bothers with that kind of thing. If she's got something to say, she comes right out and says it. 'In this weather?'

May checks the window. A sky like smoke, but the trees are calm. 'It's not bad.'

'Yet, Mother. It's not bad yet. Didn't you hear the news this morning? There's a major storm on the way. Eighty-mile-an-hour winds. You've no business going swimming in that.'

'If I leave now, I'll miss it,' May says, in as firm a voice as she can manage. She replaces the phone, gently, in its cradle.

Breda means well, but really, she's like an old woman herself, the way she goes on. May keeps meaning to get one of those phones that tells you who's calling. Not that she'd stop answering Breda's calls altogether, of course she wouldn't. May is of a generation that respects the phone, its urgencies, its excitements, its surprises. She wouldn't dream of ignoring it when it rings. But she might not have picked it up this morning, when she was already halfway out the door, if she had known it was only Breda trying to stop her in her tracks. She checks the kitchen clock and *tsks* at her own foolishness. If she doesn't hurry, she'll miss the others.

When she gets to the harbour, Ruth and Joan are already in the water, doing the sidestroke, faces turned to each other. Frank hovers at the ladder. Sara is still getting undressed.

'There you are, May.' Frank winks at her. 'We thought you'd decided to spend the week in bed.'

Now that she's here to keep Sara company, he sets off down the ladder. Frank is a sweet man. Considerate, but not in a showy way.

May fumbles with the buttons of her lilac cardigan. Her fingers aren't as sure as they used to be. She folds the cardigan into her bag and pulls off her elastic-waisted trousers. Underneath, she's wearing her swimsuit. She tugs her swimming cap over her hair. It squeaks a little, pulls at the skin of her forehead. A sudden gust of wind knocks her bag over. She straightens it, pushes the trousers further in.

'Are you ready, Sara?' she asks.

Sara nods and stands up. Together they walk to the iron ladder. 'You go first,' Sara says. 'I'll be slower.'

May likes the pressure of knowing someone is above her on the ladder. It keeps her going, down into the cold slithery grip of the water. Otherwise, she might hesitate. She might even change her mind. There's always a split-second when she has to brace herself. But when she launches herself into the sea she feels a thrill. It's like the beginning of a flight, when a plane accelerates until the force of its own momentum drives it on up into the air. That commitment. No going back.

The water is a shock. First the cold slap of a wave, then immersion. The initial icy sting warms to a glow that spreads throughout her body. She swims steadily across the harbour and back again, feeling a thrill of pride. Seventy-three years old, but she can still do this. She turns onto her back and lets herself float. In the distance she hears a car-horn and feels a quick scorn for people who cushion themselves against the elements, ignore the magic resource of the sea right here on their doorstep. They don't know what they're missing.

Without movement, the cold seeps into her. She turns onto her front and swims a firm, determined breaststroke to the ladder.

Up on the quay, she towels herself dry. Frank uncorks a flask of brandy-laced coffee and passes it around. They all take deep swallows and watch Sara's slow progress back.

'I'd worry a little about our Sara,' Ruth says.

'She's getting slower,' Joan agrees.

May turns her back on them, makes a tent of her towel and wriggles into her clothes. She shivers, straightens, reaches for Frank's flask.

'Where's Sara?' she asks.

They scan the harbour. The water is empty except for the leaky rowboat that's always moored here.

May goes to the edge and looks down. Sara's purpled arm is hooked over a rung of the ladder, but she stays in the water, bobbing up and down with the slowly rising swell.

'Sara! Are you all right?'

Frank appears beside her. 'I'll go.'

He hurries down to Sara, says something, tugs on her arm. Then he slides into the water behind her. At last she comes up: one rung, then another. Frank, behind her, urges her on. His body covers hers, shields her from the rising wind. Like a lover, May thinks, wistful.

When they get to the top, May pulls Sara into her arms and holds the flask to her lips while Ruth and Joan rub her briskly with dry towels. Her teeth chatter. They don't talk until they have her dressed again.

'I'll get the car,' Frank says.

They all get in, even though the bar they go to is only a short walk away. They huddle around the fire with hot whiskeys and toasted sandwiches.

'That was close,' Ruth says.

May shoves her elbow into Ruth's side. Joan glares at her.

'Are you all right, Sara?' May says.

'Fine.' Sara has never been much of a one for chat.

'We're none of us getting any younger.' Ruth sighs.

Frank stretches his fingers. His joints crack like pistol shots. 'Where there's life, there's hope.'

The next day, May wakes with a hacking cough. She walks down to the harbour anyway. She knows full well that it's the easiest thing in the world to stay indoors, postpone these bracing encounters with the sea. But look at what she'd miss: after the shock of contact, the powerful rhythm of movement. The afterglow.

Some mornings when she stands at the top of the iron ladder she thinks how easy it would be to turn back. She could meet the others in the pub later. But it wouldn't be the same. She's afraid that postponement would quickly become a habit. First she'd blame the weather, then there'd be something else. Next thing she wouldn't want to leave the house. From there, it's a short step to staying in bed, turning her face to the wall. If she's not careful, she'll turn into one of those old people who sit so close to a fire they might as well be *in* the damn thing. Their thighs becoming varicose and scarred while they hoard the heat, letting their energy melt from them, like wax. Like Icarus, flying too close to the sun and plunging to his death in the infinite blue of the Aegean. What a glorious flight that must have been, before he fell.

Her mind roams contradictory paths these days, surprising her with the things it throws up, the flotsam and jetsam of her life. Like this morning, walking along the seafront, a road she has known since childhood. As she looks at the grey, sullen water and the heron, who stands on the rocks revealed by low tide, holding his wings out to dry, she is struck by a notion that her childhood self still passes up and down this road, seeing the same things; that her young-mother persona is also there, carrying buckets and spades and nets, bundling Breda and her brothers up and down from the beach, their pale legs thin as matchsticks. It seems to her that all her previous journeys up and down this road are still happening, she carries them inside her, like nested dolls. And she, May, is contained within future, unseen selves. Time is only a convention, she thinks. Our puny attempt to impose human logic on the unthinkable, mortality.

The others are there before her, except for Sara. 'Her back's at her again,' Frank says. 'She had to stay in bed.'

May's cough gets worse.

'You should go to the doctor,' Breda says.

'I'm fine.'

'Will you at least stop swimming?'

'Leave me alone!'

Sara comes back. She's slower, stiffer, but she gets herself down that ladder and into the water every day. Her face glows when she's dressed again, and her eyes are fierce when anyone asks how she is.

'If I'm here and I'm upright, there's no need to ask!' she snaps at Ruth one day.

So they all pretend not to notice that Frank stays closer to her than usual, walks behind her on the way to the car, makes sure she has a good seat in the pub, away from any draughts.

Every year, in October, May and Breda go into town on a shopping expedition. They make an afternoon of it. They drive in, in Breda's car – an indulgence that even May can justify because of the load of bags they'll carry home afterwards. May does all her Christmas shopping early, on this one afternoon. If she can't find gifts for everyone she resorts to vouchers. May hates shopping, it wears her out. She feels like a damp dishcloth by the time it's over. Breda might be a fusser, but she's a good person to shop with. She has a good eye, and she knows what the young people like.

So May is all dressed up and ready to go when Breda arrives, looking shifty.

May squints at her. 'What is it?'

Breda has the grace to look embarrassed. 'I've made an appointment for you with the GP.'

A fit of coughing gets in the way of May's reply.

'You see?'

Why does she have to sound so triumphant?

'That cough sounds dreadful. And you're flushed. You might have a temperature. Come on, Mother. Do this for me. We'll go shopping tomorrow.'

May could argue that she's flushed from swimming, or from the fire in the pub afterwards, but all of a sudden the fight goes out of her.

Dr Woods is new to the practice. He's a young man, with a shaving rash and a pimple on his nose. He speaks to May in a slow, distinct voice that's just a shade too loud.

'I'm not deaf,' she complains.

'Sorry,' he says, in a more normal tone. 'I'm a little concerned about your heart.'

'What? What is it?' Breda leans forward in alarm.

May wishes she'd stuck to her guns and said yes, actually, she *did* mind if Breda came in with her. But Dr Woods had said he thought it would be useful if Breda was there, that she'd remember the details later. As if May wouldn't. There's nothing wrong with my mind, is what she should have said.

'Your mother has an irregular heartbeat.'

'I've always had that . . .'

'And her colour . . .'

They both study May's face. She feels herself flush even more, with irritation.

'Her blood pressure is up. And there's that cough.' Dr Woods shakes his head and fingers his stethoscope. 'She should rest.'

'Hello? I'm still in the room, right here!' May waves her hands at them, trying for comic effect.

They don't laugh.

'You should rest,' he says. 'Take things easy.'

'She goes swimming every day,' Breda says. "In the sea."

'Well, that has to stop.'

He goes on about prescriptions and diet, a gentle walk every day, would Breda be able to manage all that? And Breda sighs and says yes, she'll manage. Then there's talk of diagnostic tests and stress levels.

When May told Breda she needed a hobby, this was not what she had in mind. The airlessness of the room gets to her and she drifts a little, until Breda shakes her arm and tells her that it's time to go.

It's raining when they come out of the building. The cool, fine water on her skin is so lovely that May closes her eyes and lifts her face, as to the sun. Next thing she knows, the world reels and dips, the ground rushes up to slap her cheek, and her wrist is on fire.

'Mother!' Breda's anguish is genuine. 'Are you all right?'

The spinning world slows and May registers where she is –

sprawled on the wet ground with bits of gravel jammed into her face, Breda calling for help and people bustling around, helping her to sit, telling her to 'take it easy now, slowly, slowly'.

Breda brings her to hospital. Her wrist is broken. Her face is black and blue, she has a gash on her knee that needs stitches. They plaster her wrist and keep her overnight for observation. She spends the night on a trolley in a draughty corridor, which is where the others find her, after their swim the next day.

'They take "observation" literally, don't they?' Ruth says. 'The world and his wife could keep tabs on you here.'

They keep having to move out of people's way, and from time to time her trolley is bumped by others on their way past, up to a ward or down to X-ray. When a nurse comes to take her blood pressure, the swimmers regroup around a vending machine. In a hospital environment, they look elderly and a little odd, with their untidy hair and their weather-beaten faces.

'All right? When can you go home?' they ask, when the nurse has finished.

'They keep asking if I lost consciousness before I fell. I only slipped. The steps were wet.'

'They won't want to admit that!' Sara snorts. 'In case you sue them.'

Later that afternoon, she's discharged. When Breda brings her home, she realises how tired she is. Just for once, it would be lovely to sink into the armchair, let Breda make tea and bring it to her on a tray.

'You should come and stay with me for a bit,' Breda says. 'It'll be hard for you to manage everything, with your arm in a cast.'

'No, I –'

'It'll be easier all round.' Breda looks up from the prescription, the small suit of appointment cards. 'Please. Let me look after you.

If it wasn't for me you wouldn't have been on those steps in the first place.'

May's cough settles in. She's in bed for days. When she gets up, her legs are as weak as a baby's.

'Sorry you're under the weather!' Ruth booms, when they come to see her. Her voice, strong enough to penetrate any wind outdoors, is too loud in Breda's front room.

Joan puts a bowl of fruit on the windowsill, where the colours come alive in the weak sunlight. Grapefruit and oranges, lemons and limes.

'Nothing like Vitamin C to get you up and about again!' Ruth roars. 'Don't be long! Even Sara is still at it, you know – and her back is banjaxed!'

Breda frowns. 'She can't possibly swim with her arm in a cast!'

'I'll come when my wrist is better.' May's voice is hoarse, as if she doesn't have quite enough wind to push it out through the channel of her neck. She closes her eyes.

When she opens them again, Ruth and Joan have gone.

The cast comes off a few weeks before Christmas, but then the fuss of preparation begins: the cooking and baking, the puddings Breda makes for her friends, jars of cranberry sauce. May finds it soothing to be surrounded by so much activity. She sits with her back to the window, calls out ingredients, blanches almonds, stirs the various mixes, but slowly. She's building up strength in her wrist.

Joan rings to see how she is. 'Will we pick you up on our way to the harbour?'

'No thanks. I still have a bit of a cold.' May gives a small, unconvincing cough. She doesn't say that the fall has made her fearful, that she shrinks from the force of the sea.

Breda's girls come home for Christmas dinner. They have a lovely day. May makes them cry with laughter, telling stories about Breda in her unruly, disruptive teens. When they've gone Breda sighs a deep, happy sigh.

'It's good to have them back, but quite nice when they leave again.'

'I'll be going soon, too.'

'No rush.'

One day in the new year, the phone rings. Ruth's voice booms out the bad news. May's blood hammers in her ears while she tries to sort out what she's hearing.

'Sara? Did you say . . . drowned?'

She gives the phone to Breda and sags into a chair.

When Breda hangs up, she urges May into the kitchen, brings her tea. 'Are you all right?'

'I can't take it in.' Even as she says this, an inner voice sneers, *oh yes you can, you can see it exactly.*

On Saturday, the day of the funeral, there is a crashing storm, the kind that would keep anyone out of the water, even in the whole of their health. The big chestnut tree in Breda's back garden swoops and slaps its bare fingers on the windowpane.

'It's lashing,' Breda says. 'Maybe you shouldn't go.'

'I'm going.'

'Wait a minute, then. I'll drive you.'

May had intended to walk, but she's glad of the lift. The wind is fierce and insistent. It whips around her ankles, tears at her coat, the scarf she's pulled over her hair, almost as if it's trying to rip her clothes off. She has to battle her way to the car.

'You've lost weight,' Ruth growls when they meet outside the church. Her eyes are red.

Joan sniffles into a handkerchief. May slips her arm through Joan's and they all go into the church together, while Breda parks the car.

'She did it on purpose,' Joan whispers from behind her hankie when they are settled in a pew, a couple of rows behind Frank.

'Shut up, Joan.'

'No, Ruth. This is May. We can tell her.' She puts her mouth close to May's ear and goes on. 'We were heading for the other wall, so we didn't see it. She told Frank to follow us – that she'd stay at the ladder. She promised she'd get out if she got cold. When we turned back she was heading out into the open sea. There was a sun that day, the sea was like glass, it was glorious! You must remember what that morning was like.'

May is too ashamed to say that she hasn't been aware of that sort of morning for a while.

'The water was dazzling, like handfuls of fire-opals,' Joan says.

'Frank thinks the light felt like warmth to her, and she followed it,' Ruth says. 'We tried to go after her, but she disappeared.'

'And you think she did it on purpose?'

'Oh May, you hadn't seen her. She'd been in pain for weeks, could hardly walk. She said she felt free in the water. Weightless. She had an appointment in the clinic next week. She was dreading it.'

'It wouldn't be the worst way to go,' Ruth says.

It wouldn't, May thinks. So what's she afraid of? She looks around the church at the mourners. When she was younger she used to wonder how older people feel at funerals, as one by one their friends begin to die. What they think about. But now she and her friends have become those older people. Ridiculous. In her mind she's a teenager, eager for all life has to offer.

She gets a lump in her throat when she sees Breda's daughters, in a pew on the other side of the church. They're there for her. They smile at her, sympathy in their faces. She smiles back. The young have their moment in the full light of the sun, she thinks, but do they know it, at the time? She hopes they do. She's in a moment too; a moment of a different kind, but a moment nonetheless.

The storm wears itself out, passes over, leaving the world washed and new. Later that afternoon, May asks Breda to bring her to the harbour. The tide is full, the harbour brimming, alive with luminous water. Hard to resist. She walks to the very edge of the quay.

Breda hovers nearby. 'Be careful. The stone is uneven. You could trip.'

'I can swim, Breda. I'm a good swimmer.'

'I know you are.'

'Then please – stop fussing.'

A hurt, resentful silence spreads between them.

'D'you know, I think I'll go home today,' May says quietly. 'You've been generous, Breda, but it's time I got back to my own life. Time you got on with yours.'

Breda looks as if she might cry.

'It's been lovely, staying with you. I've enjoyed your company. But I can't have you fretting at my every step.'

May's not a bit surprised when Joan and Ruth appear in the distance. What better way to see Sara out than to swim together?

Their faces break into wide smiles when they see her. 'Yoo-hoo!' Ruth shrieks. 'Are you getting in?'

'I don't have my things.'

'Lucky! I brought a spare!!' Ruth pulls a pair of togs out of her bag and waves them, like a flag.

It starts to rain again, but gently, as if the air is liquefying, one state becoming another.

'It's raining!' Breda says. 'You're not really going to go in, Mother, are you?'

May touches her daughter's face, with affection. 'Why not?' she says. 'One way or another, you get wet.'

'The water is warmer in the rain,' Joan says. 'You should try it! Come in with us.'

Breda shivers and shakes her head. 'Not my thing.' She pulls up the hood of her coat. She gives her mother a despairing look. 'I'll wait in the car.'

'I won't be long,' May says.

She strips off her clothes and pulls on Ruth's togs. The sea gleams in front of her, full and inviting, drawing down fine needles of rain. It's hard to make out where sky gives way to water, where water becomes sky. The harbour brims, blue and luminous. A slow, sensuous swell shrugs like a shoulder along the harbour wall. Together they run, bare feet slapping stone, to the water's edge. Laughing, they catch hold of each other's hands and keep running.

∽ ∾

Sinead Moriarty

Sinead Moriarty was born and raised in Dublin. Her mother is an author of children's books. Growing up she was inspired by watching her mother writing at the kitchen table. At the age of thirty, while working as a journalist in London, she began to write creatively in her spare time and produced *The Baby Trail* and it was snapped up by Penguin in the UK and Ireland and has, to date, been translated into twenty languages. Sinead's books include *A Perfect Match* (published worldwide), *From Here to Maternity*, *In My Sister's Shoes* and *Whose Life Is It Anyway?* Her latest book, *Pieces of My Heart*, was published in August 2010.

In My Sister's Shoes *

Extract from her novel of the same name. (PENGUIN)

Sinead Moriarty

I woke up the next morning to my brother Derek banging on my bedroom door. Peeling my face from the pillow I shouted at him to go away.

'Yo, Mark's on the phone.'

'Tell him to fuck off.'

'He sounds kinda freaked.'

'Tough.'

'He said Fiona's locked herself in the bathroom and won't come out.'

While I had no intention of helping my selfish brother-in-law Mark out, if my sister Fiona needed me I would. Ungluing my eyes, I shuffled over and unlocked the door. Derek handed me the phone.

'Yes?' I grumbled.

'Kate I need you to come over. Fiona won't come out of the bathroom and I can hear her crying in there.'

'So deal with it, she's your wife.'

'She won't talk to me and the twins are getting upset. Maybe she'll talk to you. She sounds very distressed.'

'She has breast cancer, of course she's upset. Welcome to reality, Mark.'

'Can you save the jibes for later and please come over.'

I was tempted to leave him alone and let him deal with his family issues himself, but I could hear Bobby crying in the background and I was worried about Fiona.

'Fine, I'll be over in ten minutes,' I said, hanging up.

I washed my mascara-streaked face and threw on my jeans and sweatshirt. On the five-minute drive to Fiona's I almost crashed the car twice as I remembered the holy show I'd made of myself the night before. How could I have misread the situation so badly? I couldn't believe I'd made such an obvious pass at my ex-boyfriend, Sam. Oh God, it was toe-curling humiliation. Could my life possibly get any sadder – jobless, chubby, penniless and now social reject?

When I got to the house, the twins came running up to me.

'Mummy's crying and she won't come out,' they said in unison.

'Don't worry, she's probably just a bit sick from the nasty medicine,' I tried to reassure my five-year-old nephews. 'Now you go and brush your teeth and wash your hands and I'll go and talk to your mum. OK?' I ushered them into the bathroom and went to find Mark.

He was talking to Fiona through the keyhole. Teddy was sitting beside him scratching the door with his paw and whimpering. For once, Mark looked pleased to see me – well relieved at least.

'Thanks for coming, she won't talk to me,' he said.

'Fine, go and take the boys out to the park or something. I'll call you later.'

Kneeling down in front of the door, I tapped lightly.

'Hey Fiona it's me, are you OK?'

I could hear her crying but she didn't say anything.

'Do you feel awful? Are you having a panic attack? Because freaking out right now would be extremely normal.'

Silence.

I lay down on the floor and put my eye up to the bottom of the door. I saw her holding a clump of hair.

'Oh Fiona, is your hair falling out? Is that it? You poor thing, is it bad? Can I come in and look? I'll get a scissors and we'll fix it up. Come on, there's nothing we can't sort out.'

Silence, but a lot more crying.

'If it makes you feel any better I made a pass at Sam last night and after ricocheting off his seat in repulsion, he told me he was seeing a young one from the office. My face is still bright red from the shame of it. Come on, open up and let me hide in there with you. I'm a danger to myself.'

The lock clicked and my sister's blotchy face peered out.

'Has Mark gone?'

'Yes.'

She sighed and pulled the door back, putting her hand protectively over her head as she did. Clumps of her hair lay on the floor.

'It started falling out in the shower and then I combed it and voilà!' she said, taking her hand down and revealing a large bald patch on the right side of her head. She looked so sad and vulnerable I reached out to comfort her, but she stepped back. Clearly I was a leper at the moment, no man or woman wanted me anywhere near them.

'What am I going to do? I look like a freak. I don't recognize myself. What have I become, look at me,' she sobbed, really letting her anguish out for the first time since the diagnosis.

'Come on Fiona, don't say that. OK, the hair loss is a really rotten thing to happen, but you're still you, you're still gorgeous. We can fix this. You just need to shave it off. We'll go out and buy amazing hats and bandanas and wigs. It'll be fun.'

'Fun! I'm a bald thirty-five-year-old mother of two, with lopsided breasts whose husband hasn't gone near her in almost a year. Mark's going to run a mile when he sees my bald head. I know he doesn't find me attractive anymore and I don't blame him, I'm hideous. There's no hope for me.'

'Don't you dare say that! Now listen to me,' I said, grabbing her by the shoulders and shaking her. 'You are the most amazing person I know. I've looked up to you my whole life. You are an incredible wife, mother, sister and daughter. Your hair – or lack of it – does not make you any less beautiful. Now put some clothes on, we're going shopping.'

While Fiona got dressed I called Derek and asked him to get his mate, Gonzo, to come over with his head shaver.

'Dude,' said Derek when he saw Fiona, 'You can't be going around like that. You look like someone's attacked you with a blunt scissors.'

'I'm well aware of how appalling I look, thanks, Derek.'

'I think you need a number two,' said Gonzo. 'It'll be cool – you'll look like Sigourney Weaver in *Aliens*. She looked pretty sexy.'

'Or Demi Moore in *GI Jane*,' I added as Fiona did her best to smile.

Gonzo plugged in his razor. 'Don't sweat it, Fiona, I'm good at this. Plenty practice,' he said, pointing to his own tightly shaved head.

'Well, I can't look worse than I already do, so fire ahead,' she said, trying not to cry.

Gonzo gently and carefully shaved her head and turned her around to admire his handiwork.

'Good job,' Derek high-fived his friend. He was relieved to see that his sister now looked like a punk instead of an old woman with thinning hair.

Fiona took a deep breath and looked in the mirror. 'It's not as bad as I thought. I still look like hell, but I'm glad it's all off,' she said, fighting back tears.

'Anytime you need a top up, just let me know,' said the newly appointed Vidal Sassoon.

I looked at Fiona's bald head. There was something incredibly lonely and sad about it. It was as if her cancer was now a badge. With no hair, everyone would know she was sick. When she walked down the street, people would stare, she'd never be able to say 'I'm great thanks, how are you?' to anyone she met. It was as if she had an – I HAVE CANCER – sticker plastered across her forehead. She looked sick too. It was so much easier to pretend everything was going to be OK when she looked like her old self. But the image staring back at us was that of a sick person. A cancer victim.

'Well, I'll be off,' said Gonzo.

'WAIT!' I shouted. 'Do me.'

'What?' he asked, looking confused.

'Shave my hair off too.'

'No way,' said Fiona.

'It's my hair, my decision and I want it off,' I said, grinning.

'Awesome idea, me too,' said Derek.

'I will not allow you to do this,' said Fiona.

'It's got nothing to do with you, so sit down and be quiet,' I said, already in *GI Jane* mode. Grabbing the kitchen scissors I chopped my ponytail off as Fiona stared at me in shock. It felt fantastic. I was getting a huge adrenaline rush from doing this for my sister.

Gonzo set to and within half an hour Derek and I were as bald as badgers.

'You look hot,' whispered Gonzo in my ear and then proceeded to nibble it.

For once I didn't swat him away or insult him. I knew what it was like to be rejected. So I tried to gently pull my head away, but then he shoved his tongue into my ear, so I thumped him.

'News flash,' Gonzo, women hate having a tongue shoved down their ear,' I snapped.

Gonzo and Derek looked at each other. 'Seriously?' Gonzo asked, looking put out. 'I thought chicks really dug that.'

'Well this one doesn't,' I said. Even in my current male-famine, it still did nothing for me.

Derek looked at Fiona. She shook her head. 'Sorry guys, I'm not a fan of the tongue in ear either.'

Gonzo slouched out of the house to his car.

As Derek went to follow him, Fiona stopped him. Looking down at the floor she said, 'You both know I'm not very good at the whole emotions thing, but what you just did means . . . means . . .' She broke down.

Derek patted her on the shoulder. 'I get it that you're grateful. It's no biggie. Gotta fly. I need to get some lyrics down for my gig next week. *Adios, muchachas.*'

It was just me and Fiona and I suddenly felt awkward. I didn't know what to say and I could see that she was struggling with her emotions. She wanted to say so much, but it was too overwhelming.

343

'Kate, I –'

'Hey,' I said gently. 'I know, and you're welcome and it's really no big deal. Now come on, let's get this mess cleared up and then pick up the boys.'

Fiona was afraid of scaring the boys, so I said I'd pick them up and show them my bald head first and then they wouldn't be so frightened when they saw hers. I pulled the mirror down in the car to look at my new hair for the first time. The person looking back at me was a total stranger. I began to shake. Oh God, what had I done? I looked like a freak. It was terrifying. I began to panic. Would I ever look nice again? How long would it take to grow back? How long before I could go out in public without people staring at me and crossing the road to avoid me? I was a cross between a skin-head and a cancer patient. My hair had always been my best feature. Why oh why had I been so impulsive? I looked horrible. I suppressed the urge to wail. I had done the right thing. It had meant a lot to Fiona. After all what was the big deal? It wasn't as if I had a job that required me to look good or a boyfriend that I wanted to seduce. Gulping back the sobs that were threatening to escape, I tried not to think about the fact that my hair would take years to grow back and that no man would ever fancy me again.

'Where's your hair?' asked Bobby, wide-eyed, when he saw the alien that had once been his aunt.

'In the bin,' I said as casually as I could. I wondered if I could take it out of the bin and bring it to a shop to have it stuck back on. They could do wonders with hair these days. 'I decided to shave it off. What do you think?'

'You look scary,' said Jack, giggling nervously. 'Like an Alien.'

'Well, boys, Mummy's hair is the same and so is Uncle Derek's. We all cut our hair off.'

'Why?' asked Bobby.

'Because we wanted to look like Kojak.'

'Who's Dojak?' asked Bobby.

'Bob the Builder's dad,' I said, pulling it out of thin air. I was getting good at this.

'Bob doesn't have a dad,' said Jack looking confused. 'He has Scoop the Digger, Dizzy the Cement Mixer and . . .'

'Pilchard the Cat and Wendy and JJ,' shouted Bobby.

'And Roley the steam roller, but no dad,' added Jack.

'OK, well, maybe that's because Bob's dad, Kojak, lives in America.'

'Oh,' said the twins.

'Where does Bob live?' asked Bobby.

'In England,' I said.

'Is that where you used to live?' asked Jack.

'Yes, you clever boy, it is.'

'But you live with granddad now,' said Bobby, not wanting to be shown up by his brother.

'Exactly,' I said.

'Can I touch it?' asked Jack, reaching up to feel the scalp that was formerly my lovely hair.

'Sure.' I knelt down so the boys could feel it. They squealed with delight as they touched my fuzzy head.

'Cool,' said Jack. 'I want one.'

'When you're grown up you can.'

'I want it now,' whined Jack. 'I want to be like Bob the Builder and Mummy and Uncle Derek and Dojak.'

'Me too, me too,' said Bobby, slapping my head.

'First of all you have to let your hair grow and then when it's finished growing, when you're eighteen and you have a good job like Bob the Builder you can have it all cut off. But not now. Besides I don't think Mrs Foley would let you go to school with no hair.'

'Is Daddy bald too?' asked Jack.

'No, sweetheart, but I think we should ask him to cut his hair off tonight when he comes home,' I said, grinning at the thought of Professor Mark Kennedy shaving his head.

⸜⸝ ⸜⸝

Joseph O'Connor

Joseph O'Connor is the author of seven novels and a number of bestselling works of non-fiction. He has also written award-winning film scripts and stage-plays. His novel *Star of the Sea* sold more than a million copies in 38 languages. *Star of the Sea* also won several international literary prizes. Joseph was recently voted 'Irish Writer of the Decade' by the readers of *Hot Press* magazine. He broadcasts a popular weekly radio diary on RTÉ's *Drivetime with Mary Wilson* and writes regularly for the *Guardian* Review and the *Sunday Independent*. His latest novel, *Ghost Light*, was published in June 2010 to great critical acclaim. It quickly made the No. 1 slot on the bestsellers list – and stayed there for several weeks.

The Courage of Being a Father **

Joseph O'Connor

Every Father's Day I find myself remembering a poem I first heard when I was five or six. It's the famous extract from *Idylls of the King*, by the great Victorian, Lord Tennyson, and it tells the mythical story of King Arthur's death. Fatally wounded in battle, the king beseeches his faithful knight, Bedivere, to take the magical sword Excalibur and cast it into a nearby lake. But the sword is so beautiful that the poor knight can't bring himself to be rid of it.

There drew he forth the brand Excalibur,
And o'er him, drawing it, the winter moon,
Brightening the skirts of a long cloud, ran forth
And sparkled keen with frost against the hilt:
For all the haft twinkled with diamond sparks,
Myriads of topaz-lights, and jacinth-work
Of subtlest jewellery. He gazed so long
That both his eyes were dazzled, as he stood,
This way and that dividing the swift mind,
In act to throw: but at the last it seemed
Better to leave Excalibur concealed
There in the many-knotted waterflags,
That whistled stiff and dry about the marge.
So strode he back slow to the wounded King.

Instead, he hides it in the rushes and returns to his dying master, lying to him that he has followed his orders. In the end, after three tries, he finally does as he was told, and the hand arises from the lake, dragging Excalibur down. It's an astonishing moment, but also a powerfully poignant one, for it's an image that speaks to something very deep in us: the pain of saying goodbye, moving on. The language is sumptuous, haunting and strange, but the main reason I love the poem is personal.

My father, Seán, a lover of Victorian poetry, would read it to me at night when I was a child. So I associate the happiness of those memories with something in the poem. It was part of my childhood, and whenever I read to my own sons, I feel the poem connects me to the past as well as to the future. And I feel my father's presence in the room.

Seán, my father, was born in the Liberties of Dublin, a place that means a great deal to him still. It was a place of stubborn independence, of trade and commerce of one kind and another, of survivors, adapters and realists. Seán's mother, as a child, had seen the black bunting draped from the tenements in commemoration of those hundreds of her neighbours who had died in Britain's armies. From Bloemfontein and Spion Kop and Gallipoli and Suvla, from countless unpronounceable battlegrounds of empire and its desires, many sons of Francis Street had never wended home. As a child, I used to imagine their phantoms walking the Liberties, along with the ghost of King Arthur.

Seán started work at the age of twelve, in a Dublin engineer's office, located in one of those crumbling Georgian townhouses of which the city still has a great plenitude. Once inhabited by the well-to-do, many were sold come Independence, as their proprietors removed to more amenable locations, and some were simply abandoned to the weather. I find it haunting to think of him, a boy not yet old enough to shave, on his walk through the pre-dawn streets of his town, past the chapels and the pawnshops, past the curtained facades, to that house of lost prosperities and cracked old plaster, where he would let himself in, the first to arrive, and build and light a fire against the damp. That is my picture of my father in childhood. A boy greatly loved, working to help his family, alone in that house, his hand on its banisters, his footfalls on its floorboards, his body moving slowly through its spider-webs and spectres, as he waited for his life to begin. The smell of mattering finished, on the landings, on the staircase, and the stucco discoloured by time. The knife-grey light of the Dublin dawn, glimpsed through the bones of the fanlight over the door. Were there moments, I have wondered, when he imagined a future: a girl, perhaps; a family of his own? Was I somehow there with him, as the coals glowed in the grate of a child's hopes and the rain smacked the windows outside? That is my picture of many of our fathers. Strong, tough, loving, hard workers. We might need their spirits these days.

What might be gleaned from books – this was always his fascination, as he worked to help support his family. It was a curiosity he shared with the beautiful girl he would marry, who was complicated, eloquent, mercurial, gifted, a trainee dress-designer, a reader. Yeats writes that Maud Gonne had 'beauty like a tightened bow' and my mother in her youth had something of that willow-sprung hauteur and something of that unpredictability too. They had arguments and makings-up, went cycling and I think dancing, attended the theatre and concerts, loved music. I know *Long Day's Journey into Night* was one of their dates. They married in their early twenties.

My father studied endlessly, did exams, worked by day. In time he qualified as an engineer, began a practice in Dublin, consisting, as I remember it, of my father and one secretary. Often, at the weekends, he would visit a building site someplace, taking me with him as he compiled a report. We would wander those deserted hives of concrete and steel, making measurements among the brick-ends and gutterings and flues, a battered yellow cement-truck observing our wanderings like God keeping watch on the faithful. And I remember doodling at his desk in his office while he worked, a comradely, companionable feeling between us, like the flow of underground water. He worked in every county in Ireland, in the Republic and in the North. He went where the work was, as he always had since his childhood. That's what Francis Street people did.

Churches, schools, office-blocks, factories – they formed themselves on the drawing board he kept at the house. Often, when I went to bed, he would be working at that board, in shirtsleeves and tie, his restless eyes wearying. And often in the mornings, as I readied for school, he would be there again, measuring angles, drawing columns, so that it seemed to me, as it may have seemed to him, that he had worked all night for his family. He sang as he shaved, little nonsenses or love-songs, or the skipping chants learned in his Liberties childhood, and he asked me the irregular verbs of the Irish language as he drove me to school every day. Of such tender observances is fatherhood made. And he would read to me a while before I slept.

His taste was for the Victorian, those old-fashioned poems and epics to which he had been introduced by Brother Thomas Devane, in Francis Street School in the Liberties. And I can never read Tennyson without hearing my father's beautiful Dublin voice, its inflections and subtleties, its colour and hesitance, and its peakings and fallings away. Calming as a hearth on a rainy night, it was a voice that opened worlds, speaking of possibilities, of language, and the counterpane saw empires arise and slowly fall by nothing but a father's solidarity. It was how I had learned to read, or certainly why I wanted to; his finger tracing capitals on a yellowed old page, by the light of a lamp that was shaped like a toy soldier, bought by my parents on a London holiday. The words were a comfort to me, certainly, but now I am a father myself, I can see they must have comforted him, too.

Every Father's Day, I read that poem again: the 'Morte D'Arthur', from Tennyson's *Idylls of the King*. I look at it as though I expect it will somehow have changed, but the words on the page never do, of course. Arthur, fatally wounded, is still dying near the lake and he wishes to be rid of his sword. The false knight, Bedivere, still cannot fling it away, despite his orders and the honour of his code. The poem is all about his reluctance, the humanity of his weakness. It says the world is full of troubles, incomprehensible evils, wolves in sheep's clothing, lost battles, dead hopes, and all we have to counteract them is one another in the moment, and all else is gaudy illusion. In these times of economic challenge, the poem seems even stronger. It says our beautiful trinkets are only gaudy baubles, and that they will be thrown from us, to be grabbed by the brandishing hand of fate and drawn back to the depths they belong to. There is no destiny waiting, no preordained path to safety. It is only that those we love become that destiny; it is simply a matter of being true to them. In that sense, finally, it is a poem about fatherhood. It is a poem about love and courage.

My father is seventy now. He reads every day. He retired from his work in 2002. An engineer, then a lawyer, an activist, an arbitrator, by the time he retired he had worked five decades and more, finishing his career by managing the structural design for the new wing of Dublin's National Gallery. For me, it is one of the most beautiful recent buildings in my city. My father says he intends to haunt its corridors. I thought he would find it difficult to leave a working life behind, but he has never returned to the office and says he doesn't miss it. He likes to read poetry, short stories. He is a lover of music. And a friend of mine, a lawyer with an office in the Liberties, tells me he has seen my father now and again going into a café on Francis Street, where he sits with a book, sometimes gazing out through the windows at the world that was once his childhood.

My eldest son, aged nine, was recently in a children's production of Dickens's *A Christmas Carol*. He played one of the urchins, Tiny

Tim's brother, a role that required a costume of photogenic raggedness. 'It's great fun being poor!' he chirped to me as he rehearsed, dancing in his tatters, pointing gleefully to his patches. The perfect innocence of a nine-year-old's laughter. '*I wish we could be poor all the time*!'

I thought about my father, at the age of my son, standing in Francis Street, perhaps with his mother – the two of them silent as the people passed by, or pushing a pram through the rain. I felt close to my nine-year-old father; grateful for his strength and courage. The child is father to the man.

∽ ∽

Vanessa O'Loughlin

Writer and mum of Sophie (10) and Sam (6), Vanessa O'Loughlin is the director of Inkwell Writers Workshops. Inkwell's aim is to bring new writers closer to publication through their one-day workshops (facilitated by bestselling authors), newsletter and range of services. The credits in many new books attest to Inkwell's success. Vanessa is also involved in organising the international One Stop Self Publishing Conference (*www.onestopselfpublishing.com*) and is the driving force behind *www.writing.ie*.

Every Second Counts: Kyra's Story **

Vanessa O'Loughlin

I'm lucky. I was lucky the day Robyn was born, a healthy 7lb 6oz, and, I'm convinced, already smiling. I was lucky the day I put the kettle on when she was sixteen months old, but didn't wait for it to boil. I was lucky that I heard a sound, like the TV remote hitting the floor maybe, or a toy falling, and went to investigate. Lucky that I didn't wait a second, finish what I was doing before going to see what was up. Because, that day, seconds counted. Every single second.

It was a Thursday, about five o'clock. August. A beautiful sunny day, all the windows open, the birdsong loud even inside the kitchen, dust particles fairy-dancing through beams of sunshine. Our accountant had popped over for a chat with my husband who was on his way home from work early to meet him. He was sitting in his shirtsleeves at the kitchen table and I was just putting the kettle on as Robyn ran into the living room to play. We laughed, she had only just learnt to walk, was still tottering, delighted with her new-found freedom, had greeted him with a pirouette in her new summer dress and a cheeky *hi-ya*.

Even today I still don't know what made me rush to her. She's my first-born so I was as protective as any first-time mum, but little ones make lots of noise when they're playing, and the odd crash certainly wasn't unusual. But that day something was different. There was a silence after the crash that wasn't normal.

Before I reached her I knew something was dreadfully wrong. She was lying on her back beside the fireplace, her long dark hair tumbled across the floor, a blue duck egg of a bruise already appearing on her forehead. Shaking all over, she looked like she was having a fit, hands clenching and unclenching like a pulse. And she wasn't breathing. I tried to stick my finger into her mouth, thinking she was holding her breath, an old trick. No go. Before my eyes she began to turn blue, her soft brown eyes open, glazed, unseeing.

I screamed. Scooping her up into my arms I ran screaming back through the kitchen, instinctively heading for my dad who was in the stable yard washing his car. Whenever I think about that day, I thank God that I wasn't alone. My husband had just arrived, met me in the yard and immediately took Robyn into his arms, laying her on one of the garden tables, trying to clear her airway. Years before he'd done a first aid course, practised on a doll not much bigger than our baby. And as my dad called an ambulance, Henry started CPR.

I ran for my own phone trying to call my brother (a junior doctor) and my uncle (a GP). I couldn't even focus on the numbers, let alone make the calls. I'm normally the cool one in a crisis, but not today. Our accountant tried to calm me, made me stand still, control my breathing. But it wasn't any good. And as a breeze picked up clouds of dust in the yard, the dogs running around yapping wildly, reacting to our stress, Henry continued to work on Robyn.

But I'm lucky. Lucky my husband was there, lucky I wasn't on my own in the house. Lucky Henry knew how to do CPR. Lucky he got her breathing again. Lucky my dad was there to dial 999. Lucky an ambulance was on its way to another call, was already halfway to our house, able to prioritise our call.

We live right on the N11. The paramedics were at Robyn's side in I'd guess about three minutes. Bags open, equipment spilling over the cobbles, two professionals bending over her. A rapid assessment of what had happened. No time for pleasantries, no time for hypothesis. Oxygen mask on.

She was still shaking violently.

I remember them lifting her tiny body like a ragdoll onto the stretcher, me scrambling in behind her. Then the doors slamming, the sound of tyres on gravel, the smell of disinfectant. I gripped her hand tighter. Sirens on. Four minutes to Loughlinstown Hospital. She needed to be stabilised before she could be taken anywhere else.

Robyn was violently sick in the ambulance, inhaling the vomit under the mask. But that was the least of our problems. The nightmare was only beginning. I felt so totally useless, talking to her, cradling her cold hand in mine, my eyes fixed on her face, on her blank lifeless eyes, willing her to fight, willing her to come back from wherever she had been taken. Could she even hear me?

With no paediatric speciality at Loughlinstown it took the emergency team who waited for us what felt like an age to find a vein. We watched as they cut off her new dress, trying her feet, arms, groin and even shaving off her beautiful hair to try her scalp, but with so little oxygen in her system, the veins were closing. And she was only sixteen months. A baby with tiny baby veins. She moaned at every attempt, feeling the pain, lost and confused somewhere where we couldn't reach her. Eventually an anaesthetist was called from theatre and managed to get a line in. We both breathed a shaky sigh. An hour and a half later she was heavily sedated, stable enough to move to a paediatric hospital.

But there were no Intensive Care beds available in Crumlin or Tallaght so they couldn't take her. Standing in the heat of the corridor, burying my head in my husband's chest, gripping his arms, I stamped my foot in frustration, screaming into his shirt. What could we do? I didn't care if she was on a trolley for a week once she was somewhere where they could treat her. How could this happen? How could they have no beds? She was a baby for God's sake, she'd fit under someone's desk.

Then the call came that Temple Street had a bed.

With the anaesthetist from Loughlinstown and the emergency transfer team on board there was only room for one of us in the ambulance. Henry went with her. I felt like a failure, but I couldn't do it, felt like he was holding it together, would be more use to her than I could be. So I missed the drama that was to unfold on the way.

With our baby hooked up to a confusing array of equipment, Henry held her hand, the reassuring pip of the heart monitor giving him something to focus on as the medical team chatted about mundane things, the weather, the soccer, anything to keep him calm. The summer evening traffic was relatively light ahead of them, clearing as they headed for Blackrock. It was one of those sticky evenings when everyone wanted to get home to mow the lawn, have a few friends in for a barbecue, wind down into the weekend.

Then the pip stopped.

Flat line they call it on *ER*. Because that's what it is. A flat line on the screen, a long high-pitched flat beep. No output. No beat.

To this day, every time Henry passes the spot in Blackrock where the ambulance pulled over he goes cold. Each member of the medical team registered the change and reacted simultaneously. Heart massage. Adrenaline. More oxygen. A top-class trauma team thinking as one, working as one. Doing everything they could. Doing more than they could.

But it was no good.

Flat line.

Henry watched as they exchanged glances, reading their expressions. Willing them to be wrong. This was it. After everything, she'd gone. How could it happen like this, how could her little life end on the Rock Road? The anaesthetist turned to him, the sweat running into his eyes,

'I'm so sorry, we're trying . . .'

Pip Pip Pip. As quickly as her heart had stopped, it restarted. A microsecond of complete astonishment, and then they moved. Fast. Lights, sirens and a call ahead to clear the Toll Bridge, straight through to Temple Street.

I was waiting on the pavement with my dad outside the hospital, but she was rushed past me so fast I didn't see her. Henry climbed out of the back of the ambulance shaking, white.

I never smoked in front of my parents, but up in the Relatives' Room my dad asked if he could get me anything. I asked for 20 Marlborough Lights and chainsmoked them over the next two hours, pacing the floor, waiting for news. My dad rang everyone he knew who might be able to help. My brother and uncle arrived. No one was smiling.

Then my uncle called Dad outside. He'd been updated by the team looking after Robyn. Dad's face was ashen as he closed the door gently and gestured for Henry and myself to sit down with him,

'You've both been such wonderful parents . . .'

He didn't get any further. Henry rushed from the room, his amazing calm finally cracking.

Dad had been told to prepare us for the worst.

Ten minutes later a doctor came to see us. I don't know exactly what she said, how she said it, all I remember is hearing, 'Your daughter is very very very sick . . . swelling or bleeding on the brain . . . it is very likely that she will be severely brain damaged or brain dead . . . the next 48 hours are critical.'

They didn't think she'd survive the night.

I couldn't think about losing her. Perhaps it was a coping mechanism, but her leaving us, dying, just wasn't on the agenda. Through the cigarette smoke in that hot, stuffy little room, I looked at my dad. Images of spoonfeeding Robyn at eighteen crowded into my head. Of life with a severely brain-damaged child, of growing old with a baby locked in an adult's body.

Then they said they needed to get her to Beaumont to do a CT scan. It was the only place where they could assess the extent of the damage to her brain. We couldn't go with her because of the equipment, the personnel that was needed to transport her. And they thought that she might not survive the trip.

The doctor spoke so softly, so gently that I almost couldn't hear her. She was in the Intensive Care Unit, it would be a shock, but the equipment was essential, and she was still heavily sedated so couldn't feel anything. I finally tuned in . . . this could be our last chance to see her. She might not survive the trip to Beaumont. Henry and I followed the doctor's white coat through the long white, bright corridors to say our goodbyes.

Wrapped in tinfoil, tubes and wires everywhere, she looked nothing like our baby. Her face was blue, swollen dramatically, a collar supporting her neck, two tubes protruding from her mouth. I felt like she wasn't mine, like I'd lost her already, like my life had changed completely and utterly in a few short hours. We'd never get her back the way she was – there was no way of getting out of this without some level of loss.

So Beaumont next. Another ambulance, another transfer. This time on her own, with a dedicated team, but without her mummy or daddy. We arrived ahead of the ambulance, drank more coffee in cardboard cups in the Relatives' Room, smoked more cigarettes, waiting again to find out how sick our baby was. I was cold, exhausted, almost comatose myself with shock, wore a path on the carpet tiles with pacing.

But the news was better. At eleven o'clock we were told that there did not appear to have been any bleeding on the brain. But she wasn't out of the woods – she'd had a forty-minute seizure that had deprived her brain of oxygen. There was no way of telling how it would affect her.

1.30 am and we were back in Temple Street, assigned a room beside ICU, huddling together in the small bed. Henry closed his eyes and instantly fell into the deepest sleep of his life. Pure exhaustion. I slept fitfully, sweating in the airless room, listening to fights on the street outside, my imagination in overdrive, waiting for the phone to ring, waiting for a nurse to arrive and tell me she'd gone . . .

At 6.20 I woke up and went to check on Robyn. Pulling on the scrubs, tucking my long hair into the cap, I prepared myself for the worst. As I walked around the corner of the ICU a nurse met me, a serene smile on her face. I looked over her shoulder and saw

Robyn, still pale and sickly but sitting up in bed. Waking up moments before, she had started to pull the tube from her mouth, demanding her bop bop and the *Teletubbies*. I looked in disbelief at the nurse and she smiled.

I'm lucky. I cried like I've never cried before. I held Henry so tight he thought he was going to need a respirator, but I'm lucky.

Robyn is eight now, in second class, and has just done a test at school that puts her intellectually in the top 2 per cent of children in Ireland.

I'm lucky that Henry came home early that day. I'm lucky he'd done a first aid course. I'm lucky the traffic was light. I'm lucky that they had an Intensive Care bed in Temple Street. I'm lucky Robyn is a fighter. I'm lucky.

Kyra would like to thank everyone who helped save Robyn's life, from the workmen on the N11 who cleared the traffic to allow the ambulance through, to the paramedics and doctors who treated her. She is particularly grateful to the team at Temple Street Hospital.

First published in *Mum's the Word*, New Island, 2007

Brian O'Connor

Brian O'Connor is the author of *Add a Zero* and *Kings of The Saddle*. He works as the racing correspondent of *The Irish Times*. He lives in Wicklow with his wife and two sons.

The Foal *

Brian O'Connor

The foal was light brown with one long white sock on her back left leg. She also had a white blob in the middle of her forehead. It wasn't shaped like a star or a heart or anything schmaltzy. It was just a blob. Even now, just three weeks after being born, the foal liked to have it rubbed. She would drop her head, stick her neck out and look offended if the boy didn't run the tips of his fingers up and down her face. It was as if she wanted him to shine the blob and make her pretty.

But the boy knew the foal wasn't pretty. He knew the rules about a horse's looks. The white sock was okay, as long as there was only one. More than one and buyers might think those fragile legs could surrender to strains and pulls and tears. Then she wouldn't be able to race, and what use is a racehorse that cannot race? Even the blob didn't really matter compared to that. The boy thought the blob made the foal look goofy but he liked her anyway.

Her mouth was the problem. She had an overbite. The nose of her light brown mouth overshot her bottom jaw and curled down. The lads in the yard called it a parrot mouth. 'Jaysus, that's a pity,' they'd said. When the foal was to be sold a year and a half later, the parrot mouth would be held against her; it would be considered unsightly. It wouldn't stop her running but she might pass it on to her own foals when she had them. The boy remembered the foal's mother. She hadn't had a parrot mouth. She had been almost

367

entirely black and very good-looking, but with a leery eye. That's what the lads said. She was leery. But he didn't like to think of her.

It was dark in the stable but the boy's eyes had got used to it again. At the other end of the small box he could make out the still shape of the tinker pony steadily munching her way through a forkful of hay. The sound had its own steady rhythm. The initial frenzy had worn off. Now she was getting used to being spoiled. The boy smiled at a white tinker pony with various black blotches on her hide getting the same three meals a day as some of the bluest blooded in the country. The mare didn't move her head, kept it down and crunched every mouthful without stirring.

The foal was standing in front of him. He could see her clearly now his eyes were working properly. The yard light from outside peeped under the bottom of the stable door and through the cracks that bordered its closed top half. She was standing to attention. Her ears were forward and she was staring at him.

Her tail was flicking. It didn't look like a horse's tail. It seemed like there were no separate hairs. The boy was reminded of a foot-long tickling stick, as if some tiny Ken Dodd was conducting her backwards. She looked at the boy, sitting in his usual spot in the warm straw. It covered the stable floor and piled up a couple of feet against the sides of the walls. He was leaning against one of the corners, as far as he could get from the draughty door.

The foal gave a tiny squeal, then another and tossed her head. The boy smiled. She was bored and wanted to play. She hadn't been outside in one of the paddocks for five days. All she'd known was the inside of this box: and she'd known him and the strange black and white mare for three of those days. Now she wanted to play. But he couldn't play with her yet. The foal didn't know that and squealed again as she bunny-hopped on her two front legs. The boy laughed quietly but didn't move. Not yet.

He stared at her, still standing in the same place, but now busily nibbling at one of her knees that bulged absurdly from those gangly front legs. She stopped suddenly, ears pricked, and a couple of seconds later Johnson the night-watchman walked past the stable door. The boy knew it was Johnson even without the faintly tuneless whistling that gave him his nickname. He had heard Whistler's Alsatian padding past for the previous two nights as well. Bang on every hour there was whistling and padding.

This would be the last night. Thompson had said so. Thompson was not a likeable man but everyone accepted his knowledge of horses. Three nights the farm manager had told the boy: if she's still all right after three nights, she'll be okay. That's what he'd said and while the boy didn't want to presume, he was pretty sure the foal would be all right.

Except now she was tired. She turned stiffly on those comical legs and faced the stolidly munching mare. It was all about the mare now, not some great classic stallion who had routinely horsed yet another trussed mare at 30,000 a mount. Nor the multi-billionaire squireen tax exile who had been hoping for a colt foal that might eventually do his own high-cost horsing. It wasn't even about a two-hundred-year-old studbook, or sweat and guts or glory on a racecourse. Instead all that mattered was a thick-haired, sad-eyed pony that had been brought in from the tinker camp up the road.

He watched as the foal put her nose on the hairy black and white flank, briefly inched her way along it, and then her nose found the teat. She drank steadily. The boy fell slowly to his right with his cheek almost touching the straw to get a better look. He saw the white of the foal's eye as she kept track of him before concentrating again on her milk. The foal and mare were relaxed. Her steady munch hadn't stopped or checked, even with those sharp little teeth searching for nourishment. The foal's tail shook briefly with satisfaction.

The boy knew she was just another foal. By the end of the season there would be close on a hundred of them on the farm. In four months' time everyone would be sick of foals. Now was the best time, he thought. There were no more than ten of them around. Later they would be the big boys and girls. This foal would be one of the big girls now.

She finished her drink and was bored again. One hard blade of straw stuck out further than the rest and the foal looked intently at it. She used her nose to push the blade. It sprang back, her ears pricked, and she did it again. The blade didn't come back as far this time. She lost interest. Instead she turned to the hay her new foster-mother was munching. The boy looked but he knew now the mare was kind. The youngster's confidence around her proved that. The foal stuck her nose into the hay and was lost in happy ignorance.

He knew this would be the last night in the box. Tomorrow night he would be in his own bed, or at least the bed the farm owned. He supposed they owned the bed. After all it was their house. His father said they were lucky to have found a job that provided a house free of charge. The boy always agreed. But the box wasn't too bad. It couldn't be or else he wouldn't have fallen asleep on the two other nights. He had tucked his heavy jumper into the top of his jeans, pulled his socks over the bottom of them and then plunged his legs into the straw. His face had been cold but the heat from the two animals quickly generated the box's own central heating.

The tinkers would probably expect their mare to be put in foal. When she came into season, Thompson would tell his father to drag out Billy and the little Connemara pony would sniff and nibble her ass and then jump on her. Except he wouldn't be dragged down this time. Billy deserved it, the boy reckoned. Even a teaser's optimism needed boosting sometimes.

He hoped Billy did the job properly. This little mare deserved that. She was very quiet and gentle and she'd saved the foal. Her life must be rough, being with the tinkers and all, but she'd be fine for the next few months until it was time for the foal to be weaned. That was far enough away.

The foal decided to lie down, snorting with boredom as she stretched out in the middle of the box. Her head lay near the boy's foot. Slowly he raised his back from the wall and moved himself towards her. He could see her following his progress in the gloom. He stopped when he got his bum almost in line with her head. His hand moved slowly, and always so she could see it, onto her blob. She let him scratch it. The boy became aware that the methodical munching from the corner had stopped. The straw rustled and the mare moved to stand over them. He tried to move his left hand to the mare's cold nose but she shied. He tried it again with the same result. But she didn't move away from looking down at the foal who had closed her eyes with the pleasure of the boy's scratching.

He was glad he hadn't seen the foal the night her old mother had got sick. The thought of it was enough. The foal had been a week old and left in a box on her own. It wasn't anybody's fault. The mare, the one everyone called the leery mare, had got sick. That was all. But the foal had been on her own. He didn't like to think of the terror that must have been in her calls.

The phone call had come in the middle of the night. The boy did not know why he had been awake but he had. His father had answered the phone. That's why they had the free house, to be on call all the time. Johnson had rung to say one of the mares was acting up. His father had got up and dressed too quickly for it to be something normal. So the boy got up too and tracked him to the yard. It had been cold. He could feel the frosted grass crunching when he walked on the verge of the road.

The lights were on in the big covering shed and he could hear his father shouting. There was a soft thudding noise on the wood shavings and then he saw his father come into view through the shed's open door, running alongside a black mare. He had put a head-collar on her, the one with her racing name etched into the little brass tag, and run a lead through it. The boy could hear his father's breathing begin to struggle. He was running the horse around in circles. And then the mare tried to stop. She put her head in the air and looked down her nose, stepping back quickly as she did so. His father roared at her. But what really made his stomach knot was the sweat dripping from all over the horse. She couldn't be that warm from trotting. He knew that. On her black skin, the white sweat spread like an ugly lard. Despite the cold, steam rose from her under the shed's harsh lights and when she trotted past again, he heard her groan with pain. He didn't know a horse could groan.

'Get in here!'

The boy started. His father had seen him but hadn't stopped running and dragging the trotting mare behind him.

'What's wrong with it, Dad?' He saw the sweat on his father's face and heard the rattle of his breath. The weekend's drinking was starting to take its toll.

'It's a colic, I think. Johnson's phoned the vet and he's bringing the horsebox around. We might have to move her.'

The effort of speaking had brought him to a halt and he handed the lead to the boy. 'Run her! Run her!' he shouted and the boy started running as hard as he could: except the mare wanted to stop. She pulled back against him and he had to jump and drag while in mid-air to get enough impetus to make her move again. 'You can't let her stop!' he heard his father shout. 'If she stops, she'll lie down, and if she lies down, she's dead.'

The boy pulled on the lead as hard as he could. He closed his eyes with the effort and she moved after him. She groaned as she trotted but she trotted. His father shouted 'Good boy!' and disappeared. The sweat and steam from the mare seemed to fill the entire shed and soon he was sweating himself. The mare did not try to lie down or even stop. She kept up the trot but his arms were tensed all the time for when the pain might get too much for her again. It wasn't long before his legs started to ache but he couldn't stop. He knew it had to be colic. His father had told him about it. A horse eats too much and there's a blockage in the gut, he'd said. Except a horse has a huge gut. 'And there's no point slapping its back,' he'd laughed. Anyone who worked with horses knew about colic, except this was the first time the boy had seen it.

There was the noise of a jeep outside and lights reflected into the shed from the stable wall outside. The boy could feel his legs aching and he knew he wasn't running as he had done ten minutes earlier. He ordered himself to up the pace.

'Good boy,' he heard and his father and Whistler ran towards him.

Whistler grabbed the lead and started to jog. The boy's arm tingled with freedom but his father walked him to the jeep outside that had a horsebox hitched to it. He told him he hadn't time to waste. His father hated to do this, he said, but there was nobody else around. He'd phoned and phoned but couldn't reach anyone or wake them up. Whistler had to stay or the farm would be unguarded and that would be when the scumbags would turn up. It was just the two of them and someone had to drive.

'You'll have to stay in the horsebox and make sure she doesn't lie down,' handing the boy a yard-brush. 'If she tries to get down, you'll have to hit her. If she lies down, she's dead.'

The boy took the brush. It stood almost as tall as himself. It was the one with the red needles, the one that Thompson liked to lean on when supervising the lads mucking out the boxes. He let the timber handle drop through his fingers and the brush bounced when it hit the ground.

'Get in and grab the lead!' his father shouted.

The boy ran up the lowered ramp and into the small box that still had the wet straw left behind by the previous horse in it. He ducked under the iron bar at the end and waited. The two men outside shouted at the mare whose steel-shod hooves clattered onto tarmac and then thudded onto the ramp. His father led and Whistler shouted and waved his arms behind. The mare threw her head up at the boy but got in. He tried to grab the lead but his father tied her to the bar.

'You're going to have to hurt her,' he told the boy. 'When the pain gets too bad she'll try and lie down. You can't let her. Do you hear me?'

The boy could feel his father looking at him when the mare started tossing her head. He watched him reach for the brush, stand on it, and rip the long, slim handle clear. The horse tossed her head even more and his father changed grip, bringing it down on the mare's back. She rushed the bar in fright, ramming her chest off it and stepping back quickly again. The boy thought the lead would snap. His father hit her again on the side of the head. Her feet reverberated through the straw from the timber floor. He pressed against the walls, as far from the horse as he could get. But his father didn't seem to care.

The mare's heavy feet rattled on the floor and her arse tried to swing around in defence but his father didn't move. And she stayed on her feet.

He stopped only when she got too tired to react to the beating. Then he walked down the ramp and lifted it. He had it half closed when he nodded. The boy nodded back and then the ramp was up and shut. The boy turned on the torch his father had given him along with the brush handle. There was also light from the covering shed but it disappeared as the jeep started and lurched down the long drive to the road. Whistler had given directions to the Curragh, where there was a horse surgery. But it would take an hour to get there.

He soon needed the torch when the floor beneath him grew even more alive as they picked up speed. The mare seemed okay now. Even in the darkness he could see the sweat still steaming off her. But her eyes were more tired than terrified. He was glad of that. It had been scary back there at the stables. He had never seen agony before.

Nothing happened for ten minutes. The boy stayed behind the bar and didn't shine the torch for fear of jinxing this momentary calm. He began praying to himself, asking God to get the mare to the hospital without her acting up again, and that his father would drive quickly. And he prayed that he wouldn't have to hurt this horse. But it didn't work.

They were driving through some housing estate, street-lights illuminating the box interior, when the mare started to lower her head. He changed his grip on the brush handle. Suddenly she moved slightly backwards and the boy could see her knees begin to bend. She was trying to lie down. And then she groaned. It sounded even worse than in the shed. The boy looked around desperately, as if his father could see through to him. He knew that was silly but he shouted for him anyway. The jeep didn't slow down and he shouted twice more only for the mare to groan again. The boy knew she wanted to lie down. He didn't want to hit her but he had to.

The Foal

When they arrived at the hospital, the exhausted boy hated the horse. He didn't care if she died. He had stopped beating her because he didn't care and he hated her. He had begun to think this horse hospital was imaginary. No hospital took so long to get to. But then he looked at his watch and he saw it hadn't been that long at all – just less than an hour. There were footsteps outside and when the ramp was lowered his father swore. He watched as the mare was untied. Another man helped his father back her out and he swore too when he saw the weals and bruises on her hide. The boy stood up and walked out into the cold night air. The sweat froze on his face. He watched his father trot the mare into a large white building but didn't follow. Instead he turned and went back into the horsebox, lay down on the wet bed and slept.

The boy remembered how he hadn't cared how the shit-soaked straw had drained into his clothes as he lay on it. His father had said nothing hours later when he'd shaken him awake just as the sun was starting to hint at morning. The mare had died on the operating table. They had opened her up, taken out yards of gut and tried to find the obstruction. It hadn't mattered because she had died anyway. They had driven back and his father wondered where they might get a foster-mare for the foal. The boy hadn't thought about the foal.

He felt a snort of hot breath on his cheek and his start scared the tinker mare's nose away from him. He hadn't expected that. The foal still lay stretched with her eyes closed and the boy's fingers scratching her face. She hadn't even noticed. But the mare still stood above the pair of them and resolutely lowered her head again. The boy took the hint. He slid back and resumed his position against the wall. The foal briefly opened her eyes but soon went back to sleep. The tinker mare stood above her and prepared for the night with her back left foot arched so the toe was pointing down. She would sleep standing up. The boy had always wondered how they could do that. He thought the foal had the right idea.

375

Niamh O'Connor

Niamh O'Connor is the true crime author of *The Black Widow, Cracking Crime* and *Blood Ties*. Her first crime novel, *If I Never See You Again,* was a bestseller. She is the True Crime editor of the *Sunday World*. Her second novel, *Between the Lies,* will be published in 2011.

Virginia Whaley's No. 2 Ladies' Detective Agency *

Niamh O'Connor

When my Spanx shrunk in the spin-dry on the day I was due to interview James Bond, I lost the will to live.

'What do you mean you put *all* of them in one wash?' my twin sister Vanessa quizzed, as if she was Jeremy Paxman quizzing MI5 on how the entire royal family ended up on the same flight.

'What are Spanx, Mummy?' my three-year-old, Harry, cut in.

'Grim,' Vanessa pronounced, shaking her head as she inspected the knickers one after the other. She held them up to Harry's waist for size. Vanessa has to park leftover dinners in the fridge for two days before she can bring herself to throw them out.

'Bicycle shorts, darling,' I told Harry, tousling his hair.

'For bikes,' Vanessa added, giving me a meaningful stare.

I covered Harry's ears. 'Language,' I clipped.

'What's all the fuss about?' Mum tinkled, from the kitchen. She craned her beady eye into the single inch of space left in the utility room.

'Virginia's got to do her big interview this morning,' Vanessa replied. 'With a giant arse . . .'

'Who's the Giant Arse?' Mum asked. 'Do I know them? What were they in? You know I'm no good with names.'

No need to panic, I thought. It was true I was about to be sacked from my job in the celebrity magazine, *Shooting Stars*, for cocking up the interview of a lifetime, but we didn't have any brown-paper bags to hand that didn't stink of vinegar. That was when the previous night's episode of *The No. 1 Ladies' Detective Agency* hit me like a Road to Damascus moment. 'In every butter stall, in every bar and market, behind every window and door . . .' Mma Ramotswe had said, looking out the car window and right into my eyes, 'there are so many people who want to know the truth about some mystery in their lives, some mystery they cannot solve themselves. That's what I will do.' That's when it occurred to me that I could always set up a Ladies No. 2 Detective Agency.

For the life of me I could not think of a single way of putting my talents to better use than getting paid to snoop, either. Not to mention the spooky parallels: I too drove a white Hi-ace, and had been engaged forever.

Only one thing now stood in the way – getting fired. Since I'd only been allocated ten minutes for the interview with James Bond to discuss him landing the lead role in the Hollywood remake of *Casablanca*, that seemed like a dead cert. When she found out, Thomasena my editor was going to kill me. I'd had a major battle on my hands, persuading her I was up to the James Bond interview in the first place.

'Receptionists belong on reception,' she'd carped, only caving in when I used one of Harry's most successful psychological ploys to wear her down, 'Please, please, please, please, please,' times one hundred. We both knew it was an act of sheer genius to take a man who looks *that* good in a black tuxedo, and put him in a white one.

Thomasena finally caved in only after I'd reassured her that I had no journalistic integrity whatsoever.

'It's a poisoned chalice for the rest of us,' Bethany, the *Before & After Makeover* editor pooh-poohed, when I started strutting around the office hi-fiving everyone.

'James Bond hates journalists,' Claudine, the *Do or Diets* editor added, shoving her empty mug into my hand for a refill and sniggering, '*You* might stand a chance.'

But as I said to Russell, the *True Life Tragedy* editor, temping is something you can be proud of in your early twenties. When you hit thirty-seven, it's about as humiliating as Kate Adie chatting to Ant and Dec about dodging Scud missiles while chomping on a kangaroo testicle.

'As if James Bond would be bothered checking out her arse anyway,' Vanessa sniped, bringing me back to the present.

'Oh, you'd be amazed what men find attractive, darling,' Mum replied.

I started putting into play the techniques learned in my *Yoga for Beginners* DVD – counting to ten, scrunching my face up and squeezing my fists, when I realised the real reason my entire body was not relaxing was because Harry was swinging from my jersey.

'Mummy,' he declared, now eye contact was finally established. '*Poo!*'

'Fuck, fuck, fuckity fuck!' I flapped, looking round wildly.

Harry covered his own ears.

'Good, good boy,' I shrieked, hoisting him up at arm's length and sprinting in the direction of the toilet.

The royal flight was veering towards the Bermuda Triangle.

'Mr Bond,' I schmoozed, as his PR woman, Peachesncream, took my hand, and led me over to do the introductions.

Confidence is half the battle, Thomasena had instructed.

He looked at his watch. I ducked dramatically. He gave me a puzzled stare.

'Sorry,' I blustered, holding my hand out stiffly. 'Thought it might be one of Q's gadgets.'

He shook my hand.

'Ooops, sorry, poo finger,' I blurted, whipping it back and offering him the other.

'Baby poo,' I explained, but his deadpan expression just sort of twitched a bit. 'At least, my former-baby-now-turned-toddler poo,' I clarified proudly, shuffling awkwardly from one foot to the other.

His stony mask was starting to annoy me.

'Don't you have children?' I asked, at which point James emitted a strange '*humph*' noise. 'Oh come on, what are the odds when you've shagged that many women?' I joked, trying to dig myself out of a hole, at which point he sort of shooed me away.

On the far side of the room Peachesncream took up the cue and came mincing over to have a not so polite word in my ear. I tottered along after her towards the exit, pleading with her to give me another chance. I wanted one single published article to put in No. 2's swanky reception area. I might even attract some celebrity clients . . .

'Don't worry about it, he hates all journalists,' Peachesncream replied, hurrying me out and ushering the next sacrificial lamb on and in.

'Jesus wept!' I despaired. 'How am I supposed to fill two pages about 007 when he goes all premenstrual at the first mention of his sperm count?' I demanded.

Talk about a David Dimbleby moment – Peachesncream U-turned on the spot, grabbing my wrist, muttering something about not wanting the IVF treatment to have a negative impact on Bond's box-office image.

Ten point five minutes later, A-list interview in the bag, and hopeless situation salvaged, I was full of the joys of spring and bounced back into work, thinking if my other half, Mark, would only answer the bloody phone I might be able to tell him all about my No. 2.

'Do you make a habit of going commando?' Thomasena tackled, in a manner which, combined with the blue stains on her lips, and the fact that it was just past lunchtime, could only mean she was about to become dangerously dehydrated.

I was repeating the question to try and make sense of it when she handed me the photographer's snaps from my Bond interview. Once my ego had come up for air three times, waved frantically, then disappeared for good, my eyes dropped in horror to the place where my Spanx should have been.

'Christ,' Jeff the Airbrush Editor exclaimed, peering over Thomasena's shoulder. 'I thought I'd seen my fair share with Britney, and Lyndsy and Cheryl Cole's mum, but *that* one could bring down a small animal.'

'Congratulations,' Thomasena said, wrapping her arm around my neck. '*You,* Virginia Whaley, are exactly what we need in *Shooting Stars*. The common touch. Someone who can give the ordinary woman back her impossible dreams – flashing James Bond, ho, ho!' She pinched one of my cheeks. 'You're hired.'

Ripping an advertisement for a part-time Junior Reporter's position off the notice board, she flung it in a wastepaper basket, declaring, 'Virginia has just raised the bar for the rest of you.' She looked around the office malevolently. 'What have we all learned today?'

'Release the inner slut?' Bethany suggested, looking like she was fit to be tied.

'A Brazilian is so nineties?' Claudine cut in.

Russell put his arm around my back and gave me a reassuring squeeze. 'Don't worry,' he whispered. 'We can run a black bar there, like across a criminal's eyes.' He gave me a pitiful smile, like a climber about to truck over a prostate body lying at the summit of Mount Everest.

'It's time to up our game, people!' Thomasena went on, clapping her hands. 'I want you to make Virginia look like a superstar,' she told Claudine, who had sort of propped herself up against a table for support. 'Think *The Swan* meets *Nip/Tuck*. I want every woman who's ever left the house with yesterday's pair of tights dangling from her trouser leg and following her along the pavement, to believe she can turn her life around, just like Virginia.'

Obviously, I ought to have been feeling ecstatic having now been offered a secure job, and a pay rise, but I was just too gone on the idea of being a PI. Also, it would have helped if it had all happened before Colin Farrell went and made a big deal out of Irish women's grooming habits.

I spent the rest of the day pretending to type up my interview, but actually switching screens so I could Google 'Office space to rent' whenever Thomasena was on the move. I didn't want to pack in the job until I'd consulted Mark first. We'd both moved to our respective homes after I got pregnant, so we could save for a place once the baby was born. I wasn't able to get Mark on the phone, but as Harry is minded by Mark's parents when I'm in work, I thought I'd get the chance to talk to him when I picked Harry up.

But Mark's mum, Alice, opened the door announcing, 'He's not here,' before I'd so much as had the chance to say 'hello'. 'He still doesn't look a bit like him, does he, Fred?' she added, studying Harry.

'Not remotely,' Fred agreed, shaking his head.

'Okay, fine, you've got me, he's actually the postman's,' I joked hysterically, putting my hands in the air and, grabbing Harry, made a bid for freedom down their drive.

Vanessa was chopping an onion with psychopathic gusto (to give the impression she was cooking dinner) when Harry and I arrived home. Vanessa always busies herself prepping veg whenever she intends drinking like a raging alcoholic during the evening.

'What's for dinner?' I asked, pulling Harry's coat and hat off.

'Lasagne,' she answered, sounding slightly unsure. 'How did you get on?'

I plonked myself on the settee facing the butcher block and rolled my eyes.

'Eugh! I hate lasagne,' Harry said, snuggling up beside me for a cuddle.

'Super,' I said, starting to strangle myself silently as soon as she had turned her back to show Harry how much I agreed. He took off into the hall and I was vaguely aware he'd opened the phone-table drawer, where we keep the takeaway fliers.

'Where's Mum?' I asked Vanessa. I wanted to know if Mark had rung earlier.

'That Womens' Studies course in college,' Vanessa said, refilling her glass.

'Oh God,' I said. Mum always turns into Nell McCafferty after that one. Give me pole-dancing any day, even if she insists on wearing tap-dancing shoes with her leopard-skin leotard.

'Oh stop it. Just tell me how it went,' Vanessa stropped. Giant tears started rolling down her face. 'Damn onions!' she blasted.

I hurried over and put my arm around her. 'Whatever's the matter?' I asked.

'HRT causes cancer . . .' she blubbed.

'You and I are nowhere near the menopause.' I took the Kitchen Devil out of her hand and pushed her towards the sofa.

'And my boss is going out of his way to force me to file for constructive dismissal,' she heaved.

'Lucky you,' I said, 'You hate the bank. Actually there's something I've been wanting to talk to you about, something both of us could do together . . .'

Harry darted in with a Chinese menu, sized up the situation, and U-turned out again with equal speed.

Vanessa wrung her hands together, 'That bloke I slept with on Saturday . . . he never rang!' she bawled.

'They never do. You know that,' I said, patting her hands. 'You've always known it.'

'But why do they always have to be so, so, so,' she looked around desperately for the word then dropped an octave, 'irresistible.'

'You need to find someone like Mark,' I said, vaguely aware that Harry had just said 'No anchovies', in the background.

Vanessa snorted. 'I thought you just said one-night stands were *my* problem.'

'Hel-lo! I'm only staying here until we buy our own place,' I argued, feeling peeved.

'How long since you shagged then, hum?' Vanessa drilled on. 'Or even talked for that matter? Bet it's weeks, I know it's months since he darkened this door. You need to wake up and smell the coffee! He hasn't even had the decency to – to – to make a proper single mother of you and dump you,' she said, breaking down again.

I put my finger up to my lips to warn her to refrain from any further comment in case Harry had in fact dialled Childline, before marching out into the hall, seizing the handset off him and apologising to Domino Pizza on the other end.

Just then Mum arrived back from college.

'What's up with her?' she asked, nodding her head in Vanessa's direction, slinging her khaki satchel covered in graffiti on the floor, kicking off her maroon Dr Martens boots, and swiping Vanessa's glass of wine.

I frowned exaggeratedly to warn her to go easy.

'Men,' I said, grabbing two more glasses.

'Well, she's hardly going to pull anyone in the box-room of her mother's house,' Mum ribbed.

'*She* happens to be in the box-room,' Vanessa exclaimed indignantly, pointing her finger straight at me. 'I've got the double.'

'Hel-lo! LATs are all the rage right now.'

'LATs?' Vanessa asked.

'Living Apart Together,' I mimed, so Harry wouldn't hear.

Mum and Vanessa snorted simultaneously.

'Anyway, you're all going to have to find somewhere else to live,' Mum said with gusto. 'I'm selling up to fund my gap year.'

I didn't pay the slightest bit of attention. *Who ever heard of a gap year on an evening course?*

'Mummy,' Harry asked me suddenly, standing straight in front of me and taking my face in both his little hands to make sure he had my undivided attention, 'when are we going to start living with Dad?'

The absolute last place on earth I intended to wind up the following morning was jangling a tambourine at a mothers and toddlers playgroup.

But after Mother ambushed me at 9 am, with an actual family of strangers in tow, that's where I ended up.

'Say "yes",' she had hissed, happy-slapping the duvet in a very angry manner.

'Go away! Saturdays are sacred.' I peeked over the covers.

'You'd fit a double in, with a bit of a squeeze,' Mum was telling a middle-aged couple and a bored-looking teenage girl. 'Meet the Browns,' she said to me. 'They're here for a house viewing.'

'Where's Harry?' I asked, glancing over at his empty cot.

'Right here,' Mum said. 'He's had his breakfast, and we've even done some face-painting, haven't we, darling?'

Harry appeared from behind the sets of legs, and shot me a baleful stare, batting hard through his mascara and blue eye-shadow.

'Pastels are so passé,' the teenage Brown droned, eyeing the walls.

'Rosemary White's daughter, Judith, is holding a mother and toddlers playgroup in the Parish Hall this morning,' Mum announced, smiling through her teeth while winking frantically from behind the couple's back. 'You know Rosemary, darling, she's the second cousin, once removed, of my friend Jane, the parish secretary, who booked Harry's christening. It's all for a very worthy cause – disabled children blown up by those dreadful landmines, I think. Chop-chop, now, Virginia!'

I jumped up, and dragged yesterday's clothes off the floor. 'Do you mind?' I asked Mr Brown, who put his hands in the air with spectacular dramatics.

'And when you come back, I've organised Harry to play with Amy, the little girl across the road,' Mum called as I headed for the bathroom. 'She's just got a magician's set and her latest trick is sawing people in half.'

I slammed the door behind me.

Twenty minutes later I was in the Parish Hall, allowing some flatfooted woman with a clipboard to grill me so she could fill in a form.

'Married or single?' she demanded, over the pitch twenty-odd children can only make if they have consumed additives intravenously.

'Almost,' I announced proudly, wishing I had a ring to display.

'Home address?'

'Can I answer that one next week?'

'How would you describe Harry's personality?' she demanded.

'Hmm, let me think,' I stalled, realising 'eats, drinks and potty-trained' was not going to suffice. I prised a Solpadeine free from the bottom of my handbag, fired it into the crook of my neck, and went onto autopilot: 'Well, he's a complete perfectionist,' I began. 'He pushes himself to the absolute limit, even when it is to his own detriment.' I was getting quite into it. 'But he's the first to put his hand up and admit when he's got it wrong.'

'Can't you just ring his father and find out?' she replied.

Mma Ramotswe was back before my eyes. This time painting the words 'Cheating Partners?' to the sign listing her specialities. Come hell or high water I was going to have my No. 2 . . .

Jim Power

Jim Power, Chief Economist at Friends First Group, is a graduate of University College, Dublin. He was previously Chief Economist at Bank of Ireland Group and Treasury Economist at AIB Group. He currently teaches economics on the Executive MBA at the Michael Smurfit Graduate School of Business, UCD. Jim writes a weekly column in *The Irish Examiner* and contributes to numerous other newspapers and magazines on an occasional basis. Jim also operates a consultancy, Jim Power Economics. Jim's first book, *Picking up the Pieces*, was published by Blackhall Publishing in November 2009.

The Correct Choices Can Rekindle Hope **

Jim Power

> *Hope is the thing with feathers*
> *That perches in the soul*
> *And sings the tune*
> *Without the words*
> *And never stops at all*
>
> EMILY DICKINSON (1830–1886)

Hope represents an expectation of something better to come. Having an expectation of something better is very important to keep people going, particularly during challenging or difficult times. For those without hope, life becomes a major chore and getting out of bed in the morning to face into a new day poses extreme difficulty. When one hasn't hope, one only has despair and that makes life very challenging and difficult to bear. Of course despair or the lack of hope can be a transitory affair determined by the particular circumstances one finds oneself in. For example, a sporting defeat or some career disappointment can render one devoid of hope, but only on a very temporary basis. On the other hand the death of a close one or a serious illness can have a more profound and more lasting impact on one's expectation of better things to come. One thing is very clear, however, everybody deserves to have hope and it is incumbent on society to do the utmost to ensure an environment of hope.

Hope and the lack of it can mean very different things to different people and varies from person to person. Personally, I generally feel most hopeful late at night or early in the morning. On the other hand my darkest or most hopeless periods tend to occur when I wake up in the middle of the night and start to think about the issues or problems that are topical in my life, both at a personal and business level. During these periods everything tends to become a major chore and a source of deep worry and concern, and the longer I lie in bed thinking about them, the worse they become. During those dark periods, the only option for me is to get out of bed and tackle the issue head on that is concerning me.

When I confront the problem head on and cease prevaricating, hope tends to return and the sense of hopelessness tends to evaporate very quickly, that is at least until I wake up in the middle of the following night with different issues to worry about.

The moral of the story for me is that the only way I can dispel the deep sense of concern that turns into hopelessness is to get up and tackle and take control of the issue rather than let the issue take control of me. Once I feel I am back in control of any particular situation, my spirits improve and my sense of hope grows again. These dark spells in the middle of the night are frequent, but I suspect are not unique to me. A problem tackled is very often a problem solved.

When I worked in the world of banking I frequently drove myself into a sense of deep despair when I thought too much about what I was doing and what was ahead of me. I observed those career bankers around me, who joined the institution at an early age and whose only real ambition was to take the salary on offer, hopefully progress as far as possible up the career ladder, and then retire on a decent pension, often when still relatively young. Many of them became totally institutionalised and lived for and were controlled by the bank. This situation obviously suits the bank or indeed the majority of employers and indeed suits many people. However, for me the notion of spending a working life with one organisation and never taking any real risks was tantamount to hell and did little for my expectation of better things to come. Finally, in a fit of desperation, I removed myself from that world and took greater control over my own life and over my own destiny. This was the best thing I ever did, although the pension and general financial implications were not exactly what a personal financial adviser would recommend. However, there is a lot more to life than money. Freedom, choice and being in control of one's own destiny are the factors that are important to me and which tend to give rise to hope within me. When any of these are threatened, hope tends to evaporate, but then it is time to act and regain control. Inaction is not an option and, for anybody in despair, it is always worthwhile taking a proactive approach and exploring the options by thinking outside the box. It may not work on every occasion, but in many cases it just might.

For many people the general economic environment and how it impacts on one's employment and earnings potential are extremely important. Unfortunately we need money to live and financial security is of extreme importance, particularly if one is raising a family. After a period of unprecedented economic growth and prosperity in the fifteen or so years from the early 1990s, the past couple of years have come as a major shock to many people and have certainly created a sense of despair for many. Unemployment has increased sharply, incomes have fallen; unemployment and financial insecurity have become the order of the day.

One of the very positive features of the so-called Celtic Tiger period was the choice and opportunity that opened up to many people, particularly young people. Back in the 1980s there was not much in the way of choice open to the majority of people. However, in the more affluent environment that characterised the Celtic Tiger period, young people had much more choice and opportunity opened up to them in relation to their educational and ultimately their employment opportunities. Indeed, for older people the new environment also presented much more in the way of opportunity and choice, and for example the ability to switch employment to enhance income potential or to broaden one's horizon became a very real possibility. The increased affluence also presented greater opportunity to travel and improve the general quality of life. This sense of choice and opportunity did not exist back in the 1980s and forced emigration was the order of the day if one wanted to create opportunity and hope. Thankfully this changed and we definitely became a more optimistic and hopeful people, but dark clouds have now appeared on the horizon.

Unfortunately, since 2007 the period of unprecedented growth and opportunity has come to a shuddering halt and much of the progress has now been blown away. Many people are now struggling financially and emotionally in the face of severe wage cuts, job losses and excessive levels of personal debt. Homes are being repossessed, job uncertainty has become the order of the day and disposable incomes are coming under increasing pressure as businesses are forced to cut costs to survive and as government struggles to control a mounting national debt. Most worryingly of all, forced emigration has re-emerged as employment opportunities diminish, particularly for the thousands of young people exiting school and college. This is a real pity, particularly as it need not have been so.

The simple fact is that in the face of unprecedented growth and prosperity, Ireland got totally carried away with itself. The notion had developed at the peak of the Celtic Tiger that Ireland had become a self-sustaining economic entity that could survive on its citizens building houses for each other and buying goods and services from each other. Government was more than happy to go along with the charade because it put a very healthy complexion on the overall economy and spawned billions in tax revenues. The model of Ireland as a small open economy where exports are the lifeblood of economic activity was forgotten and neglected. Ireland became fat and arrogant and we allowed the cost base of the country to get totally out of control, and with it the general competitiveness of the country. This has now ended in tears.

Policy-makers, and indeed the rest of us, became totally caught up in the booming economy. Unfortunately, very few with influence actually stood back and questioned whether the emerging trends in the economy were actually sustainable. If they had, the answer would be no. The whole focus was on quantity in terms of the number of jobs being created and the level of economic growth. The quality and sustainability of the economic and employment growth were never considered and the country is now paying a heavy price for that lack of vision.

An inordinate dependence on the construction sector, along with the government's general economic illiteracy, mismanagement of public finances, flawed fiscal policy, pandering to vested interest groups and inability to make tough decisions led to Ireland's heightened vulnerability.

The sad and annoying fact is that we can be sure that before the whole process of cleaning up the discredited banking system will have run its course, it will have cost the Irish taxpayer an awful lot of money. Future generations will be paying the bill directly or indirectly for years to come. The other harsh reality is that, from being the darling of Europe and the world just a couple of years ago, Ireland has become a source of embarrassment to people who care about the country. Our international reputation has been seriously tarnished.

From a social and economic perspective, Ireland simply cannot afford another brain drain of the type that devastated Irish society and the economy in the 1980s. It is incumbent on our policy-makers to show courage and vision in addressing the problems facing the country. The thing that we must remember is that this did happen before, in the 1980s, and we did manage to extricate ourselves from that particular mess due to a combination of good luck and strong leadership. We can do it again, but we need to make it happen rather than wait for it to happen. We need to take control of the situation, address the problems, put better systems in place and re-create opportunity and with that will come hope again.

In the midst of an unprecedented economic crisis it is hard to see where economic recovery could possibly come from and there is a strong temptation to plunge into the depths of despair, but that is not in the nature of the human spirit. The reality of course is that there are still many individuals and companies operating in the Irish economy and in Irish society who believe in the future of the country and who will continue to try to make it happen. The challenge for policy-makers is to create an environment where such individuals and companies are facilitated to the greatest extent possible in order to create high-quality economic activity and employment, and help Ireland realise its economic potential in a manner that can be sustained. The bottom line is that there is no easy solution to this crisis and there is no painless way out of it.

Hopefully, as happened in the 1980s, the political leadership will show the way, but more is required. More active citizenship is now very necessary. The people of the country cannot sit back and wait for the political firmament or the permanent administration to solve the problem and restore hope in Ireland. We have all now got to get more actively involved in how our society is managed and directed and take control of the rudderless ship that is now Ireland. We owe this to the next generation and to future generations. We have got to have hope ourselves, and we have got to ensure that we give a sense of hope to the generations that are following us. Despair is not something that we can pass on.

One thing to note about the last decade of Irish economic and financial history is that there would appear to have been very little in the way of strategic planning or thought guiding the evolution of the economy. The attitude towards the management of the public finances was cavalier. Once the money was around it was spent, and the tax base was decimated by ideological blindness and short-term thinking, not to mention political populism. Furthermore, successive governments were prepared to ride the construction boom for all it was worth and grow the public sector as if it were the highest value-added sector in the economy. There was no real attempt made to develop other sectors of the economy to ensure that we had a diversified and sustainable economic model. Clearly, a different approach is now required.

To create hope and an expectation of better times ahead, we have got to create a strategic plan for our economic future. I believe that it is now incumbent on Ireland's policy-makers to plan for a more diversified economic offering. This strategy has to revolve around identifying a number of economic sectors in which Ireland can actually compete and ensuring that, insofar as possible, an environment is created whereby those sectors can develop. The economic plan for Ireland will have to combine the modern with the traditional, the old with the new, and the indigenous with the foreign-owned. It is not a case of either/or, but rather some of both.

The foreign-owned multinational component of the economy has got to remain an important part of the model. The ability to attract new foreign direct investment into the Irish economy and holding on to what we already have is becoming more challenging. The 12.5 per cent corporation tax rate is a necessary, but no longer sufficient, condition for Ireland's continued success in the foreign direct investment arena. To remain a player in the foreign direct investment arena, the following will have to be addressed: the quality and accessibility of infrastructure, the level of broadband penetration and our cost competitiveness across the board. Most importantly of all, Ireland must continue to supply a highly trained and educated workforce. These are the minimum conditions necessary to ensure a continued strong contribution by the multinational sector to the Irish economy.

I have always lamented the fact that mainstream economists rarely, if ever, mention the agri-food industry when analysing the Irish economy. It is as if it is regarded as a poor relation of the 'star' sectors of the past decade, particularly construction and financial services. The agri-food industry includes everything from farming to food manufacturing and much more in between. I have a vested interest of sorts in the agri-food industry as I was brought up on a farm in County Waterford and have always passionately believed that it is an industry that is undervalued by policy-makers. However, it makes a huge contribution to rural economic activity and, more importantly, can make an even greater contribution in the future. The key to unlocking the obvious potential of the Irish food industry is through new products, quality and strong brands.

Without new products, Ireland will be condemned to be a simple producer of commodities.

The Irish food industry is now under serious threat. Adverse currency movements, a high domestic cost base and increased overseas competition are all putting serious pressure on the industry. However, recent developments at retail level pose an even greater threat, particularly the 'tescoisation' of the Irish retail sector. Government needs to get serious about the farming and food sector and allow it to realise its undoubted potential as a high value-added component of the Irish economy. There is no reason why Ireland cannot become the Silicon Valley of food production, given its natural advantages as a food producer and the green image of Ireland. An artisan food industry, such as the thriving one in France, is capable of being developed in Ireland, provided of course that red tape and bureaucracy are reduced. The over-application of health and safety regulations in Ireland makes it difficult, if not impossible, for small local producers to sell produce at local markets. In France, such small markets happen in every village around the country and, as well as supporting local producers, they make an enormous contribution to the French tourism brand. Why can this not happen in Ireland?

Tourism is another slightly 'old-fashioned industry' that was somewhat forgotten and perhaps taken for granted during the boom times. The growth potential of tourism will now have to be explored and exploited to the greatest extent possible. There is nothing that the Irish tourism industry can do to influence the value of the dollar or global economic activity, but it can and must improve the competitiveness of the product. The cost of living in Ireland must be addressed and the quality of the tourism product must be improved. For policy-makers, investment in the tourism product makes economic sense because, without ongoing upgrading and investment, the quality of the product will just deteriorate and the decline of the industry will be inevitable.

Creating an alternative energy future is also very important. In terms of future planning, the safest assumption to make is that oil and gas prices will be considerably higher in the future than they have been in the past. Working on the basis of that assumption, it is imperative for Irish policy-makers to ensure that alternative energy sources are explored and delivered. Alternative energy, such as nuclear, wind, solar, wood and marine biomass energy are all possibilities.

It is not clear where quality employment is going to come from in the Irish economy over the coming years, so it is imperative that our policy-makers create a plan outlining the sectors that offer longer-term potential and create an environment where they can thrive and prosper. I have identified some of the sectors that I believe represent the future of Ireland, but clearly areas relating to the so-called smart economy, research and development activities, and professional service exports will also have a key role to play in Ireland's future development. These sectors would support other activities, such as retail, financial services, the public sector and construction. Ireland also has a strong competitive advantage in music and the arts. These sectors should be encouraged to flourish and develop.

The important point is that a more diversified economic base needs to be created, combining the modern with the traditional and the domestic with the foreign-owned. If we fail to adopt this more strategic approach, Ireland will be stuck in a time warp of low-quality employment, high unemployment, high levels of emigration and economic under-performance. Having had a taste of what is possible and having blown much of it away, it is now time to go back to the drawing board, learn lessons from past failures and get on with creating an alternative future based on hope, opportunity and an expectation of better times ahead . . .

Mainstream economic commentators are frequently criticised over their preoccupation with the notion of 'economy' and the lack of attention they pay to the concept of 'society'. Such criticism has some justification, because economic growth is not something that should be pursued for its own sake, but rather for the societal benefits that it might bring. There is little point in having massive levels of economic growth if that growth coexists with low-quality services such as health and education, serious income inequality, widespread poverty or high levels of substance abuse and crime. All of these issues have now got to be addressed in a serious and meaningful way. We must take control and we must never again accept second best. We deserve better.

Once we get the economic model right, we must ensure that the fruits of economic growth are used to improve the quality of life. This includes the quality of public services such as health and education, a good physical infrastructure, a safe society where substance abuse is not all pervasive, and an appreciation of the finer things in life, rather than a quest for Mammon regardless of the consequences. For the young generation, the best advice is to maximise educational attainment, as that will help create greater choice, which in my view is key to hope.

Ireland is in a difficult situation, but provided we do the right things as a society, we can get back on track and create a better future. The choice is ours, so let us make the correct choices.

ᔓ ᔕ

Sarah Webb

Sarah Webb worked as a children's bookseller for many years before becoming a full-time writer. Her series for young teens, *Ask Amy Green,* is hugely popular internationally, and she also writes for younger children. She has written nine novels for adults and her next book, *The Shoestring Diaries,* will be published in 2011. As well as writing, Sarah facilitates workshops on creative writing with Inkwell Writers Workshops, visits schools, and is the children's reviewer for *The Irish Independent.*

Hope and JK Rowling **

Sarah Webb

As a writer I'm often asked to speak to readers and would-be writers of all ages, from babes-in-arms at mother and toddler groups, to fantastic older women in mother's unions all over the country.

I am so grateful to have this wonderful job – even after seven years I still get a kick out of printing 'writer' in the occupation box on official forms – and I do these visits with a joyful and willing heart, even though I should really be at my desk, working on the latest book.

However, most of my visits are to schools and to groups of children and teens in libraries and writing centres like the mighty Fighting Words Centre near Croke Park in Dublin, an oasis of a place: bright, airy, the kind of building that supports and encourages both creative activity and a sense of peace.

But the real reason I do so many school visits is this – spending time with some amazing youngsters gladdens my soul and gives me genuine hope for the future.

Sometimes I tell the children my own stories, true stories, about my life as a child and about growing up in Dublin in the 1970s and 80s, ancient history to them. About Monchhichis, the Top Hat Roller Disco, my mega-crush on John Taylor from Duran Duran and his chiselled chin. I read to them from my teen diaries, cringe. It's mostly angst about boys, friends, family, school, and more boys.

I show them my favourite books as a child and young teenager – *Ballet Shoes, The Secret Garden, The Silver Crown, The Island of the Great Yellow Ox, New Patches for Old, Forever* – and explain how books changed my life, gave me confidence, self-belief, and a whole army of new friends between two covers.

I talk about the problems I had as a young child in school. I hold up my tatty old copybooks hosting my backwards Ss, my scribbled and torn-in-anger pages. I couldn't read until I was nine, which I found deeply upsetting and frustrating. But I was one of the lucky ones: I had parents who read to me. AA Milne's jaunty poetry featuring Christopher Robin and Winnie the Pooh, *Where the Wild Things Are, Busy Busy World* by Richard Scarry, the whacky rhymes of Dr Seuss.

My parents knew I wasn't stupid and they believed, like another of my favourite characters, Leo the Late Bloomer, that I'd read in my own good time. They were right. But without hearing stories every night, without the daily doses of Pooh, Max, Early Bird and the Cat in the Hat, I may never have discovered the wonder of fiction.

Books played such an important role in my childhood; they were my comfort, my 'home'. On black teenage days I'd meander along, reading on the hoof, tripping over dog leads, stumbling over cracks in the pavement, my head buried in a book.

When all around me was a swirling, hyper-emotional mess, books were my salvation. I don't believe my teenage years were any more difficult than anyone else's – I had parents who loved me, a safe home and good friends who never turned – but even so I had severe mood swings, and dark, dark thoughts, and it gave me comfort to know that Margaret in Judy Blume's *Are You There God? It's Me, Margaret,* was having an equally tough time, that the family in Virginia Adams's attic managed to stay alive despite the odds, that even after battling giant mutant rats/zombies/mad dogs Stephen King's heroes and heroines lived to fight another vampire.

These days I'm an avid Stephenie Meyer fan, and often wish the Twilight books had been around when I really needed them. No teen heroine has suffered like Bella! And oh, the swoony romance of it all.

I've never grown out of two things – my love of Abba and my love of children's books, from picture books right up to teen novels. In college (Trinity College, Dublin) I used to call up gigantic Maurice Sendak prints from the stacks, much to the horror of the handling librarians. They filled two desktops and more. Poring over his Wild Things, I got lost in Max's extraordinary world and marvelled at Sendak's technique – pen and ink hatchings over watercolour – his work grave, traditional yet utterly original. Remembering that he'd based the 'monsters' on his Brooklyn relatives, I chuckled away to myself, running my fingers over their warty, whiskery faces. I'm sure the librarians thought I'd lost it.

After college I landed my first 'proper' job in Hodges Figgis, Dawson Street, Dublin, and eventually worked myself across the road and became the children's buyer at Waterstone's and then at Eason's Head Office, then in Santry, the dream job for someone so kiddi-lit obsessed. Through my work I've met and even dined with dozens of extraordinary children's writers and illustrators, from our own Eoin Colfer, Derek Landy, Oliver Jeffers, PJ Lynch, Marita Conlon McKenna and Darren Shan; to Jackie Wilson, Judy Blume, Helen Oxenbury, Anthony Horowitz, Philip Pullman, Lauren Child and JK Rowling. I've listened to them talk about their work to hundreds of Irish children, just like I have the privilege of doing today.

While a bookseller, I also organised children's readings and events for many years in my bookshops, every one memorable. But of all the children who have ever attended the readings, I'll always remember one girl in particular: Hope, from St Kevin's Girls' National School in Kilnamanagh, Tallaght. Even thinking about Hope, with her blonde Irish dancing curls and her cheeky smile, makes me smile.

I'd like to share three stories about Hope with you: Hope and the cotton wool, Hope and the tomata ketchup, and Hope and the bishop. First the cotton wool. In 1996 American children's author Judy Blume visited Dublin and I was asked to arrange an event for her with a local school. I immediately invited the St Kevin's girls as their Head at the time was a huge book fan and loved getting her students enthused about books.

The event was held in the Dublin Writers Museum on Parnell Square. We crammed over a hundred and fifty girls into the lecture room and they could barely contain themselves with excitement. Judy strode in and started to address them in her jaunty, inclusive manner, illustrating her talk with slides from her childhood. She explained how she based some of her stories on things that had happened to her growing up. How bra shopping and then stuffing a bra with cotton wool, as her character Margaret does in *Are You There God? It's Me, Margaret* was part of her own teen experience.

Judy was petite, with twinkling eyes and a real way with children; the girls took to her instantly, gazing up at her in awe. She told them about living in New York and they all gasped at the wonder of it all. New York! The glamour.

After her talk she asked if there were any questions. Hands waved in the air.

'Me, Miss!'

'Here, Miss!'

She picked her way nimbly through the 'Where do you get your ideas?' and 'What's your favourite colour/animal?' until she came to Hope.

'Miss!' Hope said, jumping to her feet and wiggling around like she wanted the loo.

'Hand down, please, Hope,' one of the teachers said. 'You're banned from asking questions, remember?'

Judy smiled at the teacher. 'It's okay.' She smiled at Hope. 'Go on.'

'Do you still stuff your bra with cotton wool?' Hope asked with a grin.

Her teacher groaned and put her hands over her face.

Judy's eyes twinkled. 'What do you think, my dear?' she asked gamely.

'Na,' Hope said. 'You're flat as a pancake.'

The whole room broke into giggles, including, to the teacher's relief, Judy. Afterwards Judy told me it was an event she'd never forget.

JK Rowling was an unknown writer whose Harry Potter books were just starting to break through in the UK and Ireland when Bloomsbury asked me to organise a school event for her. I said we'd be delighted to have her at Eason's, O'Connell Street, Dublin, and invited, you guessed it, my favourite school, St Kevin's, to meet her.

JK Rowling (Jo as she asked everyone to call her) was charming, thoughtful and very funny. She gave a rousing reading from her second book, *Harry Potter and the Chamber of Secrets,* and then answered questions.

Hope was on her best behaviour. Her hand shot up at question time but her teacher frowned at her and she put it down again. But Jo had noticed.

'What did you want to ask?' Jo said sweetly.

'Doesn't matter, Miss,' Hope mumbled.

'No, go on.'

'I was just wondering if your hair's natural, Miss? Only it's the colour of tomata ketchup.'

Her teacher spluttered. 'Hope!'

Jo just laughed. 'It's called henna.'

When Hope and the St Kevin's girls made their confirmation some time later, the first Harry Potter film had just come out, the third book had become one of the fastest-selling books in history, and everyone knew exactly who JK Rowling was. Including the bishop confirming them.

During his sermon he even referenced her. 'God is all around us but you will never meet him,' he said. 'Just like the lady who wrote the Harry Potter books. You will hear the name JK Rowling on the news, read about her in the papers, but you will never meet her. Like God.'

A hand shot up and waved around in the air. 'Your Grace! Your Grace!' It was Hope. Apparently she could barely contain herself.

He ignored her, but she jumped to her feet. 'But we did, Your Grace!'

He gave up. 'You did what, young lady?'

'Meet JK Rowling, Your Grace. In Eason's. Ask Teacher.'

He looked over at her teacher who smiled and nodded.

And then Hope just had to add: 'Does that mean we might meet God one day, Your Grace?'

The whole church erupted with laughter, the lads from the boys' school stamping their feet and whistling.

In all my years as a bookseller and writer, I have never met a girl quite like Hope – funny, fearless, and a great little reader to boot. I bumped into her once, a few years back, on O'Connell Street. Someone ran up behind me and I felt a tap on the shoulder. I swung around.

'Remember me?' She grinned, the small gap still between her two front teeth.

'Hope! How could I forget?' I smiled back, delighted to see her.

'I'm still reading, Miss,' she said. 'Like you and that American one and JK Rowling told us to. Cecelia Ahern's my favourite. And Marian Keyes. She's a gas woman, must have some weirdo mind to be writing books like that, wha'? Have you ever met her?'

I nodded. 'She lives down the road from me. What are you up to, Hope? College? Working?'

'This and tha'.' She winked. 'See ya.'

With that she ran off, giggling, a Harry Potter rucksack bouncing up and down on her back.

To this day, if I need an instant pick-me-up I remember Hope and the poor bishop, his sermon ruined. Hope and JK Rowling.

❧ ❧

('Hope' is a pseudonym)

Kate Thompson

Kate Thompson is an award-winning actress and bestselling writer. Her most recent novel is *The O'Hara Affair*. The next – *That Gallagher Girl* – is due in November 2010.

Pandora's Legacy *

Kate Thompson

Bella was bored. Her parents were wandering around her grandpa's house with a man with a beard and a tie with pictures of fishes on. The beardy man was telling her dad how much money he might get for bits of furniture that he was going to sell in a place called an auction. The money was important. Her dad needed it to pay the owners of the old people's home that her grandpa had just moved into because her grandpa had gone mad. Except Bella wasn't allowed to say that he had 'gone mad'. She had to say instead that her grandpa had something called Alice Simor's disease. She sometimes wondered who poor Alice was, and why she had to have a disease named after her.

Bella could tell that selling the furniture wasn't going to make very much money because her mum's mouth was a bit turned-down looking. There was a 'For Sale' sign outside her grandpa's house, and her mum had said that if the sign had been there when she had first suggested it, it would have been gone by now, which Bella didn't think made much sense. Bella sometimes wondered why grown-ups didn't play with toys to cheer themselves up, instead of moaning all the time and listening to awful stuff on the news. If her mum had a Barbie like Bella's, her mum could make her Barbie do the splits or slide her up the banisters the way Bella's Barbie was doing now.

'Is there an attic?' the beardy man asked her dad.

'Yes.'

411

'Show me. That urban myth about uncovering treasures in attics holds more water than you might think.'

Treasure in an attic! Bella had a picture in her head of piles of gold coins and jewels and stuff like in the *Pirates of the Caribbean*. Her grandpa had been something called an art historian before he had gone mad. Maybe he had famous paintings like the ones in the National Gallery that Bella's school had gone to. But when they climbed the staircase to her grandpa's attic, they could see that it was just full of crap. Trunks, boxes, old shoes, books, clothes, broken furniture – all lay as if they had been flung there by a giant in a bad mood.

'Nothing much here, I don't think,' said her father to the beardy man, who looked well pissed off. Bella could bet that the man had expected to find treasure here, too, because of her grandpa having been an important art historian.

'Oh, look, Bella,' said her mother, 'there's an old doll's house. It must have belonged to your aunt when she was little. Shame we didn't know it was here. It's a tad more tasteful than that Barbie monstrosity.'

Bella hated it when her mum called her Barbie Diamond Castle a monstrosity. It had been a birthday present from her very rich aunt and uncle, and Bella loved it. With its pillars and balconies and framed photos of Barbie's horse and all her friends, it was the best crib a Barbie's pretty little heart could wish for.

'Why don't you stay up here and play with it?' suggested Bella's mum. 'We'll call you when it's time to go.'

'Cool,' said Bella, as the grown-ups turned and made their way back down the stairs.

The doll's house was a big one. It was three floors high, and it was furnished Victorian style, with velvet upholstered armchairs and sofas and a dining table set for a formal dinner. There were tiny silver ornaments on the mantelpiece and miniature books in the bookcase, and a dotey little pet poodle snoozing in a basket in the kitchen. In the topmost bedroom was a four-poster bed, with curtains draped around it. Bella reached out a hand and drew them open.

On the mattress lay a little naked doll, and as Bella went to touch her, the doll blinked her eyes open and yawned. 'Go away,' she said crossly, pulling the sheet over herself. 'You're only going to tell me to get up, and I don't feel like it today. I'm worn out from all the housework I did yesterday. I even polished the silver!'

'Oh!' said Bella. 'You can talk!'

'Of course I can talk,' said the doll, rubbing her eyes. 'What do you think I am? Some kind of dummy?'

'I thought you were a doll,' said Bella.

'How dare you!' said the doll, sitting up and tucking the sheet under her arms. 'I am not a doll, I am a demi-goddess, and I will have you know that I am extremely articulate. Who are you?'

'I'm Bella.'

'Bella. What is that effigy you're clutching?'

'It's Barbie.'

'Is she a goddess?'

'Well, she's . . . Barbie.'

'She must be a goddess. Only full-blown goddesses are allowed to wear gold.'

'Who are you?' asked Bella. She performed a little bow as an afterthought, somehow thinking that it might make the doll look more kindly upon her.

'I'm Hope.'

'Hope? Is that your name?'

'Yes.'

'What are you doing here . . . Oh Mighty Hope?'

'I'm in hiding. Even if I wasn't, I could hardly go out and fly around the streets in the nude, could I?'

'Don't you have any clothes?' asked Bella.

'No. Those bitches wouldn't allow me any. Aphrodite and Artemis and Athena and all those other so-called goddesses parading around in their golden robes – pah! But I showed them. I said, "If you won't give me a golden robe and confer goddess status upon me, then I am not going to show up for duty, my dears." But they refused to, and I ended up locked up in a box instead. But I have been true to my word. I never showed up for duty. I've never even set eyes on a mortal face, apart from the old man who took me out of the box and set me up here in this quaintly charming house.'

'The old man? Did he have kind of wild grey hair and a smiley face?'

'Yes. He was barking mad, though, in spite of the smiley face.'

'Then that was my grandpa. He has Alice Simer's disease. He's gone away from here to live in an old people's home.'

'Oh, what a shame! I liked your grandpa. He was kind to me. He decided I would be much more comfortable here than in the box.'

'How long were you in the box?'

'Oh – millennia. It was really horrid to begin with because I was locked in there with all the miseries in the world. Zeus! How glad I was when Pandora opened the lid and let them out – it had been like living in a madhouse until then. Those bastards were completely unhinged.'

'Pandora? I know that story. Pandora opened the box and out flew all the bad things that ever were.'

'That's right. And what a relief that was for me! I finally had the pleasure of my company all to myself.'

'Didn't you get awful bored?' Bella asked.

'Not remotely. I am a very interesting person, and I never get bored with myself.'

Hope tossed her hair back, in a kind of haughty gesture, and turned away from Bella to look at herself in the mirror. She had wings, Bella saw now! Proper wings like the Flower Fairies, or the butterflies that flitted around her grandpa's garden. She really was extremely pretty: gold all over, as if she'd been sunbathing in the nude, and her hair was as long and as glossy as Barbie's. She wasn't as curvy as Barbie, but she was easily as beautiful – more beautiful, even.

'So you're the actual Hope,' Bella said with awe. 'The very first Hope that ever was.'

Hope gave a pleased smile, and prinked a wing. 'I'm glad to know that I'm still famous after all these years.'

'You're legend!'

Hope slanted a look at Barbie. 'Am I as legend as your goddess?'

Bella knew that in the celebrity stakes Barbie would win hands down over Hope, but she didn't want to risk offending her new friend.

'Yes,' she said, crossing her fingers behind her back. Bella always did this when she told a lie, so that no harm could come to her. 'Tell me – when Pandora opened the box, why did she decide to leave you in there?'

'She was probably jealous of my beauty. She was a very vain and stupid girl. Anyway, she didn't leave me, per se. I elected to stay on.'

'Why?'

'I didn't want to go out in the world and consort with Old Age, Labour, Sickness, Madness and Vice.' Hope shuddered. 'Have you any idea how monstrous they are?'

'But you liked my grandpa, and he's old and mad.'

'Your grandpa looked after me. Old Age and his cohorts just ignored me and palled around together, moaning and muttering imprecations. Sickness did try and befriend me a few times, but I suspect he had ulterior motives. Also, he had the most appalling halitosis.'

'Did you never think of coming out and just taking a peek at the world?' Bella asked.

'Stark naked? I don't think so. Besides, what's to see?'

'There's some nice stuff out there.'

'Such as?'

'Um. Kittens and Coco Pops and Disneyland and stuff. And Barack Obama and Barbie.'

'Hmm.' Hope narrowed her eyes at Barbie again. 'I have to admit I like your effigy's gown.'

Bella thought that she might be beginning to have a brilliant idea.

'Why don't you try it on? It matches your hair.'

'But would it fit over my wings?'

'We could leave the back open.' Bella started to unfasten Barbie's

415

evening dress. It suddenly seemed stupid that a plastic doll should be wearing the golden frock, instead of this beautiful, fairylike being, who lived and breathed and moved – and even flew!

'Tell me more about the Goddess Barbie,' commanded Hope.

'Well, she lives in a place in my bedroom called Diamond Castle, and she has a wardrobe full of the coolest clothes. She has a horse and a carriage and a boyfriend and a sister and lots of friends who love her, and she goes to loads of parties. She has her own amazing website –'

'What's a website?'

'Um. A kind of virtual place where you go to admire all things Barbie.'

'Like a temple?'

'Yes. And she even has a special song of worship.'

'A hymn? Well, well. I do like the sound of this.'

Bella stripped plastic Barbie of the dress and handed it over to Hope. She watched as the tiny golden creature stepped into it and slid the gleaming straps over her shoulders.

'Oh!' she said, clapping her hands. 'It's lovely on you! Have a look in the mirror.'

Hope turned and regarded herself in the fly-blown cheval glass.

'Hmm,' she said, striking a pose. 'I do look good! I could give Aphrodite a run for her money.'

'You'd look even better in Barbie's mirror in Diamond Castle. It's got lights all round it, to show her beauty off to full effect.'

'Do you think that Barbie is more beautiful than me?' asked Hope.

'No,' said Bella immediately, then added: 'Hey! I've got an idea! Why don't you come and live in Diamond Castle?'

'Do you mean Barbie's Castle?'

'Yes! I'd much rather have you living there than stupid Barbie.'

Hope gave Bella a shrewd look. 'You mean you'd depose Barbie?'

'Depose?'

'Kick her off the throne?'

'Yes!'

'And strip her of her goddess status?'

'Yes.'

'And I could have all Barbie's – um – what did you call her effects?'

'Her stuff?' hazarded Bella.

'Yes.' Hope nodded eagerly. 'Her stuff. The horse and the suitor and the apparel and everything?'

'Everything! It would be like living in Paradise. It's every girl's dream come true!'

'Ha! I'd be the envy of Aphrodite and Artemis and Athena and all those pathetic demi-goddess groupies like Thetis and Echo who hang out on Mount Olympus, thinking they're the bees' knees.'

'And you could take over Barbie's job of saving the planet from all the miseries you used to live with. What were their names again?'

'Old Age, Labour, Madness, Vice and Sickness.'

'Yay! You and the Barbie Thumbelinas could kick their asses!'

'Who are the Barbie Thumbelinas?'

'They're like fairy Barbies – they've got wings like you, and they're all working really hard to save the planet.'

A suspicious look crossed Hope's face. 'Working hard? Like that sad old git Labour?'

Yikes! thought Bella. This goddess in training obviously didn't like the idea of hard work.

'No, no!' she assured her. 'They have fun doing it! And they wear the sweetest clothes.'

'Nicer than Barbie's?'

'No – never in a million years. Barbie always gets the best of everything.'

'So you reckon that if I came into the world, I could rule over even the mighty Barbie?'

Bella nodded earnestly. 'Barbie's a wimp compared to you,' she said.

Hope turned and regarded herself critically in the mirror. Then she turned back to Bella.

'Done deal,' she said, extending her tiny hand.

Smiling, Bella took it and shook.

And that is the story of how Hope finally arrived on Earth from the confines of Pandora's Box, and came to reside in Diamond Castle in Bella's bedroom in Clontarf, Dublin. Occasionally Bella takes her goddess to Toys 'R' Us and sets her on a shelf next to row upon row of inferior effigies for a joke, but mostly Hope just lives in the lap of luxury, riding in her carriage, changing her outfits, attending parties and going to the beauty salon.

As for Old Age, Labour, Madness, Vice and Sickness? They're being pursued by the Thumbelina Barbies, who are forging ahead indefatigably with their Herculean mission: Saving the Planet.

Anne Gildea

Anne Gildea is a Dublin-based writer and performer. In a varied career, she has toured internationally with her all-girl comedic songster group The Nualas; has written and performed comedy material for radio and television for both RTÉ and the BBC and is a published novelist. Since February 2007 she has been a weekly columnist with the *Irish Mail on Sunday*.

Tea ✶✶✶

Anne Gildea

Written many moons ago under my Celtic-Earth-Mother-Idiom pseudonym, Maura ní Práta (Mary, Daughter of Potato), below is a piece that expresses the traditional Irish equation:
   Hope = Tea. *

Tea
Boiling Kettle
Wolf whistle of Ireland
At the ready in the steady hands of Mammy
Oh wet the tea and comfort me
With the steam of your care
In a cup
That's never big enough
To not need a top up
Oh Mammy
Re-boot me with the caffeine kick of your cha
Loosen my tongue with the heat
Balm to all troubles
The hot gulp
Beverage perfection of 100° tap
Over a bag per head
Plus 15 for the pot

Tea so strong that Jesus could walk across the top of it
And it wouldn't be a miracle
Fermented five minutes under your tea cosy
Knitted by your Great-Great-Great-Grand-Mammy
Fidelma
During the famine
She made it in the shape of a woolly coffin
It looks lovely on the pot
It reminds us of a million dead
While it keeps the infusion hot
But no crying over spilt milk, Mammy
Just a splash in the cup
In the hand
And I'm grand
Or, oh, go on, so
If you're pushing
I'll take a slab of brack
Big enough to pave a garden path
Or even a Marietta
(That penance of a biscuit)
If that's all that you have
And while I get stuck into that
Mammy, stop the clock
In times of worry, doubt, confusion, celebration and remorse
And yes, sometimes, even thirst
Mammy in the kitchen
Do your little ceremony
Pick up the boiling kettle
And wet the font of everlasting hope
A lovely pot of tea.

* *This is not, strictly speaking, true.*

Mr Modern Office Fella

Anne Gildea

This is a piece that expresses the traditional Irish equation:
Hope = A Hero.*

When there's a wet spate of Irish weather
You respond with your golfing umbrella
Mr Modern Irish Office Fella
And when it's hot you're like a lobster screaming in a pot
Sweat pouring from your armpits down to your Fair Isle socks
Oh
I've seen you in the park
Battling with your Tesco tie
To reveal your hairless chest
To innocent grannies going by
At lunchtime
You nibble at your little lettuce sandwich
Like the rabbit that you are
Mr Modern Irish Office Rabbit.

Did you ever think if Cúchulainn came back
The sight a' you'd give him a heart attack
He who faced all kinds of weather
Wearing only half the skin of a hairy wolf
Cúchulainn knew how an Irishman should eat

A McNugget never even crossed his mind
When he was hit by a hunger pang
He just swallowed a bullock
And it did him for a year

Unlike you
Sitting there
Look at you
You pay a million pounds a month for your modern Irish flat
You think you're so sophisticated
'Cos you bought a cushion in Habitat
You fool on a futon
With a rock for a pillow
And a sheet of rain on his back
Cúchulainn made his bed all over Ireland
And never paid for that privilege

Unlike you
Sitting there
With your bottled beer
Watching the soccer on Saturday.
You couldn't play the great ancient Irish football game
Where half the men of Ireland played the other.
They didn't pussyfoot around a puny little ball
No, they took the Bladder of a Mammoth
Blew it up
And that was the *liathróid* that they fucked
Up and down the length of Ireland
Leaping over mountains in the way
A game would last for months on end
And who ever dropped dead first the other side would win
And they didn't go crying to a referee
If a leg or two came off in a tackle
They did not
No